Assessing Writing Across the Curriculum

Assessing Writing Across the Curriculum

Charles R. Duke
and
Rebecca Sanchez

Carolina Academic Press
Durham, North Carolina

ISBN 0-89089-740-9
LCCN 00-108406

Carolina Academic Press
700 Kent Street
Durham, North Carolina 27701
Telephone: (919) 489-7486
Fax: (919) 493-5668
email: cap@cap-press.com
www.cap-press.com

Printed in the United States of America.

Contents

III. Staff Development

Appendices

Foreword

As classroom teachers, we are hearing more and more from the public about the need for accountability, the importance of standards, and the role of assessment. We also hear calls from employers for authentic performance tasks, learning opportunities which reflect, as much as possible, what students will encounter when they enter the workplace. We have Presidents' agendas in education, and national education goals set by state governors. We also have new content standards in math, science, English language arts, history, art, and other fields, all of which are based on the assumption that students will be able to use writing as one of the major means for showing their knowledge and skills in all of these areas. State-wide and district-wide testing programs also are requiring more extensive samples of writing performance from students as part of an evaluation of the effectiveness of curriculum and teaching.

This added emphasis upon writing across the curriculum (WAC), however, has spawned an increasing anxiety among teachers in content fields. Many of these teachers never had any formal training in the teaching of writing, have little idea of how writing might be used for learning in addition to evaluating and, in many cases, are using strategies which become barriers to students who may wish to demonstrate that they can perform at satisfactory levels in many of these fields.

Couple this concern about how to use writing effectively to support learning as well as demonstrate it with almost an equal unease about assessment in general, and we have the ingredients for considerable confusion among both teachers and students on what is possible, and what may be important. Admittedly, it may be much easier to rely upon standardized examinations, and nationally normed assessments like the National Assessment of Educational Progress (NAEP) but, unfortunately, little useful teaching information can be gleaned from such assessments. From the classroom teacher's viewpoint, then, we need to refocus our attention upon what might be accomplished with assessment inside the classroom.

We would like to suggest that one powerful way to engage students in learning and to assess that learning is through writing. In making this suggestion, however, we also want to make clear that writing represents only one of a number of ways that student learning can be assessed, and teachers need to equip themselves with a broad understanding of assessment in order to determine which may be the most appropriate assessment strategy or approach to use at any given time. Our choices depend upon our goals—what is it we wish to assess? Richard Stiggins (1995) explains that "assessment-literate educators—be they teachers, principals, curriculum directors, or superintendents—come to any assessment knowing what they are assessing, why they are doing so, how best to achieve the assessment of interest, how to generate sound samples of performance, what can go wrong, and how to prevent those problems before they occur" (p. 240).

As we look across the school curriculum, we see at least one common theme related to assessment. All teachers expect that students will master considerable subject-matter knowledge; in fact, teachers probably will agree that mastery of knowledge provides the basis upon which all other performance can be built. But the question of how students learn not only that knowledge but the application of it remains. We believe that writing is one effective way for students to master content and demonstrate their application of it. Leon Botstein (1989), for instance, says that "the bridge between technical and specialized worlds of modern mathematics and science and daily life and experience must be constructed out of ordinary language" (p. xv). Besides speech, writing is our only other primary means for providing that translation. Botstein also points out that "ordinary language can also reach beyond the utilitarian, by opening up the beauty of science and mathematics" (p. xv). The real answer to effective learning and performance does not lie with more lists, more facts, more drill, but with teaching approaches which engage students in discovering what they know and what they can do.

We have chosen to focus this book on the assessment of writing to learn. We use the term "assessment" in the broadest sense possible to encompass both formative and summative views of student learning. We see assessment as a process for gaining useful information about student learning that can assist us in making appropriate decisions about our teaching. Equally important, however, is how we communicate with our students about the results of the assessment. So, readers will not find a discussion of norms, standard deviations or statistical validity. Instead, we hope to present writing assessment as an integral part of the teaching and learning process in content areas. We also subscribe to the viewpoint that not all writing has to be graded—in fact, the philosophy of this text is not to emphasize the collection of grades in writing but instead to emphasize the role of assessment in communicating with students about their progress and growth. As Neill and others in *Implementing Performance Assessments: A Guide to Classroom, School and System Reform* (n.d.) assert, "Assessment is therefore about the 'how' of learning as well as the 'what' and 'how much'"(p. 3). Consequently, we cannot separate assessment from teaching; they are, or should be, inextricably interwoven.

What readers will find in *Assessment of Writing Across the Curriculum* is a forum for discussion of practical, classroom-tested instructional strategies that encompass effective writing assessment of learning. Central to this discussion is the exploration of a variety of what might be called alternative assessments, alternative, at least, to the traditional multiple choice, fill-in-the-blank, end-of-unit, end-of-course tests. We also have chosen to focus upon the classroom teacher's role in this process because we believe that the most important relationship in learning is that which evolves between teacher and student and, that when it comes to using writing as a means for learning and assessment, most teachers—and that includes many English language arts teachers—have not received much assistance.

Adopting this stance calls for accepting some basic assumptions:

1. Students must be asked to show their understanding of what they are learning through writing.
2. Students should be asked to perform in a variety of modes of writing to match the variety of writing tasks they will encounter outside of school.
3. Writing should be used as a means of building a bridge between new knowledge and prior knowledge and experience.

4. Teachers who use writing as part of their overall assessment package in the classroom will need to accept new instructional and assessment roles.
5. Growth in writing performance is developmental and takes time as well as practice.

We hope that readers will not overlook any of the chapters in this book. Although there may be a temptation to look only at chapters that address a particular content area, readers will find in each chapter ideas, strategies and assessment tools which can be adapted easily for any content area. The book has been divided into three sections. In section one, the focus is upon rethinking the methods by which we use writing in our classrooms; here readers will find a clear focus upon what it means to emphasize writing to learn as opposed to writing to test. The authors in this section draw upon their own experience in finding ways to integrate writing into their teaching. In section two, readers will find an emphasis upon crafting assignments in various content areas and upon ways of assessing the products which emerge from these assignments; again, the emphasis is upon practical, how-to-do-it approaches. Finally, in section three, the focus is upon staff development and the ways that schools can make a commitment to helping teachers learn how to use writing effectively. Total school commitment to writing to learn can have a tremendous impact upon student achievement.

We do not suggest that the presence of writing is a new one in the classrooms across the curriculum, but we do know that for writing to be an effective part of the teaching and learning process, teachers need to know quite precisely what their goals are and how to gather evidence from student performance in writing that those goals are being met. We hope that the chapters in this book will prove useful in undertaking this effort.

Works Cited

Botstein, Leon. 1989. Foreword: The ordinary experience of writing. In *Writing to learn mathematics and science*, ed. P. Connolly and T. Vilardi, xi-xviii. New York: Teachers College Press.

Neill, Monty, and others. n.d. *Implementing performance assessments: A guide to classroom, school and system reform.* Cambridge, MA: FAIRTEST: The National Center for Fair and Open Testing.

Stiggins, Richard. 1995. *Assessment literacy for the 21st century.* Phi Delta Kappan (November): 238-245.

Acknowledgements

We would like to acknowledge the tremendous assistance provided by Janice Dotson-Voss and Kristen Benson in putting together the manuscript and seeing that the final copy was carefully formatted and accurate.

Chapter 4, "Giving Students Control Over Writing Assessment" originally appeared in the April 1994 issue of English Journal. Copyright 1999 by the National Council of Teachers of English. Reprinted with permission.

Chapter 5, "Making Portfolio Assessment Work in the Classroom" originally appeared in the Oregon English Journal. Reprinted with permission.

—Charles R. Duke and Rebecca Sanchez

Chapter 1

Strategies for Stimulating Informal Writing to Learn

Charles R. Duke

Common wisdom suggests that if students write more, they will become more fluent with the written word and better thinkers because writing is thinking. Our emphasis in having students write more, however, is not always to generate finished products, although that is an important part of students' writing experiences, but more importantly, to help students understand that writing is a process which leads to clearer thinking and understanding. An equally important principle to understand, from the teacher's point of view, is that not all writing necessarily has to be assessed in the same way. If we accept the principle that writing is a means for stimulating thinking and for revealing what we know and don't know, then a much broader array of writing opportunities and assessments open before us as teachers.

Student writing in content areas does not have to result always in a finished product to be useful both for the student and for the instructor. The emphasis in this chapter is upon strategies which can be used to stimulate writing while providing assessment of learning, either for short term efforts or for more developed assignments leading to a final product which will be assessed in a more formal and traditional manner. A number of strategies can be used to incorporate writing into content area classes while keeping the workload at a manageable level. Some require virtually no teacher time, others require minimal effort and others only a reasonable amount of time. If a teacher already requires some writing—essay exams, several papers—then the strategies suggested in this chapter will provide additional ways to increase student writing without overburdening the instructor or student while also providing very useful assessment information about student learning.

Frequently there is neither time nor the need for student writing to go all the way through the writing process; instead, if the student engages in informal writing to learn, the teacher and student can quickly and easily assess what learning is occurring and where further attention needs to be devoted for better understanding of material. The strategies outlined here might be compared to those exercises performed by dancers and actors as they begin to work on new pieces or performances, or the practice activities which athletes use to focus on certain skills they need in order to become more effective.

A key consideration in introducing writing to learn strategies to students is helping them understand how such writing can be helpful to them, even though it may not be graded in the conventional manner to which they are accustomed.

A brief hand-out such as the one below or an in-class discussion can be useful for this purpose.

* * *

> In this class, you will be asked to do a variety of writing; much of this writing will be short and what we call "exploratory"; it will not result in fully developed pieces of writing but instead you will be providing snapshots of your understanding of the material you are learning; this kind of writing might be thought of as "warm-ups," similar to what a musician does in getting ready for a performance or what an athlete does on a regular basis to develop his or her skills for major games. The warm-ups help us see where you are in your development as a learner. Sometimes these warm-ups can lead to fully developed pieces of writing, other times they serve only to stimulate your thinking and understanding. The main emphasis will be on showing what you know and don't know, not merely how well you do or do not use commas or understand correct sentence structure; these items we can address when you are engaged in more formal writing, which will also be a part of this class.
>
> Some of this warm-up writing will occur during class; other times you will be asked to do the writing outside of class and bring it in for discussion. Sometimes the writing will be assessed by you, other times by your classmates, and also at times by me. We will keep all of this warm-up writing in your portfolios because much of it may become useful when you are called upon to develop more formal writing pieces. In these warm-ups, we will be looking for evidence of your thinking, that you have done your reading, and have paid attention to class discussion, but it will also be an opportunity for you to let yourself and me know what you may not understand fully and where we need to spend more time in class clarifying what you are trying to learn; so, it is okay to get mixed up at times, to admit that you don't understand something, or that something is getting in the way of your moving ahead with your learning. Not all of us learn the same way or at the same rate so the warm-ups will vary to help you discover which ones work best for you.

* * *

In talking with students about this kind of writing, you will undoubtedly want to set a few ground rules. For example, having them keep all of this kind of writing in a portfolio where they can access it for use with more fully developed writing assignments is important to help them see that such writing is not isolated from other written expression. (See Chapter 5 for information on how to set up portfolios and assess them). You may also want to establish some guidelines as to the number of such activities they must complete for a given unit or marking period. Frequently teachers establish a "participation grade" to reflect the active participation of the student in the learning activities of the class. Whatever approach is used, students should be informed in advance and eventually should be encouraged to participate in setting the standard of expectation for this kind of activity.

Visualization

Most content areas are print driven; that is, most of the required learning calls for reading and responding to texts in some way. Some students, of course, have little difficulty with this mode of learning because they are good readers and good thinkers; others, however, sometimes find the line after line of print overwhelming and frequently get lost within the thickets of prose. As a result, students fail to make connections among details, concepts or major ideas. Not infrequently, such students respond well to opportunities to visualize aspects of text or to create graphic representations of ideas. Again, these visualizing efforts can be short, direct explorations or they can serve as springboards for more extended writing. Here are a few samples.

Listing

Everyone should be familiar with making lists, probably the most common kind of writing that we all experience, so it is not much of a stretch to suggest to students that becoming effective at list-making is one way to visualize a subject and find ways to explore and create meaning. Again, listing need not take a long time. To introduce the idea to students, you may want to engage in a learning activity such as the following:

What Do You See

Pair off with someone. Take a moment to study the person carefully; make a visual inventory of what the person is wearing, including things like rings, belts, shoes, as well as color of eyes, hair, etc. After you have done this—take no more than a couple of minutes—turn your back on each other and make three subtle changes in your appearance; perhaps you shift a ring from one finger to another, you remove an earring, you roll up a pants cuff, untie a shoe, etc. Do this as quickly as possible; then turn back to each other and take turns identifying the changes that each of you has made in your appearance. Talk briefly about which were the hardest changes to spot and why.

Next, sit down and on a sheet of paper list all of the details you can recall about your partner; do not look at your partner while making the list and write items down as quickly as possible without worrying about order. When you have written yourself out, draw a line at the bottom of that list; then look at your partner and see if you have missed anything. If you have, jot those details below the line on your paper. Discuss with your partner what you missed and why.

Pulling It Together

Now that you have your list, take some time to examine it in detail and see if you can figure out how you might cluster similar details. Look for some kind of way to organize your information. Identify your organization by categories and indicate what details belong under each cate-

> gory. What do you learn about your powers of observation from the amount of information you have under each category? Share your findings with your partner or your class.

Such an activity can emphasize to students the importance of detail, especially specific detail or facts. Without them, they could be describing, analyzing or reporting on anyone or anything. Class discussion can then focus on what they have learned and also what may be missing from their observation. A useful outgrowth from such thinking and writing is to ask students then to develop a paragraph about their subject, drawing on the data they have collected from observation to make a specific point. Ask that they develop a main idea that their data suggest to them. Students, with some guidance from the teacher, should be able to move from this kind of "practice" exercise into content-focused observation; working individually or in pairs, they can work from pictures in art classes, from specimens in science classes to shapes and maps in mathematics or social studies classes. The critical component is paying attention to details and determining what they tell us. Here is a sample paragraph developed by a student after participating in the practice exercise and then applying the principles to a painting in an art class:

> The man looks tired. The medium-length blond hair that covers his head is lifeless and thinning and looks as if it might not have been combed for days. His blue eyes are only half open and his lower lids sag down beside his large pockmarked nose. His large mouth droops at the corners. As he sits at his desk, he props his head up with both hands while the rest of his body slouches low in the chair.

Clustering

Many variations of clustering can be found in study skills texts. The strategy is useful both as whole class activity as well as for small groups or individual thinking and can serve a dual purpose of promoting discussion and stimulating writing. Frequently key words show up in a lesson, and the teacher wants to find out how students may be defining the word, or what associations they have with it which may affect their learning. The strategy is simple. For example, an art instructor used this strategy with her students before they were to view a painting by Paul Klee entitled "Burden" (Zimmerman 1985). Wanting to know what her students understood about "burden" as well as how they might associate it with the painting, she placed the word on the chalkboard in large print. She then invited her students to provide other words which they believed explained "burden" or perhaps were related in some way from their own experience. Here is what the students produced:

health sickness

friends | no friends
news house | not going home

people BURDEN car

brother | boyfriend staying out too late

smoking (trouble) | parent's pressures

alcohol | school

drugs | law

no money

Students can explore their own personal explanation of the word from this visual clustering or they might be encouraged to apply their interpretation of the word directly to the painting after they viewed it. This teacher worked with her students after seeing the painting to connect their viewing back to the title, asking them to list the details which helped them understand the meaning of the title. The class produced the following list:

His head is hung down.
His arms are between his legs; no hands
The objects above his head are on him.
His legs are crossed; he's skinny.
Arrows point downward.

Discussion could cease at this point and move on to other topics or a teacher could elect to ask students to develop a piece of writing which perhaps addresses the connection between their visualization of the man and how they, themselves, feel when "burdened." Or, for more advanced classes, students could be asked to comment on the painter's style and use of color and arrangement, drawing upon their observations as well as perhaps other knowledge they had gained about the painter.

Cubing

Students are accustomed to looking at a subject from at least one perspective but there's no need to stop there. Why not go for six? The best way to visualize this is to think of a cube, a six-sided figure often encountered in geometry classes. Students can be given a topic upon which to base their cubing or they can use the strategy on their own. Often teachers like to do cubing in class so that students can take turns sharing their discoveries but it can also be assigned for outside of class. A good working pace is to allot about five minutes for each side of the cube (see Figure 1 below). Students should not worry about editing or revising at this point. A sequence is suggested below but actually one can start with any side of the cube (Duke 1983).

Fig. 1 Cubing

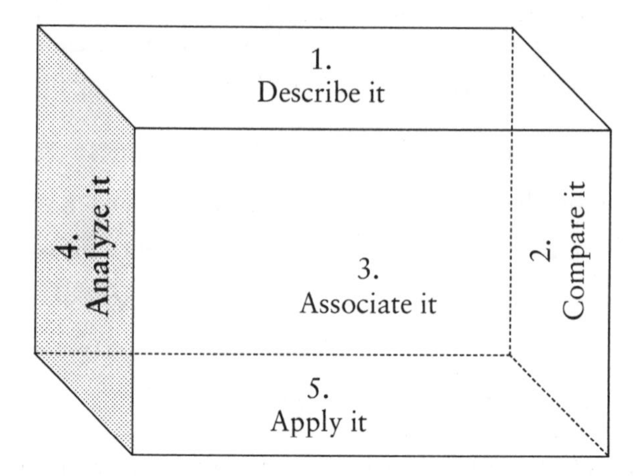

Side 1: **Description.** Describe your topic; look at it closely and describe what you see. Give as many details as you can. Describe it from all sides—top, bottom, sides, near, far, sideways, etc. If your topic is not a physical object but an idea such as violence or an event, describe the physical aspects you see in relation to it. At the end of 5 minutes of free writing, stop and move on to Side 2.

Side 2: **Comparison.** What is your topic similar to? What is it different from? List as many similarities and/or differences as you can; don't worry too much about developing any one similarity or comparison in depth; just keep listing and writing about them as much as you can. Write as rapidly as you can. Stop at the end of 5 minutes and move to Side 3.

Side 3: **Association.** Most subjects remind us of other things or of experiences we have had related to a subject. List all the associations—memories—you may have about your subject. One particular association or memory may come to your mind and you find yourself eager to get down as much as possible about it. If this happens, don't fight it; go ahead and concentrate on recording as much information as you can. Stop after 5 minutes and move to Side 4.

Side 4: **Analysis.** What makes up your subject? Can it be broken down into small parts? Can you classify it in different ways? What are the ingredients necessary for your subject to exist? If you're not sure about all the ingredients, make them up for the time being. You can go back later and check for accuracy. Stop after 5 minutes and move to Side 5.

Side 5: **Application.** What can you do with your subject? How can it be used? What are its many purposes or functions? What do you know about its uses? Which are most important? Again, if you're not entirely sure, let your imagination supply the details. Brainstorm and keep writing. Stop after 5 minutes and move to Side 6.

Side 6: **Argument.** Argue for or against your subject; take a stand, collect your reasons, silly or serious. What are the strengths of your argument? What are the dangers? If you run out of material on one side of the argument, switch to the other side. For the sake of later understanding, though, try to stay with one side of the argument as long as you can. Argue for 5 minutes.

Once students have completed the cubing, they will want to take a breather. Having them return to the cubing material the next day will give them a fresh perspective and probably enhance their abilities to take what they have collected and make sense of it. Ask the students to look through all of the material; have them circle or underline pieces that they think they might be able to develop further. Then encourage them to look at two or more sides and see if one or more might be combined. For example, the association, application, and argument sides might be the richest in information if students have been dealing with a broad topic; on the other hand, if something physical was the object of the cubing, analysis, description, and comparison may yield more.

Cubing simply provides a visualization method for exploring a topic from multiple vantage points. We might call it "starting cold" on a topic with the hope that such exploration will help eventually to focus the writer's thinking and choice of development. If this succeeds, the writer will then be able to move into the writing process and develop a full draft. If not, the material is not wasted because it can serve as the basis for future discussions or later writing.

Jigsaws

Many students have not experienced much involvement with jigsaw puzzles these days, but the concept has been easily transferred to the classroom and has become a useful strategy for promoting both learning and also group processes. This approach may be used after reading in a text has been assigned or it can be done as part of a reading in class or as an out-growth of a discussion on a topic. The approach works especially well if the text reading is divided into sections.

Obtain a large sheet of butcher paper and divide it into pieces large enough so considerable writing and graphic illustrations can be placed on them; then give a piece to each group of 4-5 students. Assign each group a section of the text to which they are to respond. If there are more groups than sections, assigning the same section to two groups can result in some interesting and useful variations in response. Provide each group with several different colored markers. Fran Claggett (1996) suggests that teachers may want the students to first read their section to themselves silently, responding in their journals to questions such as the following (adapted from Claggett, p. 86).

1. What puzzles or confuses you about this piece; make notes about unusual terms, phrases or statements?
2. What facts, images, or details stand out in your reading?
3. What impact does the information have on you? How do you feel as you read?
4. What do you feel you need to know more about when you finish the reading or what questions do you have that you would like to have answered?

Once students have completed their individual readings, they should take time to discuss with each other their findings in relation to all or at least some of the questions listed above. They may read some of their responses aloud or talk them through but they should focus on trying to make sense of what they have read; then, they should decide on how best to communicate their understanding through symbols, pictures, and words on their piece of butcher paper, using the colored markers to offer a colorful representation of their thinking.

After each group has completed its piece of the jigsaw, each group elects a spokesperson to present its piece of the puzzle to the rest of the class. The pieces of butcher paper are posted together as each group presents its findings until the whole jigsaw has been completed. At this time, students then might be asked to produce, either as a group or individually, a piece of writing which shows how their part of the puzzle relates to others, and what they perceive the overall meaning to be of the reading assigned.

Subject Acrostics

Although not many students resort to word puzzles these days, the concept of acrostics is easily grasped and applied to any content area and provides another means of visualization which can be helpful to students when they are trying to remember basic facts; the strategy also can inject some creativity into the learning process as well. Students are invited to develop a poem based upon the letters in the name of a plant, animal, character or concept being studied. The only rule is that each line must contain some fact about the subject being described and if any questions arise about the accuracy, the student must be prepared to provide supporting evidence. In this instance, the success of the poems could be judged on the basis of the accuracy of the facts used, the correct use of key words from the vocabulary related to the subject, and creativity within the constraints of the letters in the name (Johnston 1985).

Phylum Mollusca

SQUIDS

Shells are *VESTICLE* and we call them a "pen"
Quick is the movement that caves them in again
Under their suckers is a toothed horny nail
Ink sacs protect them by making "smoke screen"
Deep sea kinds are *LUMINOUSLY* seen
Strong vicious jaws make them not like a snail.

(Johnston 1985, p. 93)

A variation on the acrostic poems is the **formula** poem which is adaptable to a variety of content areas but works especially well in English, social studies, music, art, foreign languages. The formula provides students with an easily understood framework within which to work, focusing their attention on the content rather than worrying about how poetic they may be. The work may be done individually, in small groups, or by a whole class. The pattern (Page 1987, p. 48) is as follows:

Line 1: First name..........
Line 2: Four traits that describe the subject
Line 3: Relative (brother, sister, daughter, member of scientific family, etc.)
Line 4: Lover of (identify three things or people)
Line 5: Who feels (three items)
Line 6: Who needs (three items)
Line 7: Who fears (three items)
Line 8: Who gives (three items)
Line 9: Who would like to see (three items)
Line 10: Resident of..........
Line 11: Last name..........

Such word constructions often serve to trigger students' deeper understanding of relationships, of factual content, and of their relationships to the subjects. Not infrequently, activities such as these serve as a springboard for writing assignments at later times where students, building upon what they have discovered through the word puzzles and formula poems, can develop much richer and more interesting pieces of extended writing. Some students have been known to use their acrostics or formula poems as introductions to more serious and extended writing.

Quickwrites

One of the easiest and initially most productive ways to get students accustomed to writing about their learning is to use **quickwrites.** These are short bursts of writing at strategic times during class that will help students reveal their grasp of ideas, facts, or concepts. These quickwrites do not have to be assessed in depth; instead, the teacher can draw from them to promote further class discussion, promote review, introduce new material, or restructure a class on the fly. They can be collected or not. Some teachers like to collect them and scan them as a means of assessing where each student is in the learning of the material or simply to check off for credit that the student has completed the activity. Many teachers keep numerous packs of 3 x 5 or 4 x 6 notecards in their classrooms for this purpose. Here are several strategies for quickwrites.

Admit Slips

Hand students 3 x 5 lined cards as they enter the classroom; ask them to write down immediately (take no more than 5 minutes) such things as the following: (1) What key point do you remember from your reading of the homework (or yesterday's class); (2) What especially interested you about what you read? (3) What question(s) do you have about your reading? (4) How do you explain (insert a key concept or principle here)? (5) What three things do you know about (insert topic for the day's lesson here)? (6) Why do you think (insert a character from a story read or a historical figure, etc.) chose to do what he/she did?

You can collect responses and shuffle through them quickly to get a sense of where the class may be in relation to the material covered or to be addressed and then build upon the responses for that day's lesson. You also could ask representative students to read from their cards to the rest of the class and use the reading as a means for initiating discussion; still another strategy is to have students exchange cards and ask students to identify one point or aspect of the card they agree with, disagree with, or find interesting and volunteer that information back to the writer or to the class. Some teachers even group students after the admit slips are completed and have them take a few minutes to discuss with each other what they have placed on their admit slips.

Refocusing/clarification

Not infrequently as we teach, we sense that students may not be understanding the lesson or have lost a sense of direction in the work they are undertaking or the lesson has lost momentum and needs to be re-started. Stop the class activity; ask students to pull out one of their quickwrite cards and then do one of the following, depending upon what you sense may be needed: (1)What question(s) do you have about the material we have covered this far? (2) Indicate what you think are the (insert number) key points we have covered; (3) How does our discussion connect with what we talked about yesterday? Again, a quick review of the responses, perhaps having one or more students sharing their questions while you collect and review responses from other students can help you assess where the class is and what you may need to do to refocus or clarify the lesson and get it moving again.

Exit permit

Try stopping a few minutes before the end of class and asking students to do one or more of the following: (1) Summarize what you have learned this class period; (2) What questions do you have about what we have covered? (3) In your mind, what is the most important thing you learned today?

Have students submit their responses as they leave; review them before the next class and adjust your approach and material accordingly. Often it is a good idea to group common questions that appear on these exit permits and place them on the chalkboard the next day or on an overhead projector. Doing this solidifies in the students' minds that their writing and responses are considered and acted upon. Students will approach the writing with a much more positive attitude if they can see their work reinforced this way.

Freewrites

Instructors have found that often students think that they have to have everything figured out before they start to write. Freewriting, a term coined originally by Ken Macrorie (1968), helps students overcome this traditional block to putting thoughts on paper. Originally, freewrites were intended to increase students' fluency by simply asking them to get words down on paper about any topic that interested them; the only directions were that they should begin writing at a signal and continue writing nonstop until they were told to stop. If for some reason they hit a dry spell, they should continue to write, even if it were nothing more than "I have hit a dry spell" until something pops into their minds and then they can write about this new topic. Several variations on this approach have proven useful in content area classes.

The **focused** freewrite gives students a starting point but then allows them to jump off from this point and write about anything they can relate to the focus; for example, students might be asked to write non-stop for five minutes on a topic such as "cells," or "the battle at Gettysburg"; at the end of five minutes, they are asked to share an idea or event that they have identified in their freewrite. The sharing can be done with a partner, small group, or whole class. Another variation is to have students write for five minutes, and then stop and pass their papers on to a classmate. Each student then takes a minute to read what the previous writer has put on paper and then is asked to either continue what the previous author has started, disagree with the author, or develop a new topic off the one addressed by the previous writer. This writing goes on for another five minutes; then papers are exchanged again, making sure that each student receives a new paper on which his or her own comments are not present. Students read now two freewrites and then are asked to write one more, following the same directions as for the previous one. At the end of the final five minutes, students exchange one more time, still not having their own papers.

At this point, they are to read the three freewrites which are on the papers they received and to circle or underline at least one or more ideas they like, phrases or words that caught their attention, or questions that one or more of the authors on the page raise. This usually takes no more than a couple of minutes; from here, the teacher can call on individual students to share their findings with the rest of the class. Occasionally, teachers may want simply to go through the whole class and have each student share one thing from the writings. Such an activity usually surprises students at the variety of facts, viewpoints, and ideas which their classmates have and provides the teacher with a wonderfully rich assessment of students' interests and understanding.

Still another variation on the freewrite is the **freewrite collaboration.** This strategy works well in any content area when the teacher wants to assess students' understanding of a subject in a quick way. In this approach, students share the responsibility for developing a short paragraph about the subject that is being studied. Each student will need seven quickwrite cards for this activity. Here is the sequence to follow:

1. Students should take one of their quickwrite cards and write a statement about the topic under study.
2. Students then exchange cards. Based on the cards they receive, they then should take 3 quickwrite cards and on each one write a sentence which offers specific support to the statement which has been received.
3. Students exchange the four cards with another student (having students pass their cards to the classmate in front or behind them usu-

ally works best and minimizes the time necessary for the exchange). Students take 3 more of their quickwrite cards and add a statement on each of specific support for any or all of the cards which have been received.

4. Finally, students exchange their cards one more time. Taking the 7 cards which each student should now have, each student is responsible for organizing the sentences into what seems to be the best order; transition words or phrases can be added on the cards where necessary to make the sentences read smoothly. Once students have an order which makes sense to them, they should write a full paragraph with the sentences. (This can be done for homework if time is at a premium, but students should submit the cards with their paragraphs so the teacher can see what the original statements were).
5. If time permits, students should be asked to read their paragraphs aloud to the class; this serves as both a review for the class of the subject while also providing the teacher with a quick means to assess students' understanding of the material along with their ability to organize data into meaningful prose. Writing of this nature is short and focused on content. Teachers can assess such writing as a part of class discussion or the products can be collected, reviewed, given credit, and used as a basis for either re-teaching or moving into new areas of the topic being studied. In any case, students are writing to learn and using valuable critical thinking skills along with writing skills.

Microthemes

Once students are comfortable with using writing to learn and, in many ways, to assess their own learning, they can be encouraged to move into more formal but still short pieces of writing. Many teachers have found that they can build upon quickwrites to design more formal writing assignments that help students come to grips with difficult concepts, principles, or events. The microtheme is one such approach. In a physics class, for example, the teacher decided that velocity and acceleration could be difficult concepts for students to grasp. The physics teacher developed the following write to learn assignment (Bean 1996, p. 79)

> You are Dr. Science, the question and answer person for a popular magazine called *Practical Science*. Readers of your magazine are invited to submit letters to Dr. Science, who answers them in "Dear Abby" style in a special section of the magazine. One day you receive the following letter:
>
> Dear Dr. Science:
>
> You've got to help me settle this argument I am having with my girlfriend. We were watching a baseball game several weeks ago when this guy hit a pop-up straight over the catcher's head. When it finally came down, the catcher caught it standing on home plate. Well, my girlfriend told me that when the ball stopped in

> midair just before it started back down, its velocity was zero but its acceleration was not zero. I said she was stupid. If something isn't moving at all, how could it have any acceleration? Ever since then she has been making a big deal out of this and won't let me kiss her. I love her but I don't think we can get back together until we settle this argument. We checked some physics books but they weren't very clear. We agreed that I would write to you and let you settle the argument. But, Dr. Science, don't just tell us the answer. You've got to explain it so we both understand because my girlfriend is really dogmatic. She said she wouldn't trust Einstein unless he could explain himself clearly.
>
> Sincerely Baseball Blues

Can this relationship be saved? Your task is to write an answer to Baseball Blues. Because space in your magazine is limited, restrict your answer to what can be put on a single five by eight inch card. Don't confuse Baseball Blues' girlfriend by using any special physics terms unless you explain clearly what they mean.

Writing to learn assignments like the Baseball Blues problem focus students' attention on key concepts in a realistic application. Often such problem-based writing forces students to review what they know, discover new knowledge, discuss concepts with classmates, and raise awareness about the importance of being able to communicate clearly to others what it is you may know. Teachers like this kind of writing because it is brief and because it calls for fairly large amounts of thinking before writing can occur.

The number and variety of informal writing to learn strategies available is limited only by the patience and inventiveness of the teacher. Writing of this sort often causes teachers to rethink how they are presenting information because students' response provide insights into the students' thinking processes which, quite often, are not those of the teacher. These direct channels into students' learning processes are valuable for assessing how a class is progressing. Instruction can be adjusted quickly and easily on the basis of these short, informal writing to learn activities.

Other chapters in this book provide a number of suggestions of how such strategies can be adapted to specific content areas and lead to extended writing. For example, many teachers have found the use of journals or response logs to be very valuable in helping students analyze and reflect upon their reading and learning (See Chapter 9). Others have found that asking students to record their thinking about subjects through online chat rooms or e-mail to be useful. No matter what the format, no matter what the content, asking students to engage in frequent informal writing paves the way for increased fluency and ease in handling more extended writing assignments while providing the teacher with an ongoing means of assessing students' learning.

Works Cited

Bean, John C. 1996. *Engaging ideas: The professor's guide to integrating writing, critical thinking, and active learning in the classroom.* San Francisco, CA: Jossey-Bass.

Claggett, Fran. 1996. *A measure of success: From assignment to assessment in English language arts.* Portsmouth, NH: Heinemann.

Duke, Charles R. 1983. *Writing through sequence: A process approach.* Boston: Little Brown.

Johnston, Patricia. 1985. Writing to learn science. In *Roots in the sawdust: Writing to learn across the disciplines*, ed. A.R. Gere, 92–101. Urbana, Illinois: National Council of Teachers of English.

Macrorie, Ken. 1968. *Writing to be read.* New York: Hayden Book Company.

Zimmerman, Priscilla. 1985. Writing for art appreciation. In *Roots in the sawdust: Writing to learn across the disciplines*, ed. A.R. Gere, 31–45. Urbana, Illinois: National Council of Teachers of English.

Chapter 2

Setting the Stage for Assessment: The Writing Assignment

Charles R. Duke

- For next Friday, I want you to write a paper on "The Advantages of Living in This State;" make it neat; late papers will not get credit.
- Discuss the Civil War.
- Write an essay on capital punishment. Be sure to include facts from our class discussion and reading.
- On the lab table are five plates with different substances on each one. When your turn comes, examine the substances carefully. Take detailed notes if you wish. Then, when you return to your seat, write a paragraph in which you indicate how the substances are alike. Then write another paragraph which shows how they are unalike. Finally, write a paragraph in which you provide some way of classifying the information.
- Write a report on the book you have been reading. Be sure to discuss the theme, characters, plot, and setting.

No writing exists in a vacuum. We write because some internal or external influence prompts us. In the work world, needs arise for written communication and employees attempt to respond. Perhaps an employer asks for a report or a customer service order must be completed or a response to a customer complaint must be made. Maybe advertising copy has to be written for an upcoming sale or a case history has to be compiled. These situations and, many others like them, usually contain a well defined purpose for the writing, a clear sense of the audience and appropriate form, and an understanding of the writer's role.

But school writing is unique. Most writing required in various content areas bears little resemblance to writing tasks students encounter outside of school. For example, where, in writing outside of school, does one find the traditional All-American school "theme"? Teachers cling to this form like a lifeline—one paragraph to introduce the topic and the three points to be made, one paragraph for each point, and then a paragraph for conclusion. Teachers love the neatness—and shortness—of the form; students generally hate it!

Most students have no clear idea why they are being asked to write, and see no connection between "school writing" and more authentic writing tasks they know exist outside of school. The results of in-school writing often are disappointing, especially in content areas other than English language arts. Teachers throw up their hands in disgust, announcing to anyone who will listen that students can't write, and proceed to blame English teachers, elementary teachers and almost everyone else beyond themselves for this terrible state of affairs. Based upon such experiences, teachers frequently decide not to assign writing at all.

Teachers' negative reactions to student writing, though, are unfair. Regrettably, many teachers in various content areas receive no training through their teacher preparation programs in how to develop authentic writing situations that could produce effective student writing. Teachers have even less experience or knowledge about how to treat the written products after they are received. None of this needs to be the case. Student writing can become more effective, and assessment can be easier and more consistent, if teachers remember some key considerations before assigning writing.

Part of our problem as teachers is that for too long we have viewed writing simply as a means for testing what students know. But even when we have used writing for testing, we have not spent much time examining what it is we are asking students to do, and why they might not be able to do it very well. Arthur Applebee and others (1981) suggest that "the first steps in improving the writing... of students call for more situations in which writing serves as a tool for learning, rather than as a means to display acquired knowledge" (p. 101).

But what might happen if we shifted the focus in our use of writing from merely an emphasis upon testing to one that emphasizes learning? In *Plain Talk About Learning and Writing Across the Curriclum* (1987), Judy Self lists some of the purposes for such a shift:

- To focus students' attention on subject matter
- To engage students actively with the subject matter
- To arouse students' curiosity about subject matter
- To help students discover disparate elements in subject matter
- To help students make connections between the subject matter and their lives
- To help students make their own meaning from subject matter
- To help students identify what they do and don't know about a subject
- To diagnose students' learning successes and problems
- To help students think aloud on paper in various ways: associating, analyzing, synthesizing, etc. (p. 15).

These purposes, however, remain unknown to students until translated into appropriate writing situations. At the heart of this transformation lies the writing assignment. Stephanie Pace Marshall (1992), past president of ASCD, points out, "The key to effective assessment is the match between the task and the intended student outcome" (p. vi). Hence, assessment in writing begins not with the written product but with an understanding of the elements of an effective assignment.

Our first step is to examine the writing prompt or task upon which any writing assignment is built. The term "prompt" conveys exactly what we're trying to do when we begin to construct an effective writing assignment. We want to prompt students to write. As an example, here's a prompt that appeared at the beginning of this chapter:

> For next Friday, I want you to write a paper on "The Advantages of Living in This State." Make it neat; late papers will get no credit.

A writing prompt always sends a message to students about what's important. In this case, students will undoubtedly focus on three items: *the paper is due on Friday*, *neatness counts heavily*, and *they won't get any credit for whatever they do if they do not meet the deadline.* At the same time, many unanswered questions emerge from this prompt. For example, "write a paper" provides no clue to the student as to the form for the writing and sets us and the student up for possible failure when the final writing is evaluated. Could the student, for instance, write an editorial, a monologue, or just fill a piece of paper with writing and meet the requirements? All seem acceptable based on the information in the prompt. In fact, a teacher might have some difficulty explaining to students why they had not met the requirements of the assignment as long as the writing was about advantages of living in the state.

Other questions appear. Why, for example, must the student be restricted to only addressing advantages? Might students learn more and show what they know more effectively if they were not so restricted? How many advantages will be sufficient? What level of detail should the student expect to provide? Good reasons may exist for the narrow focus, especially if this is a test situation, but the prompt offers no clue to the student. Who will be reading the paper and what will they be expecting? Students, of course, have come to assume that the only audience for school writing is the teacher—and they are usually right! But is that necessary? Might students learn more and show more of what they know if they are not so restricted?

Let's now assume we've received papers which have been written to this prompt. What criteria will we use to assess the writing? If students have passed the papers in on time, and were neat and gave some advantages, what can they expect for a grade? What will be the criteria for determining who gets a higher or lower grade if all of the students have met the criteria as expressed in the prompt? For example, if one student gives five reasons and another only four, does one warrant an A and the other a B? More often than not, teachers who give prompts of this sort seldom have any criteria in mind; instead they make the decisions about criteria after they receive the papers. Such a practice leads to "grading drift," especially if the papers are being read late at night or in batches of 30 or 40 at a time. Under these circumstances, we find students who typed their papers getting higher grades than ones who wrote them long hand, or students who listed many advantages but did not develop them getting lower grades than students who identified one or two advantages and developed them fully. No clues exist in the prompt to provide guidance to students or to teachers.

Prompts like this, unfortunately, appear time and time again in classrooms and as a result, both students and teachers grow increasingly frustrated with the role of writing in teaching and learning. Students approach teachers and say, "If I had known that's what you wanted, I could have written a good paper." And teachers go into teachers' lounges and complain about how badly students write, how they seem to have no interest or pride in what they produce, and how time-consuming and boring it is to read their efforts.

None of this needs to happen if more care is taken in preparing for a writing experience, regardless of the content area. Fundamental to this preparation is the question, "Why do I want my students to write?" Simply saying they need practice in writing is not enough. Before any writing occurs in a course or class, we need to consider the organization of the course—what are its chief elements? how do they relate to each other? and how will writing support those elements? What are the abilities of the students? Have they written frequently before? Do they understand the nature of the writing process? What range of abilities in reading and writing do students show? What seem to be the students' interests? How are they responding to the subject matter? What connections between the subject matter and their lives have become evident through class discussion? And, finally, what are the overall goals of the class—what would we like to have students know and be able to do when they finish? Once we as teachers have answered these questions, we then can focus on what kinds of tasks we are going to ask students to complete in order for us to assess how well they have met the overall goals of individual lessons, units, and even complete courses.

Teachers, of course, are assessing all the time in the classroom and are in the best position to know what will work and what will not, what students may be able to achieve and what they cannot. Effective and useful assessment has to be built on something more than an occasional piece of writing, or an infrequent speech, or an occasional quiz. At the same time, when students are asked to perform, they need to know what the expectations are and these should not be delivered in vague terms.

Elements of an Effective Writing Prompt

Assuming that general factors concerning the use of writing in the learning process have been addressed, the next step is to construct writing prompts that enable us to assess students' skill and understanding while also contributing to student learning. To assist us, we need to think in terms of RAMPS (Duke 1983), a useful scaffold for building effective writing prompts. Each prompt should contain the following elements: *Role*, *Audience*, *Mode*, *Purpose* and *Situation*. Let's examine each of these elements and their contribution to an effective prompt. Although the elements are presented in a certain order here, in most cases, teachers can develop each of them in any order that seems to work best.

Role

What will be the role of the author in the piece? Will the author be himself or herself, drawing upon personal experience and knowledge? Or will the author become a character from a piece of literature, or act as a scientist, as a public official, or as a relative? Whatever the writing is to be, the author must determine what his or her stance or role will be in relationship to the other elements in the prompt. The decision about role also dictates how the author will approach the subject matter.

For example, let's assume that as a teacher, you want students to come to understand the importance of perspective or point of view in reporting on an event. You select a news item such as the following:

> Throughout most of his 53 years and various careers, Jesse Burgess Thomas of Washington, D.C. had been a compulsive collector. As a member of the Merchant Marine, an editor for a Tokyo newspaper (Japanese was among his six languages), a naval historian, and a part-time cab dri-

ver, he had amassed a staggering collection of junk—hand-tinted Japanese slides, 30 broken umbrellas, first day issues of stamps, old cottage cheese containers, nautical charts, and oriental altar pieces. In addition, Thomas had acquired an annoying habit of not paying his rent.

His landlord gave him several warnings and then took him to court. Last week, to carry out a court-ordered eviction, a deputy U.S. marshal and a crew of twelve moved into his apartment and dragged his belongings onto the sidewalk.

There passersby and neighbors wantonly began to loot and destroy. When Thomas returned to see his treasures scattered about, he collapsed on the sidewalk from a heart attack. In half an hour, he died. His neighbors argued over who was to blame: his landlord, for showing too little compassion; each other, for showing too much greed; the local police for not protecting his property. On one point, however, all were in agreement: Jesse Thomas died of a broken heart.

Time Magazine, April 9, 1973, p. 10.

This incident contains rich possibilities for a variety of roles and perspectives. Some of these might include the following:

- A seventeen year-old boy (girl) who lived in the neighborhood and always considered Mr. Thomas an "odd man."
- A policeman called to investigate the event.
- An ambulance attendant who first arrived at the scene.
- A stranger who just happened to be passing by when Mr. Thomas saw the heap of his possessions on the sidewalk.
- An elderly neighbor who lived in the next apartment and occasionally exchanged pleasantries with Mr. Thomas and who had made the call to police when Mr. Thomas collapsed.
- The landlord who learned of the event the next day.
- A member of the crew who dragged the possessions into the street.
- The judge who ordered the eviction.
- A homeless person who was helping herself (himself) to some of Mr.Thomas's possessions when he arrived on the scene.
- A neighbor who had taken something from the heap of possessions and had it in his or her apartment when Mr. Thomas arrived on the scene.

Most students have never had the opportunity to choose from such a wide variety of roles nor have they been encouraged to identify the possibilities on their own. Yet understanding one's role in the act of writing is an essential part of the process of determining which knowledge and understanding the situation requires. Because students lack experience in identifying roles, we should spend time in class brainstorming the possibilities, modeling how students themselves can engage in canvassing the potential roles in a writing situation.

Audience

Our next consideration in developing the prompt becomes the identification of audience. Who will be reading this piece? Traditionally, of course, the teacher has been the audience for school writing. This can present a problem for students. Rightly or wrongly, they have viewed writing to such an audience as nothing more than a test. Students have difficulty telling what they know to an audience that already, in their eyes, has superior knowledge about the subject. After all, what really is the point? Outside the classroom, however, multiple audiences await students as they move into work or professional situations; on one occasion, employees may have to write to their bosses, another time to a customer, still another to their fellow workers.

Students encounter few opportunities to become familiar with analyzing audiences and determining how the identification of audience should influence what is written. Understanding an audience's needs as well as its prior knowledge is critical to successful written communication. Students need to be encouraged to raise questions: Is the teacher the only possible audience? Who else might be interested in the information? What level of knowledge about the subject will my audience already have? How will that level of knowledge affect the approach I take? What will be the relationship between me and my audience—friendly, hostile, noncommital? What will this audience need to know in order to understand the point I want to make? What will be their expectations of me as a writer?

If we return to the news item about Jesse Thomas and select one of the role possibilities, we can see the options that emerge for an audience. Assume we're the elderly neighbor who lived next to Mr. Thomas. Here are just a few of the possible audiences for the neighbor:

- another neighbor in the same building who did or did not witness Mr. Thomas's collapse
- the police who are investigating the event
- the landlord
- a relative of the neighbor who lives some distance away but who has or has not heard about the event

As we begin to make these choices or at least to identify our options, we also start to discover how a decision about one element of RAMPS leads naturally to another and the entire scope of the prompt begins to unfold for us.

Mode

Research (Britton 1975, Applebee 1981) has shown that the single most used form of writing in school settings is the essay or some variation of it; yet, in life outside of school, students quickly discover that unless they intend to write for magazines or scholarly presses, their writing will be directed to various audiences, each one perhaps calling for a different form of writing and most of which they have had no experience in developing. Much of the lack of attention to exploring different modes stems, once again, from the wide-spread view that writing is testing and the most common test form is some variation of the essay—either a short answer paragraph response or a full-blown essay response. But teachers who have experimented with using different modes of writing for testing as well as writing to learn have discovered that these modes can show equally well what students do or do not know about a subject. These modes engage students in learning and provide them with valuable experience in adjusting their writing to the form, the audience, and the role. The number of possible modes which can be used for writing is staggering. (See, for example, James Moffett's *Active Voices* series, 1992). Here's a short list to suggest just how rich the possibilities can be:

Letters	Journals/diaries
Memos	Biographies
Sketches	Profiles
Menus	Notes
Requests	Applications
Poems	Plays
TV/Radio/Movie scripts	Speeches
Monologues	Dialogues
Resumes/vita	Proposals
Lab reports	Story problems
Debates	Short stories
Telegrams	Editorials
Directions	Technical reports
Children's books	Case studies
Booklets	Cartoons/comic strips
Songs	Poster displays
Fact sheets	Definitions
Science fiction	Paraphrases
Commentaries	Fillers for newspapers
Newsletters	Job applications
Advertisements	Epitaphs
Interviews	Prophecies/predictions

Presented with such an array of choices, students may feel overwhelmed at first, but some careful modeling in the classroom can set the stage for their assuming more and more responsibility in the selection process. Let's return to the case of Jesse Thomas and use it as a basis for demonstrating how this process might work. Suppose that we have decided to view the Thomas incident from the perspective or role of a neighbor who had taken something from the heap of possessions and had it in our apartment when Jesse arrived on the scene. We're feeling guilty, especially after seeing Jesse collapse on the sidewalk. Whom might we talk to about this? We might choose to speak to another neighbor in the same building who did not see Jesse's reaction. What might be the mode we would use in this case? We could choose to develop a face to face conversation with the neighbor or we could use a phone call. We might choose not to speak to anyone; then what might be our choices for a mode—a diary? An internal monologue?

Selecting a mode does not mean all the choices are complete; within each mode may lurk still further possibilities. For example, if the writer decides to use the letter mode, then the selection process continues: will the letter be a business or friendly one? Decisions about mode often are linked to the writer's decision about role and audience and even purpose. Important also to the writer are the audience's expectations about the mode and how those will need to be taken into consideration as a part of the writing process.

Purpose

The identification of purpose in the prompt often requires us to look at this element in two ways. First is the overall *teaching* purpose of the assignment. What is our purpose as teachers in designing the writing experience? Are there certain skills we want students to develop? Are there content considerations that we want students to explore? Presumably we have spent time considering the answers to such questions before releasing the prompt to students.

From the student's perspective, the purpose consideration will be embedded in the prompt as a whole and will be attached to the decisions about all the elements of RAMPS. A number of key verbs appear in writing prompts to suggest purpose as well as the level of thinking required to complete the assignment. However, as teachers we often discover to our dismay that our students frequently have different expectations about what the verbs mean when writing becomes involved. Settling upon definitions of the key verbs with students prior to their responding to any of them will help make a prompt far more successful. Figure 1 below suggests how Benjamin Bloom's taxonomy of the cognitive domain (1956) can be adapted to remind us of the linkage between the levels of thinking and the writing actions called for in a prompt.

Figure 1

Level	Cue Words		Sample Writing Cues
KNOWLEDGE	Observe	Memorize	What do you see under the microscope?
	Repeat	Recall	Define amnesia
	Label	Recount	Recount the steps you followed
	Cluster	Outline	What were the major events in the story?
	Record	List	Record the changes in fluid levels.
COMPRE-HENSION	Locate	Report	Explain the... What does the graph mean?
	Identify	Review	What is happening in the story?
	Tell	Describe	
	Summarize/Paraphrase		

Figure 1 (cont.)

Level	Cue Words		Sample Writing Cues
APPLICATION	Select	Use	What might happen if... What other reasons might... How do you make... Imagine that you were...
	Show	Solve	
	How to Apply		
	Imagine	Dramatize	
	Imitate	Organize	
ANALYSIS	Examine	Compare/ Contrast	What did the writer mean? How would you answer... What elements are involved...
	Classify	Debate/Refute	
	Interpret	Differentiate	
SYNTHESIS	Plan	Construct	Make up... If this is all you had, how... Based on this situation, create...
	Design	Imagine	
	Create	Invent	
EVALUATION	Rank	Convince	Which choice would be most... Why would you select... How might the opposition... Decide which side you would...
	Judge	Decide	
	Argue	Persuade	
	Predict	Justify	

We need to remind ourselves, however, that when as teachers we construct a prompt, we are doing so for a teaching purpose. The student, though, gains his or her purpose from the full context of the writing situation which is presented in the prompt. Again, if we become the neighbor who stole something from Jesse Thomas's pile of belongings, the purpose of the communication may be to relieve the guilt, shift the attention to someone else, draw the neighbor into the plot—the possibilities are seemingly unlimited, once the prompt begins to develop. All of the possibilities, nevertheless, should relate back to the instructional purpose of the assignment. What do we want this piece of writing to accomplish for us? For the student? In this case, we want students to understand what influence perspective has on reporting events.

Situation

As we have said, no writing exists in a vacuum. Or another way of saying this is that all effective writing exists within a clear context, a context which RAMPS helps to define. Effective writing grows out of a sense of a particular time and place and exists within some kind of boundaries; if not, then the writing tends to wander in search of those boundaries, and we often hear the comment from readers, "What's the point of all of this?" The writer needs to decide what the context or situation for each piece of writing will be. This decision has to encompass all of the previous elements of RAMPS and bring them together into a well-defined situation.

> *Situation*
>
> You are a young kitchen boy at Valley Forge during the winter when Washington's troops wintered there; you are cold, starving, and very frightened (**ROLE**). Desperately homesick, you think of your parents (**AUDIENCE**) and decide to write a letter (**MODE**) to them, asking them to find a way to get you out of the war (**PURPOSE**).

To understand the importance of the RAMPS elements, and the information which those can provide to the writer, compare the writing prompt above with the following which students might encounter as the basis for an SAT writing sample:

> Consider carefully the following quotation and the assignment below it. Then plan and write your essay as directed.
>
> "Any advance involves some loss"
>
> *Assignment*
>
> Choose a specific example from personal experience, current events, or from your reading in history, literature, or other subjects and use this example as a basis for an essay in which you agree or disagree with the statement above. Be sure to be specific.

Analyzing the information provided in each of these prompts, we should be able to see a major difference in how clearly students will understand the situation that is being created. Let's return to the Valley Forge prompt; notice how each element focuses what we may or may not do in responding. Consider that the author is young, cold, starving, very frightened and homesick; he is in a particular location—Valley Forge—and time—winter. We might call this the "setting" for the writing. Note how the situation would change if the role called for a warm and well fed British soldier who is writing to his family back in England about the conditions in the colonies.

Now, look at the possible SAT writing prompt. What is the role of the writer? To whom are these remarks addressed? Why should the audience be interested in a response to the quotation? If students have had considerable experience with RAMPS, they actually can take this featureless prompt and probably turn out a fairly respectable piece of writing, but there will be a good amount of guesswork involved in the planning and execution of the writing which could have been avoided. Such prompts also present distinct problems in assessment because of the lack of clarity in the expectations for the writing. In fact, one of the reasons many students may have difficulty with the SAT writing sample might very well be traced to the design of the prompts. If more attention were paid to setting up a situation in which the writers could locate the boundaries and work accordingly, the writing samples might show a marked improvement. The same could be said for many of the prompts used in writing proficiency tests at the college level and on state writing assessments.

Occasionally questions arise concerning how long or detailed a writing prompt should be. The amount of information to be included in a prompt is something which needs to be considered carefully but in most instances a low information load in a prompt usually leads to little information in the student writers' responses. Compare the following in terms of how helpful they might be to writers:

Low information load:

Topic: Write about drugs in the schools

Moderate information load:

Topic: According to recent news reports, there has been a marked increase in incidents of drug use in public schools. Why, in your view, has there been an increase?

High Information load:

Topic: You are a member of an honor society in a school which has had a record increase in incidents of drug use. The principal has approached the honor society and requested that it offer suggestions as to how the school could deal with the problem. The president of the society has asked each member to come to the next meeting with a written plan suggesting what the major causes of the problem are and ways by which the council might help in solving it. What would be your suggested plan?

Some prompts can be highly specific, such as the one on Valley Forge, or they can be more open with options available to students. After students have become familiar with the elements of RAMPS in prompts, they can move easily into creating their own prompts, making the choices which will insure that all the RAMPS elements are present. Students working with the *Time* article on Jesse Thomas, for example, might receive this kind of prompt:

Situation

Select an individual who might have been aware of Jesse Thomas's difficulties.

Assume that individual's role and create a situation in which that person's views and actions related to the incident are revealed. You may select any audience, mode and purpose as long as they provide a clear perspective on the incident.

Designing the prompt, however, is only the beginning of creating an effective writing assignment. Even the best designed prompt will not work if the teacher has not also thought through the whole sequence which will move students from the task called for in the prompt to a sequence or process that naturally leads the student into writing. Failure to take this into consideration will only lead to confusion and frustration on the part of students. Compare how two versions of the same assignment could be handled and decide which one might lead to more effective writing and easier and more meaningful assessment:

Writing Prompt

Version 1

Please read the entire assignment before you begin to write.

We all feel angry sometimes and are tempted to react with violent words or actions against the person who angered us, even though we know violence is rarely the best way to resolve conflict. Violence is a real concern in the world and many people are trying to understand why so many choose to act violently, especially teenagers.

As you work through this assignment, follow the steps of the writing process. First, brainstorm and write as many details as you can think of for your topic. Then start to organize your ideas. Add important details; eliminate unimportant ones. Next write a rough draft. Skip spaces so that you have room to revise. If you use commas, review proper punctuation in your grammar book. When you have written a first draft, read it aloud to yourself, then to a friend. Make any changes you need to, check spelling and capitalization as well as punctuation, and be sure sentences are complete. Remember what you have learned about paragraphing and sentence types. On your final draft, be sure to leave large margins. Write on every line in the final draft.

As you write, imagine that you are talking to a psychiatrist who is doing research about teenagers and their problems. Your conversation will help the psychiatrist better understand how teenagers feel about violence. This assignment will require several days in class. Take your time and work carefully. As you complete the steps, check them off on this paper. Do your best work.

* * *

Version 2

Read the entire assignment before beginning to write.

Background: We all feel angry sometimes and are tempted to react with violent words or actions against the person who angered us. We do this even though we know violence is rarely the best way to resolve conflicts. Violence is a real concern in the world and many people are trying to understand why so many choose to act violently, especially teenagers.

Role/Situation/Purpose: Imagine that you have been selected to appear on a television show with other young people to discuss violence. Think of a time in your life when you allowed yourself to react violently with words or actions.

- What caused the violent reaction?
- What did you say or do?
- What was the result of your loss of control?
- What might have been some other, more effective ways to deal with the conflict?

Mode/Audience: You know that the show's host will ask you questions about this incident. Develop a question/answer written format about what you anticipate you might be asked and what you might say in this situation. Remember that your audience will be the host, members of the studio audience, and a larger, unseen audience of television viewers, all of whom probably know nothing about your situation.

Hints on How to Proceed:

In your writing process, you may want to try the following:

1. Brainstorm all the details you can remember about the incident. (Do a talk/write with a partner to make the details come easier).
2. Decide how you want to organize your information; do you want to start from the beginning or start at the end and then show how you arrived at the action by retracing your steps. Design the host's questions to match your organization.
3. Try a rough draft; write yourself out, getting down as much detail as you can. Remember that you are talking to audiences unfamiliar with your situation.
4. Test your rough draft on a classmate. Ask your classmate to imagine he or she is in the television audience. What questions might the audience have? What might they want to know more about, less about? How would you respond? Take notes as your classmate makes suggestions.
5. Revise your draft, following the suggestions made by your classmate if you believe they will strengthen the piece; add or change other parts as well based upon your own assessment of their effectiveness.
6. Check your draft once more with your classmate; any additions or deletions?
7. Polish the draft and submit it when you are satisfied.

* * *

The writing prompt should become an integral part of an overall writing assignment which takes into consideration the prewriting that needs to be done, the actual writing activity which will occur, the sharing or responding among students and perhaps the teacher during the process, the options for rewriting, revising and editing, and ultimately, how the writing will be assessed. Actually developing an effective writing assignment is not as easy as it may seem and many teachers do not analyze their writing prompts to determine just what students will need to do in order to produce an effective piece of writing. Often a prompt can call for rather extensive preparation. Consider the following:

> In one segment of the television show "60 Minutes," Andy Rooney, a CBS commentator, talked about the words advertisers use. He reported that the ten most commonly used words were the following:
>
> 1. New
> 2. Natural
> 3. Light
> 4. Save
> 5. Free
> 6. Rich
> 7. Real
> 8. Fresh
> 9. Extra
> 10. Discover/Discovered
>
> These words appear most frequently because they connect the product being advertised with values that are important to us. Locate examples of advertisements using some or all of these words. Based upon what you find in the advertisements and your own associations with the words, explain the values that these words suggest in a well organized essay to someone who believes that the impact of advertising is greatly overrated.

At first glance, this seems like a simple, straightforward prompt. But let's consider what students will need to do just in the prewriting phase. First, they have to locate advertisements containing examples of the ten words (access to the right materials, therefore, becomes an issue). Then students must have some idea of how to "read" the advertisements; for example, students might need to know how to turn the statement of the problem into a question: What are the values these words suggest? There is, of course, an inherent assumption in this prompt that students already have some sense of what the term "values" means. If they do not, then some explanation and discussion would be in order prior to their tackling the prompt.

Next students would need to identify some possible connotations for the words and to check those connotations against the advertisements and their own experience. Following this, they would need to do some categorizing, grouping words which share common meanings. This, then, is to be followed by a determination of the cultural values implied in each grouping. From this analysis, the writers would then need to decide upon a plan for writing the essay in such a way as to provide evidence from the advertisements which indicates the values being promoted; and, of course, students must remember that the essay is being addressed to someone who does not believe advertising has any impact on people. Teachers should try their own prompts and writing assignments prior to giving them to students. Doing so will quickly highlight areas which may be unclear, or which require skills or knowledge that students may not have or where more time than originally anticipated will be needed.

Often when introducing students to the concept of RAMPS, teachers may prefer to use a writing assignment which includes "controlled data"; that is, the basic information needed to complete the assignment is presented to the student. The emphasis then falls upon the skill of the student in using the data effectively in a written mode. Here is a sample of such an assignment:

> You and your neighbors are planning a yard sale. You will need to solve several problems to make sure the yard sale is successful. Here's a suggested plan of action:

1. You survey your neighborhood and collect the following information:

People participating	*No. of objects to be sold*	*Space needed*
Your family	10	30 sq. ft.
Browns	15	35 sq. ft.
Livermores	7	10 sq. ft.
Jacksons	13	20 sq. ft.
Parsons	12	18 sq. ft.

2. You call the rental store and find out that they rent tables measuring 6' x 2 1/2' for $6.00 a day. How many tables will you need for the yard sale? How do you know?
3. The yard you are planning to use measures 20' x 30'. *Draw* a diagram of the placement of the tables in the yard. Be sure to allow about 4 feet of space around the tables for movement of customers.
4. You call the local newspaper and find that the cost of advertising in the local newspaper is $13.50 for the first ten words and $1.00 per word after that. *Write* an advertisement describing the neighborhood yard sale. Be sure you include the details that customers will need to know. The items to be sold are all kitchen and garden utensils. How much will your ad cost?
5. Your neighbors are waiting to hear what your plan is and how much it will cost. Prepare a short oral presentation for them, being certain to anticipate as many of their questions as possible and provide the answers in your presentation. Develop an outline or a series of notes to follow as you give your presentation.

* * *

Setting the stage for effective assessment in writing depends upon the identification and development of appropriate performance tasks. Using the approach we have just described, teachers in all content areas can develop tasks that engage students in continued learning while also providing evidence of students' skills and understanding.

Works Cited

Applebee, Arthur N., and others. 1981. *Writing in the secondary school: English and the content areas.* Urbana, Illinois: National Council of Teachers of English.

Bloom, Benjamin. 1956. *Taxonomy of education objectives: Cognitive domain.* New York: David McKay.

Britton, James, and others. 1975. *The development of writing abilities (11–18).* London: Macmillan Education Ltd. for the Schools Council.

Marshall, Stephanie Pace. 1992. Foreword. In *A practical guide to alternative assessment,* Joan A. Herman and others, v–vi. Alexandria, VA: Association for Supervision and Curriculum Development.

Moffett, James. 1992. *Active voice: A writing program across the curriculum.* 2d ed. Portsmouth, NH: Boynton Cook Publishers Heinemann.

Chapter 3

Student Writing: Response as Assessment

Charles R. Duke

Most content area teachers will acknowledge that the kinds of informal writing to learn strategies addressed in chapter 1 can elicit useful information about student learning while also providing students with opportunities to engage in critical thinking and in learning how to express themselves in both oral and written discourse. Content area teachers also will acknowledge that designing an effective writing assignment is a major step toward helping students focus their writing and connect it with their learning. However, when the time comes to respond to student writing and move towards more formal assessment, many content area teachers show far less confidence because they have, quite frankly, had little training in this aspect of writing instruction. What should be remembered, however, is that all of the time and effort put into engaging students with various content through writing provides performance indicators and authentic assessments of student learning. In an age of accountability, we need such evidence.

Peer Response

A number of teachers have discovered that students themselves can handle a good amount of the early response to writing, relieving the teacher of having always to wade through rough drafts, searching for some kind of understanding of what the writer wanted to say or even understood. Instead of asking students to wait until a final grade is placed on a paper, which frequently is nothing more than an initial draft of an assignment, teachers have discovered that having students assume the responsibility for responding to each other's writing can improve student writing and creates a sense of audience which tends to motivate students to put more effort into their written communication. It also puts the student in a position to demonstrate authentic performance of a wide variety of skills even as the writing is being developed. The informal writing strategies which have been suggested previously offer a means for laying the foundation in the class for talk about writing as well as performance of writing tasks and this is fundamental to eliciting effective peer response.

Students, understandably, may find this talk about writing a new experience. Most of them have had little opportunity to obtain helpful responses to their ideas or material prior to writing a lab report or an essay on a historical event; perhaps even fewer students have had the experience of talking to a peer about writing. As a result, teachers should not expect instantaneous results when moving to peer response. In fact, before encouraging students to talk to each other about their writing, teachers may want to model such discussion in class, perhaps using some of their own writing or working with a student who is comfortable with his or her writing and who is comfortable in front of a group.

Initial talk/write sessions should remain brief, no more than five minutes or so for each student during the early stages of writing. While such conversations are occurring, teachers need to move around the room unobtrusively, listening to the talk, prodding a little, suggesting and encouraging but maintaining an air of relaxation and informality. Partner dialogues work well, since it is easier to focus on one response than multiple ones. Initially, students can talk to each other , taking turns telling their partners about what they hope to write. The next stage may be to respond to that initial effort. Since students often will say they have no idea what to say about someone else's writing, providing them with a few simple prompts such as the following is helpful:

For the listener/reader:

1. What is the writer trying to say—repeat or summarize the main points as you understand them back to the writer;
2. What details or examples seem clearest and help you the most as a reader/listener understand what the writer is trying to tell you?
3. What is not clear to you or what additional information would you like to have as a reader?

For the writer:

1. As your partner responds, try not to be defensive about your writing; listen carefully to what your partner tells you; do not settle, though, for general comments such as "I like it," or "it's okay, I guess." Ask your partner for specifics—what sections were clearest? Why did you think that was the main point?
2. Take notes about your partner's response so you will have them to remind you of what needs to be worked on in your next draft.

Partner dialogues should occur frequently but always in short spans of time so students do not feel intimidated by the process. Partners should be varied from time to time to help students understand that people's perspectives and needs are different and that we seldom write exclusively for one person. Eventually students may seek writing partners of their own both in and out of the classroom after they begin to experience the advantages such assistance can bring. Teachers can monitor how different duos work together and make adjustments as necessary. Often teachers are concerned about the time that such response takes in class, but students actually are learning and re-learning information and coming to understand different perspectives on a topic. Valuable learning can be demonstrated through these exchanges in ways that otherwise might never occur in the classroom if the teacher remains the sole source of information and response. The time is well spent.

Teachers need to provide feedback to students about their performance in these exchanges; useful comments can be repeated for the whole class to hear; examples from exchanges can be placed on the board and discussed for their effectiveness. Students themselves can be encouraged to offer feedback on what they learned from each other and how they might improve their performance next time.

Peer group response follows partner response. Like the one-on-one situations, group response can be intimidating at first for students. For this reason, early peer response sessions need to be carefully structured to alleviate some of the traditional problems encountered with group work. (For a practical use of writing to uncover and assess problems in use of groups in the classroom, see Chapter 8.) Initial experience in peer group response should emphasize active listening and oral response. Students do not begin by trying to offer critical evaluations of each other's work; instead, they continue to provide the listener response in terms only of what they think they heard from the writer. Each student has an opportunity to play the role of listener/responder as well as reader/writer. Peer group response works especially well once students have an initial full draft of their writing completed.

Teachers will need to decide how they want to handle the identification of peer response groups. Some teachers like to keep the groups together for several assignments so students gain confidence and trust in each other's responses; other teachers prefer to mix peer group assignments so the entire class gets to work together at various times in groups, offering a much wider sense of audience. Sometimes group membership can be identified by interest, ability, or location; other times, the traditional "numbering off" suffices. Overall, for purposes of freshness and variety, a combination of approaches usually works best and the teacher's judgment usually is the best barometer of how a certain group will work together.

Oral response and group work tend to make classrooms noisy and teachers have to determine what their tolerance level is. However, keeping group size to no more than five and actively monitoring the volume usually will keep the noise and confusion to a minimum. Students quickly learn how to speak distinctly enough to be heard within their groups. After a few times, students serve as their own monitors and can remain surprisingly well focused on their tasks.

The teacher's role in working with peer response groups is to remain unobtrusive. As much as possible, groups need to accept their responsibilities and carry them through. Teachers should avoid staying with any one group very long or the locus of control will shift from the group to the teacher and the advantage of peer response will be lost. An effective strategy for the teacher is to move around the room quietly, stopping beside a group to listen to the interaction to determine how the group is working; if necessary, the teacher can make a brief comment, raise a question that directs the group's attention to its task or suggest an alternative approach to addressing a writing problem and then move on before the group starts looking for answers from the teacher. Circulating in this manner allows teachers to monitor all groups, and make mental or even written notes about how students are working together, including which individuals seem to be having difficulties. These observations from several class meetings help teachers make decisions about what may be the most effective ways to use peer group response.

A sequence such as the following, which is really just an extension of the original pair response strategy for first drafts, works well when first introducing students to peer group response, since there will need to be an understanding of both roles and process. Size of the group may need to be addressed based on the length of students' writing and the time allotted. The process also will go much better if copies of each student's paper can be made available to each group member. With the advent of copiers, not to mention personal computer printers at home or in labs, getting four copies for each group should not be insurmountable.

Seeking Response

Writer of the Paper

1. Avoid any preliminary apologies and talk *about* your paper.
2. Read your paper aloud to the group, taking your time and speaking loudly and clearly enough for only the group to hear.
3. Pause for a moment after your reading is completed; do not say anything. The silence is good reflecting time for your audience.
4. If there is time, reread the paper aloud, remembering not to rush. (The teacher can determine if there is time for this step).
5. Listen carefully to the responses from your group; make notes on your paper as they talk; do not take time to provide lengthy explanations if your group raises questions. Your role is to find out what works and does not work for your group.

Listeners

1. Listen carefully to the reading; after the first reading, jot down words, phrases and sentences that linger in your mind; these may be items that made the listening enjoyable and clearer to you; they should also include those which confused you or did not strike you as being as effective.
2. If there is a second reading, listen carefully and add to the list you developed in step 1.
3. After the reading is completed, group members should take turns doing the following:
   a. Tell quickly what seem to be the main points: specific events, facts, people, etc. (Don't hesitate to repeat a point someone else makes but try to mention some new ones as well).
   b. Summarize the main idea of the piece in one sentence with each group member offering a version.
   c. Identify one thing about the piece you liked, found useful, interesting, etc., and one thing that was unclear to you or about which you needed more information or detail.

Note: everyone needs to have time to share his or her writing with the group and get response; if time is still available after initial readings and responses from everyone in the group, take turns as authors asking the group for more feedback on specific parts of your writing.

Ultimately, the teacher may wish to move from the initial experiences with oral response toward written response from peers, providing students with additional responsibility for displaying their learning and contributing to the learning of others. Modeling this process is critical to its success, since students' initial written comments often parallel those offered at the initial stages of partner or peer group response: "You need more detail"; "nice job." Such comments are of little use to writers when they are struggling to improve a draft. To underline the importance of fully detailed responses, teachers will find it helpful not only to model comments by taking a sample paper and working through it with the class to determine appropriate responses but also to collect students' written responses to each other's papers. A way to facilitate this process is simply to make sure each writer receives written comments, attempts to revise the paper in response to the comments and then passes the paper in to the teacher with the peer written responses attached. These responses should be skimmed and where appropriate, the teacher can make notations to draw the responder's attention to useful and not so useful comments. These early responses will probably need some kind of assessment such as the following system which can be incorporated easily into a class participation grade if that seems appropriate:

v+ = writer will find these comments very helpful
v = you have the right idea; try to be more detailed next time; see my comments.
v– = writers will find it difficult to use your response because it says so little—see comments and try to be more helpful next time.

As a guide for peer written response, questions such as the following, which parallel what students have become familiar with in oral response, usually promote useful assessments and can be adapted easily, depending upon the purpose of the writing, the content, and the format. At the beginning, when students are just becoming accustomed to their roles as responders, and writers are being prepared to receive written comments, a good practice is to assign different students different questions and ask them to read all pieces for just one question; in this way, the student is not overwhelmed and can read for one particular aspect of writing, and the writer receives multiple responses to each question. These multiple responses also help to remind the writer that not all readers read or respond alike to a text.

1. What is the main idea, finding, issue, etc., the writer is trying to explain?

   Write the main idea, finding, or issue in one sentence and then identify several places in the piece of writing where you think the writer has made this unusually clear; if you're unable to identify any place where it appears, briefly explain to the writer why this is so and suggest how the writer might solve this problem.

2. What is the pattern of organization?

   The writer may have used one or more ways to organize the material; decide how effective the organization is for you as a reader and cite some specific parts of the piece that help to explain your response to the writer. If you are unable to determine how the writer intended to organize the material, say so and suggest ways the writer might address the problem.

3. What details, facts, examples or events used in the piece are effective?

   Select several good items and explain briefly to the writer why you found these to help you as a reader; if you feel the piece would be stronger with more evidence, point out several places to the writer where as a reader you think more would be helpful. If you feel too much evidence is presented, let the writer know this as well and offer specific examples of what might be omitted.

4. To what extent does the piece give you a clear sense of a beginning, middle, and end?

   Comment on the strengths and weaknesses in the piece's structure; suggest ways for improvement if appropriate. Pinpoint specific areas for the writer so he or she can understand your response as a reader.

Feedback from the teacher helps motivate students to produce higher quality work; feedback from their peers works even better. Not infrequently, teachers will ask students to assess the usefulness of their peers' written comments and then share their assessment with the responders.

Students will need time to become accustomed to this kind of group work. Since many students may not have had opportunities to work together and because they often are unaccustomed to accepting responsibility for each other's work, the teacher will need to be most encouraging and patient at the beginning. The use of frequent short, informal writing in the classroom helps students understand the role writing plays in thinking. If students become comfortable with and more fluent in the uses of writing, they can make the transition into peer response far more easily and quickly.

Occasionally the routine can be varied. For example, some teachers like to put students in a big circle with their drafts. Each student gets a fine tip colored marker. Students begin by passing their drafts to the person on the right. The teacher also has a draft and sits in the circle and participates. Each person is to take the new draft and underline or circle one thing he or she liked or that was effective and put a star next to it. Everyone reads as quickly as possible, marking the draft and then passing it on to the next person. If time permits, students can periodically stop and take turns commenting on a particularly effective word or piece of information; then the process can resume. By the end of the period, everyone—including the teacher—has read all the drafts. Students who have experienced this process frequently report that they get so many ideas from this kind of reading that they can hardly wait to get their own drafts back and go to work on them.

Eventually most students come to accept the group response model as a natural part of classroom activity, and teachers may not have to do more than simply announce peer groups are meeting on a certain day and students will divide themselves into groups and get on with the tasks of responding to each other's writing. Perhaps the most important outcome of both partner dialogues and peer group response is that through the reading of each other's papers and hearing each other's comments about them is the stimulation of individual thought and understanding which becomes an important contribution to the information each student takes away for subsequent reflection and revision. But perhaps even more important is the confidence the writer gains. As a consequence, the writer looks upon the group as a valuable resource because they offer help while also still acknowledging strengths. When each student in a group experiences this, the group work just takes off and reduces the teacher's workload greatly.

One issue that usually causes teachers to pause when considering the expanded use of writing in the classroom is, again, time. The emphasis upon coverage of content, the high stakes accountability now present in many districts, and the myriad other responsibilities teachers have been asked to assume are often cited as reasons why more writing is not done in content area classrooms. A careful review, however, of what occurs during the kinds of writing activity being emphasized in this book will suggest that the time spent on writing can be most helpful in learning content. When students engage in peer review, they are talking about content and providing authentic assessment opportunities of both their thinking and speaking skills. They are checking their knowledge, identifying gaps in thinking and understanding that can be corrected, helping each other learn to use the language of the content area accurately and effectively, and having the importance of knowledge being reinforced for them on a daily basis. Teachers who use writing on a consistent basis report that their class discussions are richer, that students are more thoughtful in their responses, and that retention of information improves. Teachers also need to recognize that responding does not have to occur all in one day or consecutive days; it can be woven into a week or two as time and schedules permit.

The Teacher's Response

Using peer response is an effective strategy for providing students with early feedback on their writing. Such response can occur with multiple drafts of a piece, with each response session—peer or group—focusing on a specific element of the assignment, but eventually, of course, the teacher also has to respond. A teacher has many ways for responding to a piece of writing and in most cases the appropriate response is dictated by the nature of the assignment and its purpose. At times, focusing only on content may be appropriate; other times, attention to structure and expression will be the focus and, ultimately, the whole context of writing, the integration of knowledge and expression, will become a focus for the response.

One of the reasons teachers shy away from requiring writing in the content areas is that they believe they have to respond to everything on a paper. If, on the other hand, they can view writing as a process and that perhaps in each assignment the focus can be on only one or two key aspects of the assignment, then the task does not need to seem so large or overwhelming. Careful assessment of where students are in their writing abilities, how writing connects with what is being taught, and what the goals for learning are in a particular unit or lesson leads to careful selection of what method and the amount of response which may be needed.

Conferencing

Talking with students about their writing is often overlooked as a useful means for assessing their growth as learners while also contributing to helping students improve their drafts. Unlike the college instructor who has the flexibility to schedule office hours—and has a place to hold them outside the classroom—the typical middle school or secondary school teacher has to figure out a way to dialogue with students about their writing but in short spans of time and usually within the classroom. Conferencing with students, therefore, has to remain flexible.

Some teachers have found it helpful to schedule in-class days for students to work on drafts, either in small groups or individually. At the beginning of the class, students are invited to put their names on the chalkboard if they wish to talk to the teacher about a specific problem or area in their papers. They have to understand that they will have, at best, about 2-5 minutes in which to identify the problem and get some feedback. Having students focus the conference agenda gives them an opportunity to begin to develop assessment skills of their own—what is blocking me from moving ahead with this piece, what idea or concept do I not understand, what sentence structure or word choice problems do I have? Such conferences should be kept focused on one area; if a student has multiple problems, deal with one and then suggest the student work on that and perhaps schedule time after school or during study hall to work on the others. Having the student come to the conference—usually held at the teacher's desk but it could occur at the student's seat—focused on a particular issue speeds the process greatly. Although teachers express concern about not having had an opportunity to view a paper before addressing a problem, usually the problem is sufficiently clear that advance reading is not necessary and, of course, having the student articulate the difficulty is part of reinforcing an important learning process. If the teacher always assumes the responsibility for analyzing the paper, students will never learn how to do this.

A key principle to keep in mind when responding to student writing during conferences is not to address everything that needs attention. For example, if the major problem of a student's paper is that it does not address the assignment, then spending time correcting spelling and grammatical errors will be wasted for everyone; the whole paper may shift once the focus is found and sentences and words previously used very often are replaced by new choices. One way for a teacher to remain focused on this progression is to keep several key questions in mind when responding to writing. Almost all problems that students will encounter as writers will be encompassed in one or more of the following questions and they are designed to suggest a general order of review from the more global to the more specific when looking at a piece of writing. Usually one question is enough to consider at a time. Begin, whenever possible, though, with the student's question.

1. What has the writer promised to do in this draft? Does the writer fulfill the promise? Consider the assignment; does the writer understand what was to be done?
2. How effectively has the writer organized ideas and evidence?
3. What key details or pieces of information has the writer placed in the draft to increase the reader's understanding of the subject? Is there enough evidence?
4. How effectively does the writer control the subject through appropriate use of paragraphs?
5. How effectively does the writer control sentence construction and use?
6. How well does the writer have language use under control?
7. How well does the writer handle the mechanics of expression and the appearance of the draft?

These questions are generic. Specific assignments may call for attention to aspects unique to the assignment. For example, perhaps the student has been asked to respond to the following prompt:

> Write a letter to a friend who has moved away from your area and who has indicated to you in a recent e-mail that she is going to take up smoking because it is something that everyone seems to be doing. Try to persuade your friend not to begin smoking. Give at least four reasons for

your position and offer details to explain each reason. Refer to our class discussion of the dangers of smoking and also the hand-outs from our guest speaker. Chapter 4 in your health book has some useful information as well. Be sure to sign your letter with your own name.

Peer response questions for such a highly focused assignment can also form the basis for a conference although the teacher may need to address only one question in talking with the student:

1. How do I know the writer has taken a clear position on the issue? Can I identify places in the paper which show this? If I cannot find a clear position, how can I explain to the writer what is causing the problem for me as a reader?
2. What are the four reasons the writer offers? Which of these do I find as a reader most persuasive? Why?
3. What evidence do I think is especially effective? What evidence might be stronger? Explain.

Whatever the set of response questions may be (and students even can generate these as a whole class), students should have access to the questions from the beginning and be encouraged to use them as a kind of self-assessment when working with a piece of writing. When students know in advance that these questions will form the foundation of any response to their writing, they will tend to anticipate how those questions might be answered in reference to a particular piece of writing and take pains to try to have all of the questions answered as positively as possible. Again, modeling the use of the questions with a sample of writing taken from a prior class helps illustrate how the questions can be applied.

A few techniques for interacting with students about their writing texts will prove useful in keeping the conference centered on the student and the writing. **Focusing** statements at the start of a conference let the student know what is going to happen: "You've said you're having trouble with your introduction, let's look at that and see if we can get you moving again." Such comments offer a clear sense of structure, reassure the student that the conference is not going to address everything at one time, and give both the teacher and student a specific task to address. Avoided is the rambling monologue from student or teacher about everything but the main problem. From time to time, as a conference proceeds, the student may need some help in seeing what is being said or should be said in the paper; these efforts are called **clarification** such as in the comment: "Ah, you mean that when these two compounds are mixed, this..." Without resorting to technical language, the teacher helps the student clarify thinking, perhaps discovering new language or ways to structure an explanation.

Students, understandably, may be very reluctant to talk about their writing at first. Many of them may not have had much success with writing and as a result have rather poor self-images of themselves as writers. Another reason is that writing is a kind of self-identity; it is, after all, a manifestation of yourself and no one likes having someone else point out your shortcomings. Careful attention to erasing this poor self-concept is critical if conferencing is going to work, so teachers should not try to solve all problems in one conference or one series of comments. Building self-esteem in the student writer takes time, but once students have confidence in their ability to express themselves, their work and attitude often show improvement.

During conversations with students, then, attempts can be made to use **acceptance** words that reflect agreement, along with comprehension of what is being said without expressing any value judgments. Simple responses such as "I see," or "yes" as students struggle to articulate their thoughts help to set a positive mood. **Reassuring** responses such as "I always have trouble with that part of the calculation myself" or "The same thing happened to me when I first tried to . . ." communicate to student writers that they are not alone in their efforts to make meaning.

Fundamental to establishing a positive climate in conferencing is to avoid the dogmatic. Students are accustomed to being told what to do; if a teacher proceeds to tell the student exactly what to do in a draft, including the wording which should be used, the facts to be offered, and the structure to be followed—a kind of recipe, if you will—then time spent conferencing is wasted. The goal of writing conferences is to help students reach the point where they are comfortable talking about their writing and where they become willing to accept responsibility for examining it on their own, in and out of the classroom. For this reason, the **non-directive lead** is a helpful device. The simplest leads are often the most effective: "What seems to be giving you the most difficulty?" What might be another way you could say this?" "What do you think your reader needs to know about this subject" The questions should be open-ended as much as possible so students will be encouraged to accept responsibility for discussing their efforts. Writers need to think for themselves. The sooner students come to accept this idea, the better the results will be in their writing and in conferences.

Class management during conferencing can become an issue unless advance planning occurs. Rather than staying at the desk in the front of the room, many teachers choose to stake out a position in the center where they can monitor groups who are working while conferences are taking place. Students who are not conferencing will need meaningful tasks to keep them engaged. Placing one or two tasks on the chalkboard for everyone to address helps students focus on their own writing and not upon the student who is involved in a conference. For example, students might be asked to read each other's drafts to determine "why has the writer in Germany written to his sister in America?" Or it might be a series of mechanics tasks: "Check for paragraph divisions. Check for run-ons and fragments. Let's have the mechanical problems in your draft taken care of by the end of the period."

The writing conference functions as a part of the writing process; conferences can be held where the sole focus is on discovering an idea about which to write, and conferences can be held as many times as necessary to aid during the writing and revising stages of the process. In the best of situations, the student should feel the teacher is an ally, not an opponent, during the entire writing process and the conference becomes the common meeting ground.

Knowing Where You Are Going

One of the most common complaints from students about the writing they are asked to do in school is that they do not know where they are going; that is, they have no clear sense of the expectations surrounding their completion of a writing assignment. As was addressed in chapter 2, developing effective assignments is key to obtaining successful writing from students. An assignment which lays out the parameters, provides guideposts for development along the way, and offers reasonable levels of support during the writing process will go a long way toward enhancing students' attitudes about writing.

Part of this knowing where you are going, though, is tied directly to knowing how the product will be evaluated; that is, what are the criteria for success? For example, students may be writing microthemes (see Chapter 1). These short pieces of writing, often but not always completed in class, may not withstand the same kind of scrutiny as a formal research paper that has gone through multiple stages and drafts over several weeks, but most teachers will want to evaluate students' products. Criteria for success on such assignments need not be complex but they need to be clear, and if students participate in setting the standards, few questions should arise. So, for microthemes, especially those which students are given time to revise and polish, the teacher working with students might develop a rubric—categories for assessment—such as the following adapted from Bean (1996):

6/5 Writing at this level shows a clear understanding of the concept and presents a fully developed explanation which is appropriate for the intended audience; examples, details, and factual information show the writer is in control of the subject. A "6" will be well organized, and have very few, if any, spelling, grammar or punctuation/capitalization errors. A "5" will have a good understanding of the concept and will address the intended audience appropriately but will not have quite as much development as a "6" and may also contain a few errors in fact as well as in writing.

4/3 Writing at this level shows that the writer probably understands the concept but lacks clarity and a fully developed explanation for the intended audience. Details and examples are generalized and minor factual errors may be present. Difficulties with organization may occur, and spelling, sentence structure and punctuation/capitalization errors are more evident.

2/1 Writing at this level reveals that the writer does not understand the concept to be addressed and has paid little attention to the needs of the intended audience. The writing lacks detail and appropriate examples and reveals difficulty with organization, sentence structure, spelling, and punctuation and capitalization. In fact, readers may have considerable problems determining what the writer knows.

Note: writing which shows the writer does not understand the topic even though the writing is otherwise well done should be placed at this level as well.

This rubric is a **holistic** one; that is, it calls for an overall impression of the writing performance and does not assign specific values to any one aspect of the written product. Such a rubric provides students and the teacher with a good reference point for discussion about student performance. Splitting levels, such as 2/1, offers the teacher some leeway in being able to acknowledge certain aspects of a paper may be slightly better or slightly weaker, justifying the higher or the lower ranking. In some cases, teachers may wish to make the rubric much more assignment specific, dropping in specific subject matter points or areas which students will be expected to cover, perhaps identifying a particular organizational structure that must be followed, and expect more attention to audience and purpose. (See chapter 5 for an example of this kind of rubric).

Teachers who choose to use rubrics such as the one above are well advised to spend time with their students familiarizing them with the different levels of expectation. One of the best ways to do this is to take samples of writing from previous classes and ask students to read them and "score" them according to the levels; following this, a class should engage in discussion about the features of the papers and why a certain score was assigned. After such discussions and consensus building, students then feel more comfortable in approaching similar writing; in fact, most of them will do a self-scoring before submitting their writing, and teachers may want to ask for such self-assessments as part of the process for helping students assume more responsibility for determining the quality of their work.

Rubrics are not overly difficult to develop, but they are of inestimable value in helping students know where they are going. The **holistic** rubric, such as the previous one, is intended to address all aspects of writing, giving an overall impression of the writer's ability to produce an effective piece of writing without isolating specific aspects of the writing or weighting one aspect more than another. In writing which tends to be informal and often written under timed circumstances, the holistic approach is useful. In fact, most district and state-wide writing assessments use some form of holistic scoring when assessing student writing samples; the same can be said for college placement or proficiency exams. For this reason, students should have experience with holistic assessment of their work and participate in the development of the rubrics so they can understand the differences in categories. Before a **generic** rubric is used; that is, one which attempts to cover a variety of writing assignments, the teacher always should check to make sure that it does, indeed, encompass the elements of a particular writing assignment.

Analytical rubrics focus upon key aspects of the writing and/or the content and each part of the piece of writing is described at different levels of performance. By doing this, the teacher can focus on specific aspects of the writing which are working well and others with which the student is experiencing difficulty. For the teacher who wants to develop analytical rubrics, attention must be paid to all of the individual elements which the teacher believes are critical for success. Working from actual student papers and involving students, once again, in the development of the rubric, especially with the language used to describe the categories, will help students understand the criteria better. Some schools or departments have taken state-wide assessments and developed generic analytical rubrics for use with students in efforts to help them understand what the expectations are for such assessment; this effort or others which focus students' attention on the elements of good writing in any situation as well as in a content area can only lead to improved student performance on writing. For example, below is a sample of how an analytical rubric might address two key aspects of writing for any assignment. For a more fully developed example of the analytical rubric and how students can be involved in its development, see Chapter 4.

Content

SCORE 6/5:
- Shows sophisticated thinking/ideas
- Provides well developed examples and explanations related to topic and purpose

- Selects information appropriate for audience and purpose

SCORE 4/3:
- Presents ideas somewhat lacking in sophistication
- Provides examples and details related to topic but they may be uneven in development
- Selects information appropriate for audience and purpose

SCORE 2/1:
- Presents under-developed and unsophisticated ideas
- Provides examples and details as listings without development and not always relevant to topic and purpose
- Shows little awareness of audience's needs

Organization

SCORE 6/5:
- Maintains a logical order/sequence
- Focuses on one subject each paragraph
- Provides logical transitions within sentences and between paragraphs
- Offers a clear introduction and conclusion that frame the topic under discussion

SCORE 4/3:
- Maintains a reasonably logical order/sequence
- Focuses most of the time on one subject within each paragraph
- Provides transitions within sentences and between paragraphs but not always consistent in their use
- Offers an introduction and conclusion but without much clarity or originality

SCORE 2/1:
- Displays inconsistent order/sequence
- Exhibits difficulty in maintaining focus on one idea in each paragraph
- Shows inconsistency in use of transitions within sentences and between paragraphs
- Offers little in the way of a controlled introduction or conclusion

These examples are taken from a state-wide holistic assessment used in Pennsylvania. They were derived from features that were encompassed in a holistic assessment, but which schools wanted to separate so student performance on each could be more clearly identified and addressed. The scale was used for simplicity purposes, but other variations are possible or more specific descriptions encompassing levels of performance from 6 to 1 might be used. Such a scale is, of course, generic, and most teachers have found that they prefer to construct holistic or analytical rubrics keyed to specific assignments. Translation of the score points into a traditional grading scheme is not difficult, and additional weight can be given to some categories if appropriate (see chapters 4 and 5). Extensive rubrics should not be used unless students have ample time to go through the entire writing process which permits them time to research and develop a topic, seek feedback from peers and teachers during the drafting process, and have an opportunity to apply the rubric themselves to self-assess their efforts prior to submitting a paper for formal grading.

Responding in Writing

The jokes about English teachers lugging home bulging briefcases of papers to be "corrected" while their colleagues in math or some other subject area walk out swinging an empty thermos bottle are plentiful. In fact, nothing intimidates content teachers more than the image of papers piling up in stack after stack which have to be read and graded. How many times have students received papers back only to find a letter or number grade at the top and cryptic comments such as "well done" or "poor work" pencilled—usually in red—at the top or the end of the paper? And how much unnecessary frustration does this stimulate among students? What was well done? The student could study the paper for hours and still not know; or what was poor work? Again, without any further notations on the paper, the student will be hard pressed to know what needs to be improved. And, what's even worse is that the teacher may not be able to recall the original reasons for the grade because the paper offers no evidence of that thought process.

If we want students to take writing seriously, if we want them to develop good writing habits, and if we want them to continue to write in content fields, then we need to make sure our response is more than a word or two or a grade at the top of the page. Does it take time to respond to students' papers—indeed, it does. Will students pay attention to the response? Yes, if it is evident that the teacher read the paper carefully and has given some thought as to how the student might improve the next draft or use better writing skills on the next assignment. Every teacher has developed shortcuts in the responding process. But regardless of the approach, the key to successful response is focusing the comments, placing responsibility back on the writer to make appropriate adjustments, and leaving students with the sense that they can do well with writing.

The use of scoring rubrics can help both teacher and student immensely because they provide a common denominator for assessing the paper. The language of the rubric then can be incorporated into teacher comments, and this enables students to begin to place their work on the rubric to determine where they need to go to improve. Consider the following piece of writing, done by an eighth grader, after being asked to identify some famous person whom he admired and tell why he admired the individual.

> Danal Boon because of his braver and he talent aa woods man and of a guide. He is know for his braver in the face of dancer and of his curge in the face of discress.
>
> He loast 2 sons and yet cept going to bigger and better things. His life is one of history and of his love of the out doors and beccus he liked to be alone as much as possible. And to go his one way when he wanted to.
>
> He was marred to a woman at 20 years old and hat 6 or 7 children yet he cept moving west. He opeaned the gate to the west you mite say.
>
> He was a man of curge becaus of his noled of the Indians and of there way. He made peace with some and war with outers yet he lived to be a great man and a famase one to.
>
> He lost everthing and yet reganed it in the end. He lived on his land until he was 63 I think then he went to vist ge relitive and distusts.
>
> He was bured and the dug up and moved to a knew spot and there he layes till this day.

Initial response to this piece of writing might well be despair on the part of some content area teachers. They would point to it as reinforcement of the idea that asking students to write is a waste of time because they cannot write and no one has time to correct all the errors in such a piece. We might call this the "three-quarters empty" philosophy with such teachers assuming that there is next to nothing here worth salvaging. The opposite would be the teacher who understands that writing is a process and what is shown in this writer's draft is the following:

> It is probably a first draft because of the way it is structured and expressed; hence, with some peer response and conferencing, the student probably could produce an improved draft because the writer has
>
> - Identified someone that he admires
> - Identified one or two key points he wishes to make about Daniel Boone—talented as a woodsman and showed great bravery and courage
> - Lists some undeveloped examples-Boone's family, his pioneer efforts
> - Follows a general structure, identifying his main points first, and then tries to develop them

Circling all the errors in spelling, sentence construction, usage, and structure and returning the paper to the student will accomplish little except reinforce for the student that he is not an effective writer. If this student is to have a chance at showing he can produce an acceptable piece of writing, he is going to need some very focused help, and it cannot be relegated solely to his English class. All response to student writing, written or oral, should be focused, acknowledging what is working, and where the writer might direct attention next. Little need exists to write comments that are longer than the text the student produced. If teachers find themselves doing this, they probably need to build some time into class for one-to-one conferencing with students and limit their comments to one step toward improvement at a time.

So, what might be said to the student? Here is one possible way that written comments might be made to the writer.

good I know who you like

Danal Boon because of his braver and he talent aa woods man and of a guide. He is know for his braver in the face of dancer and of his curge in the face of discress.

What are some of these?

He loast 2 sons and yet cept going to bigger and better things. His life is one of history and of his love of the out doors and beccus he liked to be alone as much as possible. And to go his one way when he wanted to.

He was marred to a woman at 20 years old and hat 6 or 7 children yet he cept moving west. He opeaned the gate to the west you mite say.

useful details

why was this courageous?

He was a man of curge becaus of his noled of the Indians and of there way. He made peace with some and war with outers yet he lived to be a great man and a famase one to.

He lost everthing and yet reganed it in the end. He lived on his land until he was 63 I think then he went to vist ge relitive and distusts.

how did this happen?

He was bured and the dug up and moved to a knew spot and there he layes till this day.

—

provide a sense of your reading

acknowledge what he has done

Jimmy, you admire Daniel Boone because of his bravery and courage. As a reader, I want to know more about this. As a first step, please make a list of examples with as much information as you can—see the questions and then decide what order makes sense to you to present them to the reader. Bring your organized list to class tomorrow and let me talk with you about it; then you can work on another draft that provides more information to your readers.

steps to task

timeline

Writing of this nature may be an indication of a special needs student although this is not always the case. In many classrooms, special needs students represent an increasing population. Writing can be difficult for them but they can function well under the conditions outlined in this chapter if given the opportunity. Many special needs students tend to have a visual, tactile or kinesthethic learning style. Response groups, rubric building, conferencing—these activities offer avenues for success, since the activities parallel how they learn. These students also gain great security from knowing how they will be assessed from the beginning of the assignment. Giving them criteria or a rubric as they start the task provides the concrete direction they appreciate. RAMPS writing also works well with this population because of its organization and concreteness. Feedback from both peers and the teachers also is an important ingredient in the success of these learners. They crave reinforcement but they tend not to ask for it. Unless a teacher is aware of this need, students could just stop with one sentence and go no further. There's no need to single out the students but monitoring their progress and responding can make a huge difference in their willingness to undertake a task. The whole monitoring process can be as simple as moving around the room, stopping by a regular student to comment, then moving to the special needs student, again stopping to comment, and then moving on to the next student. An element of instruction which seems to work well not only with special needs students but also with all students is to begin discussions of a piece of writing with some word of praise—find the positive and then help the student build on that. Often the laborious act of revising can be greatly lightened if students are given post-its to use as they make changes. Writing revisions on the post-its and then sticking them to a draft to indicate where they should go in the rewrite simplifies the revising process and appeals, once again, to the visual and tactile learner.

When using group work with this population, the special needs students should not all be placed in the same group. With all the legal implications accompanying the Individualized Educational Plans for such students, teachers will need to insure that the best possible environments are present. No one wants to violate an IEP deliberately but more importantly, no one wants to be the one to turn a student off when it comes to writing or participating in all the activities which lead to effective writing

Admittedly, not all papers will have as many obvious problems as the Daniel Boone piece, but without focused feedback, this student will not improve. With it, he has a chance to show he knows something about his subject and that he can write well enough that others can understand what he has to offer. Will the mechanical errors go away? Not entirely, but the surprising thing about having students revise with the benefit of peer and teacher comments is that many of the initial errors do disappear as students gain a sense of what needs to be communicated to an audience that shows a genuine interest in learning what a writer has to offer. Once the writer has found a focus and has developed it, a willingness to correct spelling, punctuation, and other errors begins to emerge. For all of this to happen, however, and for student growth to occur in writing skill, students must write often, and must have a sense that their writing is being read seriously by both peers and teachers, The only way student writers can gain that confidence is by receiving regular written and oral response to their work.

Responding to writing is an essential part of formative assessment which allows both writers and teachers to continue with what is working well and to make adjustments to what is not. The writer, of course, does this while working on a draft. Teachers have a broader range of elements which may need to be adjusted—the design of the assignment, the peer response partner, the make-up of peer response groups, the conferencing style and length, the decision of whether to give oral or written feedback. Teaching is a complex act in any subject area. Using writing to stimulate as well as assess learning does not lessen the complexity of teaching, but it does provide a worthwhile performance by which learners can be assessed on what they have learned and are able to do.

Work Cited

Bean, John C. 1996. *Engaging ideas: The professor's guide to integrating writing, critical thinking, and active learning in the classroom*. San Francisco, CA: Jossey-Bass.

Chapter 4

Giving Students Control Over Writing Assessment

Charles R. Duke and Rebecca Sanchez

Teachers often see any kind of external assessment as an evil to be endured but certainly not embraced. And as more and more states enter the writing assessment arena, the fear and hostility indexes among teachers have risen dramatically. Some of this apprehension is understandable, since most statewide assessments have not provided much useful information to teachers or to students. In addition, the design of the assessment has not always been clear to teachers, and there has been uncertainty about how results would be used.

Pennsylvania is a good case in point. Because new curriculum regulations included more emphasis upon writing, the state department of education decided in 1992 that a statewide writing assessment was needed. Grades six and nine were the targeted population. With the help of teachers, test experts, and state-department personnel, a holistic writing assessment was designed and field tested. A percentage of districts were to be tested each year so that all districts would have been assessed within a three-year cycle (see Pennsylvania State Assessment System 1992).

The Pennsylvania holistic writing assessment was similar to many other such assessments; it used a six-point scale applied to five key characteristics of effective writing: focus, content, organization, style, and conventions. Two readers' scores provided the holistic assessment; disagreement between readers was arbitrated by a third reader. A student, therefore, could receive a score anywhere from 0 (unscorable) to 12. As a result of participating in the training provided by the state department of education, we began thinking about how our students could directly benefit from the assessment. We also hoped for a means to provide classroom teachers with ways to incorporate aspects of the assessment in their teaching.

One of our principal goals was to give students more control in the assessment process. So we began with the students' ideas about effective writing and helped them to derive assessment criteria that they could use individually and in peer-response groups. We aimed at analytical scoring which draws upon the same premise as holistic scoring—the whole is more than the sum of its parts—but which also offers a way to talk about writing in a language that is readily accessible to students and which, therefore, helps them with revision. Analytical scoring identifies the key characteristics of writing and provides descriptors of these traits in terms of strengths and weaknesses similar to those appearing in student samples of writing (see Spandel and Stiggins 1990).

Frankly, we were uncertain how students might take to designing their own assessment criteria since they were more accustomed to the teacher-driven model of assessment and the "hidden agenda" ordinarily involved in evaluating papers, which required students to guess what the teacher wanted. We determined, however, to create a different environment in which the criteria for assessment were collaboratively developed, frequently discussed, and consistently used.

Because Rebecca was teaching ninety-four tenth graders in six classes divided among both general and academic students, we focused upon them as our pilot group. All of these students were familiar with the writing process and already had worked in peer-response groups. We began by setting aside class time to consider the characteristics of effective writing. In small-group discussions, students focused on what makes writing work. We suggested that they consider a piece of favorite literature as well as an article in a magazine such as *Seventeen* or *Sports Illustrated* as sources for ideas. In addition, students generated a list of short stories, nonfiction pieces, and novels that they had read thus far in the class. Students also could consider each other's writing. Titles were placed on the chalkboard for reference. Beside these, we placed two questions: What makes the writing strong? What makes the reading enjoyable?

Scribes in each group recorded comments while students pondered over just what it is that makes writing "tick" for them. As they talked among themselves, names like Victor Hugo, Piers Anthony, Jeffrey Archer, Danielle Steele, Charles Dickens, and Edgar Allen Poe floated around the room. Both we and the students were astonished that they had read and remembered so much.

Once authors had been identified, the groups moved on to exactly what these and other authors do in their writing. Students began to make comments:

- I love it when there is a case history at the beginning of the article.
- There has to be tension and suspense.
- If I'm not hooked in the first paragraph, I won't read more.
- I hate dumb endings that just stop or pretend they are dreams.
- Fragments, I love fragments that work. Tried them in my own writing last year but lost points every time.
- I need description of characters. I have to know what characters look like. I can figure out what they are like from their actions, but please, dear author, give me description.
- I hate it when something goes off in two or three directions. Can't figure it out then.
- When I read Amy's piece the other day, what made me want to read on was the way she didn't reveal too much at one time.

The students spent two class periods in dialogue. The general classes tended to be far more topic-oriented than the academic classes, expressing distinct preferences for violence and love stories while demanding certain features in the text such as the setting in the first paragraph and language that did not perplex or challenge them and take them away from the focus of the story. The academic classes, on the other hand, tended to cite features such as foreshadowing, characterization, dialogue, and ideas that make you think.

As the dialogue continued, students began to examine and discuss their lists of characteristics. One group discovered that a "satisfying ending" meant a "cliff-hanger ending" for some, "all loose ends tied up" for others, and "happy ending" for still others. Students began to see the differences in their demands as readers and in their preferences as writers. One student remarked, "This is more reason than ever to talk about our writing with each other. One word can mean one thing to me and something different to the people in my group."

After generating characteristics of effective writing, the students spent two class periods categorizing items under the five traits of effective writing established by the Pennsylvania Department of Education (PDE): *focus, content, organization, style,* and *conventions.* When students submitted their finished lists, we combined the material generated by all the classes and grouped it under the five traits. As we eliminated duplicates, combined similarities, and refined the language, the definite characteristics of the five traits that began to emerge bore a striking resemblance to the PDE descriptions of each trait, even though we had never shown those descriptions to the students.

We put the PDE traits and the student-generated characteristics on overhead transparencies and showed them to students; we stressed that what they saw on the transparencies was the cumulative result of their discussions, their lists, and their demands for quality in reading and writing. Students quickly recognized their own or their group's contributions. Exclamations of "I said that one," or "Hey, that came from our group, remember?" could be heard around the room. We were careful to interweave exact comments from the students' work so they knew we had read their material, and we discussed each characteristic to be certain that students understood the language. For example, these were the traits that appeared for *Organization:*

- Maintains logical order
- One subject in each paragraph
- Flow—transitions from sentence to sentence and from paragraph to paragraph
- AGO (Attention-grabbing opening)
- Satisfying ending
- Not redundant
- Foreshadowing—subtle hints that create connections
- Tension

Students then turned to texts to find strong examples of any of the five traits. Their examples could come from other students' written work, readings from any subject area, or their own freereading choices—any text but their own personal writing. Leroy asked, "You mean if I find a passage from *Rolling Stone* with strong verbs, I can bring it in?" Yes. "If there's a good description of a guy in a book," asked Jenn, "can I use that?" Yes, again.

We decided to display the items on large pieces of white cardboard that could be moved easily about the room. Items had to appear with the identification of the source and the name of the student making the contribution. The next day students pored excitedly over each other's pieces, reading, talking, copying passages, and presenting. In all the classes, students preferred to work with each other's writing rather than published pieces. Gretchen, for instance, offered an item from Heather's paper as a strong example of style: "When I entered the classroom, I saw him—my stud-muffin across the room. The students stepped back, creating a corridor of love that ran from him to me. I looked up only to gaze into his eyes, wide with horror."

Nathan, making a contribution to the conventions trait, was impressed with Dustin's handling of the semi-colon, a skill which thus far had eluded Nathan: "As a little boy I walked the snow between the house and the barn with my grandfather; I loved stepping into his footprints." Reading over Dana's piece, Erika identified the beginning as a useful example of an attention-grabbing opening (AGO): "Bent over the ground, curly-topped and sweaty, I wrote my father's name in the dirt with my finger." Sheldon, also focusing on organization, offered Rich's entire piece for its paragraphing. Rich, grinning ear to ear, admitted that he had mastered that skill at least.

In this way the students assembled a collection of examples for each of the writing traits. As the assessment work continued, the display examples served as quick points of reference for our discussions. Without much prompting, students continued to contribute to the display regularly. Often students would leave their response groups to study the display of a certain trait and then report back to their groups. Others, who had located examples of their own work that seemed to fit the traits, used them as teaching tools with their peers. Their sense of empowerment in defining the traits became quickly apparent, for never before had these students approached their peers' writing with such eagerness and confidence.

Once the traits and their general descriptors had been identified, the next step was to show students a range of quality within each trait. To help them visualize this range, we used a descriptive continuum (see Figure 1 for the trait of organization), modeled on one developed for use in teacher workshops by Vicki Spandel and Ruth Culham of the Center for Classroom Assessment, Northwest Regional Laboratory, Portland, Oregon.

The next step toward analytical assessment called for breaking each of the traits into a scale of six increments because we wanted to mirror the Pennsylvania holistic rubric as closely as possible. To focus students' attention on the language of writing assessment, each increment of a trait was represented by a number rather than a grade. Each trait, therefore, had to be scored from six to one with a score of six corresponding to the most effective use of the trait. Student attention was focused on the descriptors for each increment. In this way, we hoped to disassociate students as much as possible from the old points and letter-grade game. The main purpose of the analytical rubric was to help students place their work in relation to each of the traits. Doing so would provide them with greater feedback about their writing than the holistic-scoring scheme used in the statewide assessment.

Although we originally intended to have separate descriptors for each of the six increments, students quickly decided that a "5" really was a thinner version of a "6'; once they seemed to understand this, we collapsed the scale to the version in Figure 2. Students did not seem to experience difficulty in determining whether a trait was at the lower or higher end of the range.

Figure 1
Organization Continuum

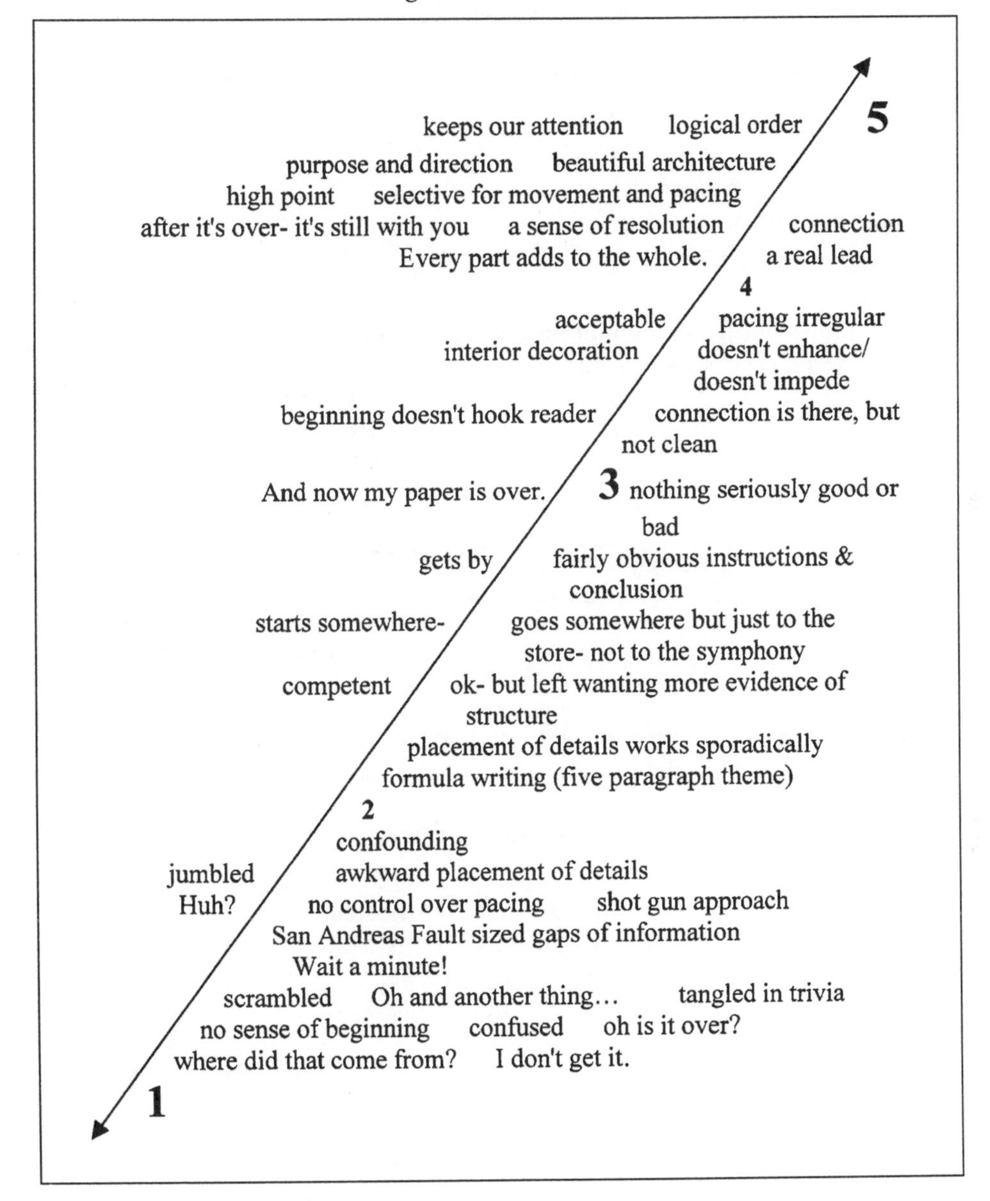

Figure 2

Focus

6/5

- establishes and keeps a clear purpose;
- shows consistency in use of transitions within sentences and paragraphs;
- shows clarity and originality of ideas.

4/3

- maintains a clear purpose most of the time;
- varies occasionally in keeping a single point of view;
- ideas are generally clear but not especially original.

2/1

- shows uncertainty about task and audience;
- has no clear sense of purpose;
- has difficulty in holding a single point of view or role;
- lacks clarity or originality of ideas.

Content

6/5

- shows sophisticated thinking and ideas;
- provides well developed examples and explanations related to topic and purpose;
- selects information appropriate for audience and situation.

4/3

- presents ideas somewhat lacking in sophistication;
- provides examples and details related to the topic but they may be uneven in development;
- selects information appropriate for audience and situation.

2/1

- presents under-developed and unsophisticated ideas;
- provides examples and details as listings without development and not always relevant to topic and purpose;
- shows little awareness of the audience's needs.

Organization

6/5

- maintains a logical order/ sequence;
- focuses on one subject in each paragraph;
- provides logical transitions within sentences and between paragraphs;
- offers clear introduction and conclusion that frame the topic under discussion.

4/3

- maintains a reasonable order/ sequence;
- focuses most of the time on one subject per paragraph;

Figure 2 (cont.)

- provides logical transitions between sentences and paragraphs but is not always consistent in their use;
- offers an adequate introduction and conclusion but without much clarity or originality.

2/1

- displays inconsistent order/ sequence;
- exhibits difficulty in maintaining focus on one idea in a paragraph;
- shows inconsistency in use of transitions within sentences and paragraphs;
- offers little in the way of a controlled introduction and conclusion.

Style

6/5

- shows precise language use;
- exhibits effective word choice that suggests originality, and a sophisticated vocabulary;
- offers a consistent voice and tone; appropriate for the topic, purpose, and audience;
- demonstrates control over variety of sentence structure, types and length.

4/3

- shows fairly precise language use;
- exhibits appropriate word choice;
- offers somewhat inconsistent tone and voice or selects voice and tone inappropriate for audience and purpose;
- demonstrates control over basic sentence structure but appears uncertain about variety, types, and length.

2/1

- shows little precision in language use;
- exhibits little originality in word choice and some choices may be inappropriate;
- offers an inconsistent voice and/or inappropriate voice/tone;
- shows little control over sentence structure, variety, types, and length.

Conventions

6/5

- exhibits few if any errors in spelling, punctuation and capitalization;
- demonstrates control of appropriate forms of usage—pronoun reference, subject/ verb agreement, etc.;
- displays control of sentence completeness (absence of run-ons and unnecessary fragments).

4/3

- exhibits a number of repetitive errors in spelling, punctuation and capitalization but not severe enough to interfere significantly with reader's understanding;

Figure 2 (cont.)

- shows inconsistency in appropriate choice of usage;
- displays inconsistency in control of sentence completeness.

2/1

- exhibits repetitive and frequent errors in spelling, punctuation, and capitalization that interfere with the reader's understanding;
- shows inconsistency in choice of appropriate usage;
- displays lack of understanding of sentence completeness.

Because this approach to assessing writing was new to the students and to us, we questioned the wisdom of trying to deal with all five traits for the first attempt and settled on using just three. *Content, style,* and *organization* matched well with the personal narrative assignment they had been working on, and students had found strong examples of these traits for their classroom display boards.

Even though the students learned to discuss and assess writing in terms of the analytical descriptors and seemed comfortable giving and receiving ratings, inevitably we had to translate the ratings into points for the grade book. It seemed ironic that after the students had gained so much from divorcing their writing from grades, we had to turn around and convert the diagnostic information into a traditional grading system.

Reluctantly, we designed a conversion grid, wondering as we did so if this move would destroy all we had gained. Using the analytical scale had thus far eliminated the usual questions about how much an assignment was worth: Will I get an A if I do this? How close am I to a B? What do I have to do to just pass? It had freed the students from the paralyzing effects of pre-occupation with grades.

Our conversion grid was composed of a six-point scale for each trait—content, organization, and style. A paper with the highest possible rating for all three earned eighteen points or one-hundred percent. The minimum score would be one for each trait or a total of three, which converted to below sixty-nine percentage points. We marked off conventional grade ranges that corresponded to the school's percentage system: 100–93 = A; 92–85 = B; 84–76 = C; 75–70 = D; 69 and below = F. (The personal narrative was graded on three traits only, converting to one-hundred percentage points; see Figure 3 for a sample conversion for 5 traits).

The system worked well. Every student paper had an evaluation sheet attached to it, featuring the three traits with their corresponding descriptors and score levels, a place for conversion into points/percentage, and a letter grade. As each paper was evaluated, we simply circled the ratings and then recorded the corresponding conversion grades on the evaluation sheet. Later, the percentage/points were entered in the grade book under the heading of personal narrative, 100 points possible.

We liked the system and learned to score from it quite quickly, but we were not certain how the students would react when the first papers and evaluation were returned. However, the response in all six classes varied little. In general, students spent their time reviewing the evaluations, constantly moving between their texts and the ratings. When the students finally spoke, they asked each

Figure 3

Sample Analytical Conversion Tool for 5 Traits
Sanchez
100 Point Base

Traits	PTS/ %	Grade
6 6 6 6 6 (30)	100	A+
6 6 6 6 5 (29)	99	
6 6 6 5 5 (28)	97	A
6 6 5 5 5 (27)	95	
6 5 5 5 5 (26)	93	A-
5 5 5 5 5 (25)	92	B+
5 5 5 5 4 (24)	91	
5 5 5 4 4 (23)	89	B
5 5 4 4 4 (22)	87	
5 4 4 4 4 (21)	85	B-
4 4 4 4 4 (20)	84	C+
4 4 4 4 3 (19)	83	
4 4 4 3 3 (18)	81	C
4 4 3 3 3 (17)	79	
4 3 3 3 3 (16)	77	C-
3 3 3 3 3 (15)	76	D+
3 3 3 3 2 (14)	75	
3 3 3 2 2 (13)	73	D
3 3 2 2 2 (12)	72	
3 2 2 2 2 (11)	70	D-
2 2 2 2 2 (10)	69	F
2 2 2 2 1 (9)	68	
2 2 2 1 1 (8)	66	
2 2 1 1 1 (7)	64	
2 1 1 1 1 (6)	62	
1 1 1 1 1 (5)	60	

This conversion is based upon a grading system of:

100–93	A
92–85	B
86–77	C
76–70	D
69 and below	F

Please note: If the student scores a sequence other than those listed, add the trait ratings and locate the total in parentheses for the corresponding grade. For example, a sequence of 5 3 3 4 4 equals 19, giving the student a grade of 83% C.

other about individual trait scores. No student asked another what grade he or she received. Instead, they were most concerned about their performance in the individual traits rather than the points or letter grade for the entire piece. Even in small-group discussions, students focused on their strengths as writers and acknowledged areas which needed improvement. They used the same language for discussion and for reflection on the evaluations as they had used to generate the analytical descriptors and to respond to each other's drafts during the development of the narrative pieces.

Once students had experienced the system, they wanted more. They sought to add the remaining traits to the evaluation of their next writing effort and eventually even created a sixth trait, *voice*, because they believed it was so important in creating a unique piece of writing. We followed a process similar to the original one in generating descriptors for *voice*: the discussions eventually resulted in a useable trait which students readily incorporated into their discussions and assessments of each other's writing. We simply expanded our original conversion grid and kept the same approach for dealing with the grading system. Student response remained constant, focusing on the descriptors, analyzing text in terms of ratings, and looking for ways to improve on traits with which they had experienced difficulty.

No assessment system is perfect, of course, and this one continues to need refinement; however, implementing the analytical assessment met our original goal: to give students more control over the assessment process and criteria. Students also benefited from increased feedback on their performance. All of this fostered a democratic atmosphere in the classroom. The ambiguity and awkwardness experienced so often by both students and teachers in the assessment process disappeared. What we didn't anticipate was that the language of analytical assessment, generated for the most part by the students, would so tightly unify the entire writing process and produce student evaluators willing to assess each other's writing, as well as their own, as they worked toward the common goal of improvement.

Works Cited

Pennsylvania State Assessment System. 1992. *Writing assessment handbook.* Harrisburg, PA: Pennsylvania Department of Education.

Spandel, Vicki, and Richard J. Stiggins. 1990. *Creating writers: Linking assessment and writing instruction.* White Plains, New York: Longman.

Chapter 5

Making Portfolio Assessment Work in the Classroom

Rebecca Sanchez and Charles R. Duke

"What are those crates in your classroom?"
"Oh, those are my kids' portfolios."
"What are you going to do with them?"
"I'll probably look at them this summer and then throw them away."
"Are you grading them?"
"No, I really couldn't figure out how to do that."

Interest about portfolios is high among teachers right now, especially since some states like Kentucky and Vermont have developed state-wide portfolio assessment programs, and other states appear ready to follow their lead. Still, most teachers and administrators remain uncertain about how best to deal with the question of assessment. This uncertainty is reflected in the current debate about what role assessment should play in determining student performance and what form it should take. Current assessment practices seem to send the following messages:

— Assessment always arrives from the outside.
— Skills that appear on tests are all that really matter in instruction.
— First drafts are finished drafts.
— Achievement is more important than the process of how one gets there.
— Students can self-assess or set goals.
— Standardizing assessment is the ultimate goal.

Not everyone, of course, agrees with these messages, and a growing emphasis upon alternative assessment practices is beginning to emerge. These practices are designed to accomplish the following:

— Capture a wider variety of student performance to provide a fuller picture of what students actually can achieve.
— Show how students work—a process orientation as well as a product one.
— Stress realistic contexts for work—make assignments more authentic.
— Assist teachers in showing where students are in their development.
— Weave assessment into instruction.

Out of this interest in alternative assessment has come a corresponding interest in authentic assessment. Art Costa defines this kind of assessment as "evidence of student performance in situations that demand application and transfer of knowledge as well as evidence of cooperation, persistence and creativity" (1989, p. 46). Portfolios are an attractive assessment option because they seem to offer a direct linkage to the goals of authentic assessment. Portfolios provide opportunities to record student performance on a variety of tasks, reveal the students' work process, involve students in using higher order thinking skills appropriate for the workplace, and offer a convenient method for documenting student progress. But most importantly, perhaps, they offer a way to involve students directly in assessing their own performance. Although several types of portfolios exist (Jenkins 1996), the one which seems to come closest to meeting student needs while also addressing teacher and district needs in assessment is the collaborative portfolio, identified by the following characteristics:

1. Students maintain control over selection of pieces.
2. Teachers and students work together to build the folio.
3. Teachers can include material but it isn't always necessary.
4. The folio contains student self-assessment and reflection as well as teacher feedback/assessment.
5. Building the portfolio includes goal setting and process.
6. The teacher assesses the quality of the student self-assessment and reflection as well as the portfolio itself.

Developing the appropriate classroom experiences to support the use of collaborative portfolios is critical to their success. We cannot emphasize too much the importance of developing a process from the very beginning of the school year that involves students in selecting and reflecting on their work regularly. They should learn through practice that reflection is a regular part of the writing process. The class also needs to develop its own criteria by which work can be self-evaluated. Ideally, then, self-assessment occurs as a natural outgrowth of reflection, because students feel comfortable with the criteria (after all, they helped to create them), and when it comes time to do a final portfolio assessment, the task does not seem impossible. The skills of selection, reflection, and self-assessment are already in place. Finally, the results of such an approach should be converted easily to fit within existing school grading systems.

But how does one conduct that final assessment of the collaborative portfolio? We have found the following sequence to work particularly well:

A. Students examine their entire working folder in which they have been filing their work for the year. From this working folder, students select their three all-time best pieces, which do not have to be graded pieces or pieces necessarily taken to their final stage. Tests, as long as they are essays, can be included in the selection.
B. Students select a colored two-pocketed folder (provided by the district or teacher) and place their three pieces inside. From this point on, students focus primarily on these three pieces but also may draw upon other items in their working portfolio for evidence of growth and improvement as writers.
C. Students then develop a written reflection that focuses upon their three choices while examining strategies, ideas for further revision, accomplishments, and a favorite line or passage.

A series of questions helps to guide the students:

1. Why did you select these pieces? Provide reasons for your selections in terms of what you have accomplished as a writer and reader.
2. If you could work on these three pieces again, what would you specifically do to strengthen each one?
3. When you were working on each of these pieces, what ideas, strategies, or suggestions did you employ to help you over any difficulties?
4. What is your favorite passage in one of your pieces? Identify it and explain why it is your favorite (for example, was it your word choice, style, rhyme, image, angle, etc.? Was it a problem place in the piece that you successfully revised? Was it an attention-getting opening {AGO} or an ending that "worked"?).

D. Students next construct a "Dear Reader" letter which allows them to explain their growth as writers to anyone who might read their portfolios. In this letter, students also explain the global changes in their work and development as writers which brought them to the success evident in their selected portfolio pieces and reference a list of class-generated goals which would have been addressed over the school year. See Figure 1 for a list of goals developed by a tenth grade English class.

Figure 1
Our Writing Goals

- learn to use details to write more developed responses
- learn to support opinions with evidence from the text
- learn the importance of having a choice as to topic and format
- try new modes of writing during the year
- develop attention-getting openings
- use satisfying endings
- use paragraphs effectively
- write effective dialogue
- work on run-ons and fragments
- take risks as a writer
- try stylistic features such as an sentence
- clean up mechanics
- blend my personal creativity with my knowledge of the text
- use brainstorming to get started
- learn to revise effectively

Figure 1 (cont.)
Our Writing Goals

- learn to tighten the focus of my pieces
- use strong verbs, images, interesting words, etc.
- learn to generate sufficient length for a piece to be developed fully
- take teacher suggestions or suggestions from others but also know when my way may be the best for what I want to accomplish
- learn how to quote from primary and secondary sources

E. Once students have selected their pieces, and developed both their Reflection and their Dear Reader responses, they are ready to use the "Portfolio Assessment Levels"; these criteria have been collaboratively developed by the students and teacher to make a portfolio rubric which permits both the students and the teacher to place the students' writing on one of four levels of proficiency. An example of such a system for a tenth grade English class appears in Figure 2. Using a "flight" metaphor, students determine whether their work is **near the airport**, which characterizes a weak level of performance; or **in the airport**, for writing which falls in the middle or average level of performance; **boarding the plane** identifies writing at a higher level of performance; or, ultimately, **in flight**, for writing that has literally "taken off" and is well on the flight path to excellence.

Figure 2
Portfolio Assessment Levels

NEAR THE AIRPORT

- Content tends to be skimpy, offering few, if any, explanations, details, and specifics.
- Little awareness is shown of organizational features such as paragraphs, clear beginning, and end.
- Pieces give the impression of little time invested; pieces often are incomplete.
- Successive drafts are rare; there is little or no evidence of willingness to revise.
- Little or no risk-taking is shown; tends to write the same mode over and over.
- No evidence appears of being open to suggestions from response group or the teacher.
- Reflections feature general statements that say nothing about the pieces or the writer's growth.

Figure 2 (cont.)
Portfolio Assessment Levels

- Language is "oatmeal"— bland, safe, colorless, immature.
- Sentence structure is simple and repetitive.
- Mechanical errors seem to multiply overnight; carelessness.
- No interweaving of historical details appears in interdisciplinary pieces.
- Tardiness or omissions are common.

IN THE AIRPORT

- Content is adequate with some explanations, details, and specifics, which may be repetitious.
- Organization shows attempts at beginning, middle, and end but often without paragraphs.
- Pieces give the impression of adequate time invested; pieces have a sense of completeness.
- Successive drafts occur, but they may be similar in appearance.
- Some risk-taking is evident; some variety in modes is attempted.
- Evidence shows writer is open to suggestions from response groups or teacher; pieces are sometimes revised accordingly.
- Reflections feature some specifics but not always.
- Some interest in colorful language and strong verbs appears, but not consistently.
- Sentence structure tends to be simple; writing shows some care in building sentences.
- Mechanical errors may be repetitive but not glaring ones.
- Some interweaving of historical details appear in interdisciplinary pieces but usually show unevenness.
- Evidence exists showing responsibility in meeting deadlines.

BOARDING THE PLANE

- Content is sufficiently developed with explanations, details, and specifics.
- Clear organization is evident with AGO, satisfying ending, and paragraphing.
- Pieces give the sense of sufficient time being invested.
- Successive drafts reflect major changes through revision.
- Risk-taking is apparent; writer uses a variety of modes.
- Evidence suggests writer is open to suggestions from response groups and teacher and revises accordingly.

Figure 2 (cont.)
Portfolio Assessment Levels

- Reflections discuss the specifics of growth and change in the pieces.
- Writing shows adequate use of descriptive words and strong verbs with an occasional image.
- Some variety in sentence structure appears; writer tries an occasional stylistic feature.
- Few, if any, mechanical errors appear.
- Interweaving of historical details in interdisciplinary pieces is evident.
- Writer shows responsibility in meeting deadlines.

IN FLIGHT

- Content is well developed with explanations, details, and specifics.
- Effective organization is evident in use of satisfying endings, and paragraphing.
- Pieces give the sense of much time and thought invested.
- Successive drafts reflect major changes through revision.
- Risk-taking is apparent; ample variety of modes is evident.
- Evidence suggests writer is open to suggestions from response group and teacher, but the writer also senses when something "works" well enough to keep it.
- Reflections thoughtfully discuss the specifics of growth and change.
- Effective and playful uses of language appear with the use of descriptive words, strong verbs, images, metaphors and other language devices.
- Clear variety in sentence structure is evident; many stylistic features are present.
- Few, if any, mechanical errors appear.
- Effective interweaving of historical details occur in interdisciplinary pieces.
- Writer shows responsibility in meeting deadlines.

F. After students have determined what level of performance characterizes their writing in the portfolio, they then place themselves on that level as to "low, middle, or high end" by using the tool "Converting Portfolio Levels to a Grade." (See Figure 3.) For example, students might place themselves at the low end of "In Flight" to show that in their view, their work has just broken into this level. After identifying the level of performance and making the conversion into grade points, students write a paragraph to explain why they placed themselves at the particular level.

Figure 3
Converting Portfolio Levels to a Grade

Student:______________________

Evaluator:____________________ Date:____________________

	—IN FLIGHT—	
upper	*middle*	*lower*
100–98	97–95	94–93
	—BOARDING THE PLANE—	
92–90	89–88	87–85
	—IN THE AIRPORT—	
84–82	81–80	79–77
	—NEAR THE AIRPORT—	
76–74	73–72	71–70

The teacher, upon receiving the portfolios, uses the same assessment tools for ranking the students, but with one change. To assess the student reflection and the "Dear Reader" response, the teacher uses class-generated criteria which fold organizational descriptors of the portfolio itself along with content-based descriptors for evidence, detail, and seriousness of purpose into one rubric. Included in the rubric is a conversion tool for translating the level of achievement into a numerical grade. (See Figure 4 designed by a tenth grade English class).

Finally, the score from the portfolio assessment and the score from the "flight" rubric are combined, and a final exam grade is recorded for each student. The results are stapled to the portfolio and returned to the student for review and discussion, as needed, with the teacher.

Figure 4
Rubric for Portfolio Organization,
Self-Assessment and Dear Reader Letter

Strong 100–93	Completes all steps in the organization and assessment requirements. Consistently uses abundant details and evidence. Conveys a maximum sense of effort and seriousness of purpose.
Good 92–85	Completes all steps in the organization and assessment requirements. Consistently uses sufficient details and evidence. Conveys a sense of effort and seriousness of purpose.

Figure 4 (cont.)
Rubric for Portfolio Organization, Self-Assessment and Dear Reader Letter

Average 84–87	May not complete all steps in the organization and assessment requirements. Uses some details and evidence but not consistently. Gives the impression of just enough effort to say, "I'm done."
Weak 76–74	Does not complete all steps in the organization and assessment requirements. Tends not to use details and evidence; tends to generalize. Conveys little, if any, sense of effort or purpose.

The entire sequence can be done in class using two forty-minute periods. By using the in-class time, teachers insure all students have equal opportunity to complete their portfolio assessment and submit it for a grade. Students who are absent can make arrangements to come in during study halls, home room, or after school. Since the final sequence is student-centered, teachers can work during class time on assessing portfolios submitted by previous classes. As a result, most of the teacher assessment work can be completed in school. If the skills of selection, reflection, and self-assessment are presented early and frequently in the classroom, teachers can create a final portfolio assessment system that is efficient and effective for both students and teachers. By the year's end, students will know exactly what they need to do in assembling the final portfolio.

As for teachers, they will have moved closer to assessing multiple performance, have involved students in establishing appropriate criteria, and provided multiple opportunities for students to reflect and engage in self-assessment. And not of least importance, teachers will have a system for using portfolios with large groups of students and a means for converting portfolio assessment into the conventional grading format of most school systems.

Works Cited

Costa, Arthur L. 1989. Re-assessing assessment. *Educational Leadership*, 46: (7): 2.

Jenkins, Carol Brennan. 1996. *Inside the writing portfolio: What we need to know to assess children's writing*. Portsmouth, NH: Heinemann.

Chapter 6

Assess Now, Grade Later

Carol A. Pope and Candy M. Beal

> *If suddenly, the admissions process were to become non-competitive, the need for grading would vanish. But the need for evaluation [or assessment] would remain.*
>
> David Bleich (1975)

We have always hated the grading part of teaching. We love the students, the planning, the time in the classroom, the time in Office Max buying materials for classes. We even have a kind of affection for the old grade book—the one where we record all the "credit" students earn for the work they have done. The part that we hate is putting the GRADE on a test, a paper, a homework assignment, a project that took three weeks to complete, or a group presentation or skit.

Why do we hate grading? As young teachers more than a few years ago we realized that grading had become a way to point out students' deficiencies, to pronounce a VERDICT on a student's learning—as if learning ever stops. We discovered that grades are often used to compare, to label and determine categories of students, even to limit them, to establish parameters around where they can go next in their student careers. The grading system is a closed one that we as adults use to control the number of students who can get "good" grades.

As we see it, grades are more of an aid to adults than to kids. Adults need grades for GPAs, and GPAs allow us a conscience-free way to label, sort, and select students for everything from college admission to class placement and academic awards. If we were college admissions directors, or politicians, or even high school counselors, maybe we would find all this labeling and sorting helpful. However, as teachers, if we are honest, we admit that grades do not really help us much. They do not help us gain camaraderie and rapport with students; they do not help us, despite the common myth, guide students to learn more or refine their work. Nor do they help us teach.

We believe that "teaching is organic"—a "bridge from the inner world outward" (Ashton-Warner 1986, p. 95). As teachers we serve both as a "bridge from the inner world outward" and as co-creators with students of a bridge to learning. We do our best work when we develop relationships with our students so that they will trust our construction and our bridges. The relationships, then, serve as touchstones for student motivation to both create and cross a bridge. As any teacher knows, the first assigning of a grade can decimate any relationship, any creation of a bridge to learning. The grade immediately places the teacher in a position of power and control, the student in a position of subordination. Co-construction of the bridges ends.

Assessment vs. grading

What helps us more than anything to maintain a relationship, to co-create bridges with students, and to encourage their own building is to put off grading as long as possible. Instead, we choose to focus on the construction of learning through bridge-building, guided learning, and informal, yet constant, assessment. In this process, we define assessment much as Stephen Tchudi does in *Alternatives to Grading Student Writing* (1997): "descriptive," "formative," and "in-process" (p. xiv). We also use evaluation when there are particular established criteria for an assignment. Instead of focusing on students' deficiencies or elements that are "missing" from their work, we focus on pointing out what is there; we adopt a proficiency model, not a deficiency one.

We emphasize instruction, not grading, by guiding students and pushing for quality. By placing more attention on quality rather than on grading, we avoid separating and labeling students or limiting the potential of their success by placing a verdict on their work too soon. We concentrate on motivating students through our teaching/learning relationship and by building scaffolds or bridges designed to help them, not to stop them. Our goal is to stimulate and encourage, not to stymie or control students through the threat of a grade. In that process we focus on quality and learning (see Figure 1).

Writing-to-learn assignments

One of the best ways we have found to avoid an over-reliance on grading is to use writing-to-learn experiences as assignments during class and during the de-

Figure 1
Characteristics of Assessment vs. Grading

Assessment	Grading
Proficiency Focus	Deficiency Focus
Instruction	Verdict
Avoid Separation	Categorizes
Motivates	Limits
Aids Learning	Aids Adults
Builds Scaffolds	Creates GPAs
Stimulates	Controls
Encourages	Stymie
Open System	Closed System

velopment of a project. These writing-to-learn assignments give us opportunities to see students' work in progress, to see their thinking, and, even more importantly, for the students themselves to see what they are thinking as well as how they are thinking.

Our writing-to-learn assignments include everything from short, five-minute writings to longer pieces that require more in-depth exploration. We use entrance slips, short 3-5 sentence writings about an assigned topic which students bring to class and either present at the door or shortly after class begins. We use exit slips, short 3-5 sentence writings focusing on what they learned in class, questions they have, or even suggestions for the next day's class. We ask students in the middle of class to write a couple of pertinent questions about the day's class focus, or we ask them to do a focused freewrite exploring their current knowledge and information about a topic under discussion. They write letters to the teacher about what they are learning or wondering, and they write letters to their peers about their own work or that of the other students. On occasion we ask them to write a brief response on a note card to another student's presentation, writing, or talk. On these note cards students might write three main ideas or points they got from the other student's presentation, or they might write three things they can describe about their peer's writing. We also write short ditties or poems about the day's topic, and in class we often create webs or clusters to generate and organize ideas. Similarly, we brainstorm, list, or categorize our ideas and discussions. And in an age of expanding technology, we also communicate with each other through email, listservs, or web sites about the class, important points to remember, or questions that need to be addressed.

We also use some long-term writing-to-learn assignments. We and the students often keep learning logs, project journals, or daybooks to record information over time. In these cumulative notebooks we take notes, make meaning of our notes, make personal connections to the text or new knowledge gained in class discussions, ask questions, try to figure out important issues, and collect class freewrites.

We do not GRADE these writing-to-learn assignments, and occasionally we do not even read them. However, the assignments are required, and we give students credit in the grade book for their completion. When we need to find out from the students' writing how and what they are learning, we read their entries so that we can learn what and how to teach. We diagnose, analyze, figure out the next steps we and the students need to take. By not rushing to grade every piece of writing-to-learn, we avoid passing judgment too soon; we avoid pronouncing a verdict; and we TEACH! We put off the grading so we can focus on teaching and learning, just as people in the world outside of school focus on learning what they need, not on being graded.

Dancing with our students in longer projects

For longer projects, ones on which students work for a sustained period, we provide continuous, ongoing assessment. To make that assessment useful to students, we try to communicate clearly and provide helpful guidance, not render verdicts or final judgments about the product as it stands. The process that works effectively for us and our students is to do a little D.A.N.C.E. with them (Figure 2). While we simultaneously assess, teach, and guide by following these steps, we do not always follow the steps sequentially.

Figure 2
A D.A.N.C.E. With Our Students

Describe what is in the student work.

Account for what is in the student work by relating it to the expectations of the assignment, the goal of the work.

Nudge students by questioning, guiding, suggesting, probing, prodding.

Compromise with students by negotiating gaps, goals.

Envision with students; set plans of action collaboratively.

Describe: The first step in our D.A.N.C.E. is to describe what we see in the students' work. We offer specific comments about what is in the writing thus far. Some typical written or oral comments include, "You're right on track here with this point" or "You have useful details that will be helpful for your project." We tend to offer this type of description all along as the longer project develops.

Account: In the "accounting" step of the D.A.N.C.E. we either write or talk with these students about the expectations or goals of the assignment. We relate —or, better yet, we ask the students to relate—what they have done so far that speaks to the original purpose or goals of the assignment. Then we describe again by talking about what we see, and we ask the students to talk about what they see at this juncture.

Nudge: The next step in our D.A.N.C.E. is to nudge the students by questioning, making suggestions, probing, and prodding. We are also careful at this point to provide a scaffold or process for the students' next step. Sometimes, however, we reach stalemates with students. They do not see what we are suggesting, are unable to make the next step, or just do not want to the put the next foot forward.

Compromise: In a circumstance when the students choose or are unable to follow through with our suggestions, we step back and consider a compromise. We discuss with them the gap we see between the work so far and the goals we have set. Then we negotiate by presenting a suggestion and asking the students to develop a proposal for moving to the next level.

Envision: Through negotiating and compromising, we and the students envision a product and a way to reach the students' or the teacher's established goal for an assignment or experience. We develop together a Plan of Action, a pathway with check points along the way, that leads to the satisfactory completion of the work.

As we work through this process during the development of a product, we take care to develop a non-threatening, non-punitive relationship with students. We try to become partners in learning with the students, although we know the power is out of balance. We will, after all, be the one who ultimately decides about the grade the students have earned. We know it, and the students know it. But we try to acknowledge that inequity and work through the tension with the students. In our view this is teaching in its most rewarding sense: we are both guiding and learning. We are learning about the students, their work, their needs, and their own process of working, negotiating, and setting personal goals.

Assessing Writing to Learn in a Russia Project

As an example of an Assessment D.A.N.C.E. with students, we describe here a specific long-term small group project on Russia often taught in sixth grade social studies. The goal of this unit on Russia is for students to learn as much as possible about Russia—its geography, culture, history, politics, economics, and everyday life. Throughout the project the teacher, Deidre, uses writing-to-learn assignments and informally, yet constantly, assesses the students' work.

Getting started

To introduce the project on Russia, Deidre asks the sixth graders to do an individual web in which they include everything they know, think they know, or want to know about Russia. They include impressions, information, questions, associations related to Russia. They address history, politics, climate, people, literature, language, current living conditions, news events, or any other area that pops into their minds. The purpose of the webbing is to focus and generate students' thinking, to use writing as a tool for discovering as well as exploring thought. If Deidre happens to have a group of students who have little background on Russia, she might do an introductory narrative lesson in which she offers basic information, poses some questions, makes personal connections to Russia for the students, and presents a table of resources. A student web might look like the one pictured in Figure 3.

Figure 3
Sample Student Web

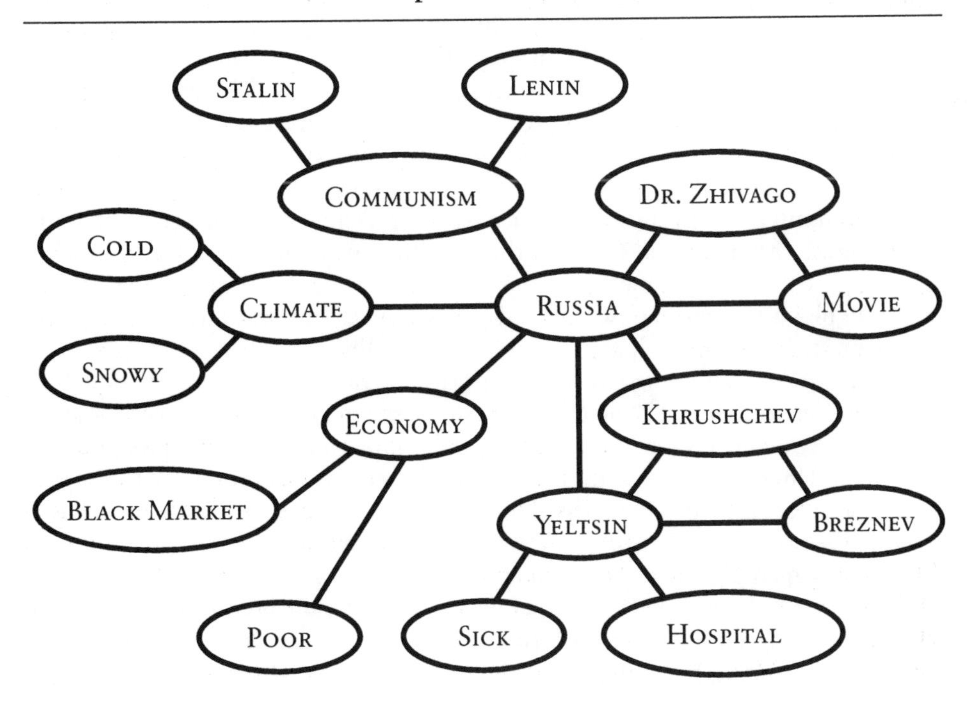

After both the students and Deidre have independently webbed for ten minutes, Deidre goes to the whiteboard and asks students to call out what they have written in their webs. She writes the students' responses, classifying the various parts of the collaborative web as she goes, creating such general categories as Culture, Geography, Politics, History, Economy, and Political Figures. She includes answers from all students and requests contributions from the more reticent students. From this co-created web, Deidre and the students develop the topics for small groups to pursue as a long-term group project on Russia. Students choose the topic on which they wish to focus, and Deidre makes notes of the various groups and the students who wish to be in them. For a class of thirty students, six groups of five students each will focus on either Russian Geography, Culture, Political Figures, Economy, History, or Politics.

To assess this writing-to-learn webbing, Deidre listens carefully as the students call out their associations, questions, and impressions, making mental note of the contributors and the contributions. To follow up the class web, she takes the students' webs, gives them full credit for doing the work, and returns the web for them to place in their own Russia Portfolio. The individual portfolio is a large folder where students keep all the materials they develop and collect throughout the project. As another introductory activity to the Russia Unit, Deidre tells the students they will be keeping a travel journal. In the journal, which will be a folder within their portfolio, they will keep their notes, research, and class activities. The first entry will be the web they have just completed.

Now that they have a travel journal, Deidre tells the students they need a passport and a visa to get into Russia. She gives the students construction paper and materials and shows them a real passport and visa to use as a model for creating their own. Their passport and visa will differ from the real ones in that students will write their name and personal information both in English and in Russian, using the Cyrillic alphabet. A Polaroid snapshot of each student completes the travel information, and the students are ready for their trip to Russia.

Deidre points on the world map to Kennedy Airport in New York and Moscow Sheremetyevo-II Airport in Moscow, Russia. Then she draws the flight path a pilot might take from New York to Moscow. During this "flight," Deidre role plays the pilot and provides some interesting historical background on Russia as well as present-day customs and their cultural origin. The students take double-column notes in the travel journals while Deidre plots information, concepts, dates, and historical facts on the timeline posted on the classroom wall. Students keep a similar timeline in their travel journals for their own reference. Deidre explains that from now on, students will place important dates, facts, and details on their own as well as the classroom timeline.

So how does Deidre assess the passport and travel journals as introductory writing-to-learn activities? She takes up the passports, looks them over for accuracy, gives students credit in her trusty grade book, and posts the passports on the Russia Unit bulletin board. She eventually returns the passports to the students for placement in their individual portfolios. Deidre also watches the students make notes in the travel journals as she presents background information; she makes a mental note about each student's participation. Later she reads and reviews the travel journals in more detail, but for now, she is content that the students are getting the necessary information recorded, ready for additional facts, details, and insights they will gain as the unit study progresses.

Group projects

After these introductory activities and the students have "arrived" in Russia, the small groups begin their work together. They start with the portion of the class web (now copied from the whiteboard onto butcher block paper and hung in the classroom) that refers to their topic, and they begin to expand that portion of the web. If, for example, their topic is Russian Political Figures, they now add more information from Deidre's discussion, add questions they want to answer, and clarify the direction of their web. Each group develops a web that serves as the ever-evolving plan of their work. Students copy the web and keep it in their individual travel journals. Deidre checks these web-writings by watching over the shoulders of the group members, by spot-checking the travel journals, and by reading and responding to the entries thoroughly at the end of the unit. In the process of reading over shoulders and spot-checking, Deidre reminds the students of other information they need to include and guides the class as a whole about the travel journals and their function in the project.

The members of the small groups become research partners throughout the Russia project. Their goal is to learn as much as they can, organize their information in an interesting way, and to teach what they have learned to the rest of the class. They become experts and display that expertise through both a group presentation and a group portfolio. The group presentation may vary in format, but must take thirty minutes and include the following: (1) a written report that has been collaboratively developed; (2) representative visuals; (3) accurate material and information; (4) an interesting format. In addition, the presentation must reflect complete preparation and involve all members of the group.

The group decides the kind and focus of their research, and the group members follow up individually or in pairs. Some students go to the Internet for information that they place in their travel journals; others interview available community resource people and make notes; others go to print sources or other text forms like videos, slides, and photographs. Students take notes in their travel journals, always reporting to their group each day.

As a means of assessing both the group's progress and information being collected, Deidre requires a daily written report from each group. She uses this report to (1) keep track of students' progress; (2) record credit for that progress; (3) offer feedback and guidance in writing and/or in verbal conferences.

Assessing in-process through a D.A.N.C.E.

Until this point, Deidre has been mainly assessing students' work by observing, making anecdotal notes to herself, and recording completion checks (✓) in the grade book. Now that the long-term project is underway, she begins her D.A.N.C.E. with individual groups of students. As she talks with the groups, reads their daily reports, and spot checks their travel journals, she **describes** what she sees in their work. A typical comment to the Political Figures Group might be:

> You have a good start by listing a number of pertinent political figures. It's great that you included both current and historical figures—everyone from Lenin to Yeltsin.

Providing this brief, yet pointed description shows the students she is paying attention and that they are proceeding appropriately.

As the groups continue over the next few days, Deidre monitors closely, reads their daily progress reports, and checks their travel journals. She reminds the groups of their goal to be extensive in their research and to become experts. As she reads their notes and reports, Deidre realizes that a couple of groups are stuck. They have done the basic reading in encyclopedias and the textbook, but they lack extensive, in-depth information that will give them the stories they will need to make a part of their presentations interesting to their peers. To the whole class she recommends more resources, reminds them to search the Internet, and also mentions how groups have found materials that might be useful to other groups. She recommends that they interview each other.

As she speaks directly to the Political Figures Group about their work, she offers the following comments.

> I can see that you've done the basic research from the textbook and the class encyclopedias. Given that you will be the class experts on Political Figures, and you will be teaching this to the class, you probably need to use some other sources. How about checking the Internet [I have a couple of sites where you can start] and the library for more information and materials?

In this response assessment, Deidre not only accounts for where the students are in their process and reminds them of their goals, she also begins to **nudge** them by suggesting that they extend their research and expand their resource list. Such a response precludes her assigning a grade at this point in the students' process; rather, she offers guidance and gives them credit for where they are, what they have accomplished.

If the Political Figures Group resists Deidre's suggestions or just does not follow through with consulting more extensive, varied resources, Deidre and the students talk about the goals of the project and how they intend to get there. The following conversation represents an exchange between Deidre and the student group.

> Deidre: I notice that you've stopped doing research and did not try the Internet. What have you found so far?
>
> Group: Well, we found these five great books on Russia, and each one had some good stuff on the Political Figures we have chosen.
>
> Deidre: And which figures did you finally select?
>
> Group: Well, we decided just to do Lenin and Yeltsin, since they're both so interesting, and we found lots on them.
>
> Deidre: I can see how those two figures would interest the class, but I'd like you to have representatives from other periods as well. If you added five more important Political Figures, who would they be?
>
> Group: Hmmm...maybe Khrushchev? Gorbachev? Stalin? Czar Nicholas II? Catherine the Great? Peter the Great? Rasputin? Maybe even Solzhenitsyn—even though he was a writer, could he also be a political figure?
>
> Deidre: Yes, certainly. Are you interested in adding any of these figures to your report?

Group: [Silence. . . .]
Deidre: How about this? Your job as a group is to teach important Russian political figures from different time periods to the class. Of course, you'll want to make your teaching interesting and informative. How about if you choose five figures—each from a different period in history—and concentrate on those? Since there are five members in your group, each of you could be responsible for one figure, but you could all help each other. I'll go away and let you decide how you will handle this process; let me know your plan tomorrow.
Group: Okay.

In this brief conversation Deidre has clearly done some questioning and leading, but she has also tried to negotiate a compromise with the students by suggesting that they do more than two political figures, but fewer than the seven they have already named. She also offered a possible vision for how they might tackle this expanded list by making each group member responsible for one political figure.

Deidre displays positive communication skills and teaching here; but she is also practicing assessment-in-process. Deidre is guiding, nudging, negotiating, and compromising with the students. She is assessing, but she is not grading. She does not give the students a "C" on their two-person political figures list; rather, she reviews the goals of the group and asks the students to respond accordingly.

Writing process in action

After the students have completed their group research, they decide on a format for the written portion of their class report. Deidre has offered the groups a number of options and has suggested that they can even go beyond the ones she has offered. They can write a dialogue between television commentators about their topic, compose a debate, develop a video complete with a script, write a play or skit, compose a formal lecture complete with visual references, develop a web site, or think of another format. Once the group has decided on a form, they collaboratively write their script. They use what they know about writing and do some brainstorming and consulting of their research notes before beginning their draft. After they have developed their first draft, they get feedback from another group of students in the class. They revise the piece, get more responses from another group, and ask Deidre to read the piece for clarity, accuracy, and coherence. From both their peer group's and Deidre's responses, they revise again and edit the piece for final copy. They may ask Deidre to do a final "teacher edit," or they may ask other students to edit their piece.

Throughout the process of the students' collaborative writing and developing the written form of their class presentation, they receive feedback from their peers. Deidre also has the opportunity to respond to the students' writing, and to make suggestions for improvement, and to give a final read and edit of the paper. As she observes and participates in this process, she sees assessment in process during the development of the paper. Again, she has not assigned a grade, but has continually assessed the content and quality of the paper.

Products and grading

Group Grading. The culmination of the Russia group project occurs when each expert group teaches its topic to the whole class. Each group gets thirty minutes to teach about Russian Culture, Economy, Political Figures, History, or Geography while the rest of the class learns and takes notes. Obviously this process takes several days. During the presentations, Deidre observes and takes notes on the accuracy, the quality of the presentation, and the degree to which all members are participating. At the end of the presentation, each group gives Deidre its Group Portfolio. The Portfolio includes the group web, the students' travel journals with notes, the final collaboratively written report, and an assessment of everyone's participation in the project. Deidre uses her continuous observation assessment notes as well as the Group Portfolio to determine a final grade on the Group Russia Project. With good conscience she can assign the grade the students have earned. Because she has encouraged quality throughout the process, she expects that all the students who have participated actively will receive good grades (Figure 4).

Figure 4
Group Portfolios

Components		*Points*
Daily Written Reports: 5 Due (3 pts. Each)		_____ (15)
Group Web*		
Completion (2 pts.); Quality (1-3 pts.)		_____ (5)
Travel Journals: Research Notes		
(Individually Evaluated and Averaged for Group Score)		
Completion (2 pts.); Quality (1-3 pts.)		_____ (5)
Final Written Report		
Group Brainstorming (5 pts.)	_____ (5)	
First Draft (5 pts.)	_____ (5)	
First Revision with Feedback (5 pts.)	_____ (5)	
Second Revision (5 pts.)	_____ (5)	
Second Revision with Feedback (5 pts.)	_____ (5)	
Third Revision with Final Edit (5 pts.)	_____ (5)	
Final Copy (10 pts.)	_____ (10)	
		_____ (40)
Oral Presentation of Final Report		
Accuracy (5 pts.)	_____ (5)	
Quality of Presentation (5 pts.)	_____ (5)	
Equality of Participation (5 pts.)	_____ (5)	
Visual (5 pts.)	_____ (5)	
		_____ (20)

Figure 4 (cont.)
Group Portfolios

Group's Self-Assessment of Process & Effort (5 pts.)	_____	(5)
Teacher's Observations—Group Efforts, Dynamics (10 pts.)	_____	(10)
Total	_____ (100 possible)	

* Group Web Quality Ratings
1 pt. = Bare Bones
2 pts. = Some Connections Made Between Categories, Some Extensions of Categories
3 pts. = Thorough Brainstorming, Numerous Connections Between Categories, Each Category Extensively Developed

Individual Grading.

Building on the group projects and presentations, individual students have simultaneously been creating their own Individual Russia Portfolio. They have their own webs, group webs, and passports from the introductory activities. As they listened to their peers' presentations, they added notes to their travel journals, have filled out their Russian maps with details of topography, economy, agriculture, cities, rivers, and surrounding areas. They have also plotted important dates, people, and events on their own and the posted class timeline. At the end of the unit they organize all these parts of their portfolio, label them and turn the entire portfolio into Deidre. Deidre assigns a grade to the students' portfolios on the basis of satisfactory completion of all its parts. Just as in the Group Portfolio, if the students have been active and have followed through with all the assignments, Deidre can expect that they will earn good grades (Figure 5).

Figure 5
Individual Portfolios

Components	*Points*	
Individual Web: Completion (2 pts.); Quality (1-3 pts.)	_____	(5)
Class Web: Completion (5 pts.)	_____	(5)
Passport/Visa: Completion (8 pts.); English/Russian (5 pts.); Picture (2 pts.)	_____	(15)
Timeline Copied Class Timeline (5 pts.) Individual Additions (5-15 pts.)	_____	(20)

Figure 5 (cont.)
Individual Portfolios

Map of Russia
Topography (10 pts.)
Economic Issues (5 pts.)
Agricultural Products (5 pts.)
Cities and Rivers (10 pts.)
Surrounding Areas (10 pts.) ______ (40)

Travel Journal
Double Column Teacher Notes (5 pts.)
Research Notes (5 pts.)
Other Groups' Presentation Notes (5 pts.) ______ (15)

Teacher Comments Regarding Effort
Spaseba (Thank You) OR
Spaseba Bolshoi (Grand Thank You)

Total ______
(100 possible)

Note: Deidre could just as easily used a check (✓+/✓ /✓-) system or a simple completion of task credit for the individual portfolios.

At the end of the Russia unit, which included both individual and group portfolios as well as presentations, Deidre gives a test to check the students' grasp of the important material and information. Her test includes a short identification section complemented by a series of reflection questions that allow students to pull ideas together from their writing and their experiences listening and learning. Below are some sample questions.

1. What two Russian political figures from our study stand out in your mind? Why are they memorable to you?
2. Russia has some distinct land features. Discuss two unique features that stand out in your mind and explain how those two features affect Russian life.
3. What period of Russian history made an impression on you? Why?

With the unit completed, let us look back at all the writing-to-learn assignments and products Deidre has required during the Russia unit (Figure 6). Each of these assignments was constantly assessed, and students received response all along the way from Deidre and from each other. In addition to her extensive assessment throughout the unit and the final Individual and Group Portfolio grading, Deidre also gave a test at the end of the unit as a final review of the material. Although the final test is the easiest product for Deidre to "grade," it is not her most important assessment. Her most important assessment has been her continuous attention to the students' evolving work, the D.A.N.C.E., and the quality products their work produced. She put off grading as long as possible but never stopped assessing.

Figure 6

Individual Portfolios	Group Portfolios
Individual Web	Group Web
Class Web	Travel Journal (includes research notes for group project)
Passport	Group Project (includes collaborative Timeline written report, visuals, presentation interest and accuracy)
Map of Russia	Participation Assessment as group member
Travel Journal (includes all of above plus notes from teacher narrative and class notes)	

A Final Disclaimer

We cannot end this article without acknowledging the "downside" to not grading. In the current climate of systematic testing, an emphasis on students' knowledge of discreet pieces of information, the public's addiction to grades, and even the students' over-reliance on grades, on-going assessment not translated into a grade on every piece of work is a challenge, maybe even a risk. However, we and Deidre are convinced that both parents and students prefer learning over grading and that students' participating in rigorous experiences like Deidre's Russia unit will make them forget about grading, focus on applying knowledge, and concentrate on learning.

Works Cited

Ashton-Warner, Sylvia. 1986. *Teacher*. New York: Simon & Schuster.

Bleich, David. 1975. *Reading and feelings: An introduction to subjective criticism*. Urbana, IL: National Council of Teachers of English.

Tchudi, Stephen, ed. 1997. *Alternatives to grading student writing*. Urbana, IL: National Council of Teachers of English.

Chapter 7

Writing and Assessment: Some Practical Ideas

Anne Wescott Dodd

In Mr. Braintree's social studies class, Jill struggled to recall what the Missouri Compromise was and what date she should write down on her paper. Mr. B always seemed to ask the pickiest questions about the reading. No matter how many times she read over the assignment the night before, Jill ended up with a very low passing or a failing grade on the reading quiz. Later that day when Mr. B graded the quizzes, he was just as frustrated as Jill; it seemed that only three or four students had done the reading. "They just don't care," he thought. "They'd rather skateboard or watch TV than do their homework"

Meanwhile across the hall in Ms. Smiley's class, several small groups of students were scattered about, engaged in conversation. Their task was to compare their summaries of the major concepts in the textbook chapter and to construct a new summary that most effectively presented the purpose of the Missouri Compromise and explained the reasons it was an important historical event. John beamed as the recorder in his group responded to his suggestion that perhaps it would be good to include the date for later reference. That afternoon, Ms. S checked off the individual summaries as having been done, but she carefully read only the five group summaries (rather than the 24 reading quizzes Mr. B corrected). On her lesson plan notes for the next day, she jotted down points that some groups didn't mention and chose one of the summaries to share with the class as an exemplar. She was pleased to see that every team had a good understanding of the major concepts although, of course, some of the group summaries were more tightly organized and better developed than others.

There are several points from these two brief classroom examples to suggest that the traditional ways of assigning and assessing student work may not be very helpful for fostering achievement or for motivating further learning. By shifting the focus from memorizing factoids to understanding concepts and from grading/correcting student work to assessing what students have learned in order to improve teaching effectiveness, teachers may get better results. And these results are likely to become more important as more states and school districts adopt learning standards for students. In some cases student achievement is already being used or discussed as a factor in teacher evaluation.

One powerful strategy for meeting this challenge is not formal writing that teachers grade, but informal writing that can be thought of as thinking or talking on paper. There are several reasons that informal writing can help teachers do a better job of teaching. However, the use of such writing also requires that teachers rethink their assessment practices. Changing one without the other may not do the job. In thinking about using informal writing, teachers should consider these general principles:

Students don't always learn what you teach.

There are many ways to misunderstand or get something wrong.

Students learn best when they are actively engaged in learning and can see the meaning and purpose of an assigned task.

One of the best ways for teachers to increase learning and to improve teaching is to understand more about the class from the perspectives of students.

Informal Writing as Formative Assessment

Informal writing, which I often refer to as "free writing,"is "working writing," writing wearing jeans and a T-shirt. This type of writing is best used as *formative* assessment (a way of finding out what students are learning along the way and how the teacher might help them improve) rather than *summative* assessment (a judgment about students' achievement on a final product, such as a paper, an exam, or a project). To extend the analogy above, formal writing for a final product can be described as writing dressed up in a suit and tie or wearing a dress and heels. Because informal writing is a way of assessing students' progress in process and students do not usually have time to revise or edit their work, teachers should concern themselves with content rather than conventions. In other words, there is no need to correct errors in spelling, punctuation, and the like. Later, of course, teachers could ask students to revise and polish an informal writing and turn it in again. Then it would make sense to grade or mark a paper for mechanics as well as content.

The reading summaries students wrote in Ms. S's class provide a good example of writing as *formative* assessment. She did not ask students to recall factoids or to write answers to the questions at the end of the chapter, which can often be done quite well without even reading the chapter if students copy the appropriate passages even when the text is written in another language! Instead she asked students to select the "big ideas" in the reading and to use their own words to explain them. Ms. S wasn't concerned with grading individual work because she knew some students might not have understood the text. A few may even have misunderstood it in important ways. However, by collaborating with classmates to create group summaries, students could teach each other. Thus, even though she had clear expectations of what students needed to know about the Missouri Compromise, Ms. S used this writing to figure out what she might do to help all students "get it."

Evaluating homework by assigning individual grades at this time, as Mr. B did, would have been counter-productive. Failing grades might discourage the students who need to learn the most and perhaps make some, such as Jill in Mr. B's class, decide it is pointless to do any work. Instead of grades, Ms. S. used checks to record the work students had done and also made notes of points to go over in the next day's class.

Of course, later in the process, perhaps at the end of a unit, *summative* assessment makes sense as a way of evaluating students' overall learning. Although some people might argue that grading is never a good idea, the reality is that some grades are necessary because schools require them. A strategy of dealing with grading will be discussed in a later section.

Informal writing in any subject can include the following:

1. writing what students know about a topic at the beginning of a new unit. This is a good way to find out what personal knowledge students have that may enrich the curriculum; e.g., perhaps a student's family has lived or traveled in the country students will study in a geography class, as well as prior misconceptions that may hinder learning of new concepts, as in a science or mathematics unit.
2. explaining the process they used to solve a problem or find an answer. This strategy is especially useful for finding out how well students understand a math concept.
3. summarizing what was learned in class along with any questions or concerns students have. Teachers often try to gauge how well students understand by asking, "Are there any questions?" Hearing none, they may erroneously assume that everyone understood. Yet who among us ever wants to look stupid? Students in competitive honors classes may be the ones least likely to let anyone know they don't understand. Another benefit of asking students to write is that the teacher gets a response from every student. There isn't enough time in any class to let every student do the same aloud. If students were all willing to speak up through informal writing, though, teachers "hear" from every student.
4. maintaining a log of their progress on a long-term project. If monitored by the teacher on a regular basis, this is helpful in preventing students from doing the whole project the night before it is due, thus encouraging them to produce work of higher quality.
5. writing some thoughts in response to a teacher's question or after viewing a video as preparation for a class discussion. The pre-writing ensures that everyone has something to share and usually leads to more engaging discussions.
6. writing a personal comment to include with a student's lab report, final test, or project. This strategy gives students the opportunity to let the teacher know of any problems they encountered (personal or academic) as well as what they liked or disliked about the assignment. The latter comments help teachers see how they might improve their teaching or task design in the future.
7. writing a note to explain why an assignment has not been done. If these notes are required, they can be an important way for teaching students to become more responsible, but they can also provide teachers with useful information for working with students to help them get or stay on track. The teacher can give extensions to students with one-time personal problems that prevented their getting the work done on time or begin to work with students who rarely get

the homework done to help them figure out how to change their bad habits.

The suggestions above are just beginning points for using informal writing to learn and communicate. Such writing can empower students because it gives them a voice, a safe avenue for sharing their thoughts and concerns with the teacher. This writing can also serve to motivate further learning. When teachers ask students to share what they think and feel, they send a message to students that they care about them both as students and as people. Informal writing also makes it possible for teachers to personalize learning for each student.

In my own experience as a high school and middle school teacher and as a college supervisor of student teachers, I have seen that the use of informal writing changes the classroom in very positive ways. Two-way communication shifts the focus from do this because the teacher says so to one of building a climate of trust and mutual respect among students and the teacher. In this environment students rarely disrupt the class with inappropriate behavior, and they begin to view what they are learning as more important than the grades they get. However, since most are working harder than they might have before, overall grades tend to be higher than in a more traditionally taught class.

But How Can Teachers Grade Without Grading Everything?

Many teachers think that students won't do any work unless they get grades, and, although that may not be completely true, there is no way in most schools for teachers not to give grades. Once they get used to the idea, my students tell me they prefer getting feedback from me in the form of comments and questions on their work to having grades on it. But having no grades doesn't mean that there is no accountability. Consider, for example, how teachers might use a Homework/Classwork Grade plan. This strategy uses positive motivation to get students to do their homework and classwork when it will not be graded. First, it's necessary to decide how much of a student's quarter grade will be based on homework. (I used 20% for my high school English students.) Then the teacher tells students that, as of the beginning of the course, they all have A's for homework/classwork grades and that these will count as 20% (or whatever has been decided) of their quarter grades. Of course, students will be delighted but suspicious!

My technique is to pause briefly to let the suspense build and then to say, "But, in order to keep the A's, you must have your homework done every day at the beginning of class and available for me to check on the corner of your desks. Each day a homework assignment is not completed on time, your grade will be reduced by one letter grade (or incrementally from B+ to B to B- instead of using a whole grade)." This method means that students get no grades on the individual assignments. They get checks if they have work done. A quick walk around the class with roll sheet in hand takes care of the daily check on homework in a few minutes. Or, if teachers want to scan the work done in class, they can check them off as they read them. When I collect the papers, I write brief comments on them to go with the checks, and, if the work is below a minimum standard (carelessly done or incomplete), I require that students re-do it to earn the check.

This strategy works well for most students, but, teachers who wish to try it should be forewarned; there will be a few students whose A's quickly become D's or F's. So what happens to them? First, I tell students that in order to pass for the quarter, they must do *every* homework and classwork assignment. When I say this, someone will always say, "You can't do that! It's not fair." I reply, "This course will be easy for some of you because you have talent in this subject, but others will have to work very hard. I don't want to give anyone who is really trying a failing grade. The way you show me you are trying is to do all of the work. If you don't do it even once, I will assume you don't care. Thus, I will guarantee at least a D- for the quarter grade if all of your work, even if late, is completed by the make-up deadline one week before the quarter ends," (I fill in the appropriate date here and note it in **bold** on the assignment sheet.) This explanation usually quells all complaints because students can see that the plan is reasonable and fair.

This strategy does require some extra work, unless teachers don't mind having to deal with an unhappy student, parent, or administrator later on. My records of work completed and the dates assignments were turned in must be accurate and up to date. I also remind students who are in danger of failing that they have work due. I either write notes on papers that are turned in or periodically issue little slips like the one in Figure 1.

Figure 1

Date ______________________
To ______________________

DON'T FORGET

YOUR MISSING WORK:

____
____
____
____
____

Don't miss the deadline indicated on your assignment sheet!

Teachers may wish to give students who have not worked their way down to D's an opportunity to bring their homework grades back up to C's (and maybe B's, but I don't allow this for moving up to an A). I indicate what will count as extra credit for this purpose but also explain that the extra credit must be done in addition to the original assignment. Some activities I have counted in high school

English classes include extra reading and a written reflection on it, special research on a relevant topic which they will share with classmates, or a written reflection on a relevant TV program (PBS, Discovery channel). I also encourage all students (even if they have homework / classwork grades of A) to do this type of extra work because it encourages them to make connections between what we do in class and the real world outside school.

A caveat for teachers who wish to try this approach: call the parents of any student who is in danger of failing *long enough before the make-up deadline so that the student can get the work done* if the parents put on the pressure. If parents aren't notified, preferably with a phone call rather than a note or progress report, teachers may find they'll have the extra stress of dealing with an angry parent.

Some students may try to call a teacher's bluff the first time they use this strategy by failing to do one assignment just to see if the teacher meant what was said. If a teacher has notified the parents in each such case, the student should get the failing grade. The word will get around that the teacher means business, and no one will likely try that again. I used this method with my high school students for several years, and the only students who failed were those who rarely came to school. They would probably have failed no matter what method I used. On the other hand, once I began grading homework and classwork in this way, I found that more students were doing assignments on a regular basis.

By using checks instead of grades, teachers can focus on what students need to know or learn how to do and change their lesson plans to address the needs. Feedback, either presented orally to the whole class or in notes to individual students on the informal writing or paper drafts, helps students see what they need to work on. When a problem is too complicated to communicate in a short note, I write "See me please" on the student's paper. Then I meet with the student privately during class or at some other convenient time to discuss the problem in more detail.

The Benefits of Using Informal Writing and Fewer Grades

By using informal writing as a way of talking or thinking on paper, teachers begin to think less about grades and more about how they can better help students learn what they need to know. Because they gain important information about students' perspectives from these writings, they can better understand how they might change their teaching methods and lesson plans to focus specifically on what students have difficulty with. As every experienced teacher knows, what works with one student or one class may not work as well for others. As more and more states and districts adopt learning standards that students are required to meet, teachers will find that informal writing, if used consistently and thoughtfully, can be a very useful tool for diagnosing student weaknesses and targeting those in their teaching *before* the final (summative) assessment, whether that be a standardized test, portfolio, or student exhibition.

But for me an even more important result of using these strategies has been that teaching itself has become more rewarding and enjoyable. I have found that my students have become more motivated to learn and much more likely to do the required work than they were when I used more traditional methods, such as the ones Mr. Braintree did. As students follow my lead and shift their attention from grading to learning, they begin to become more intrinsically motivated.

In addition to fostering intrinsic motivation, informal writing offers another important benefit. Even though I usually write only brief comments and many notes that say "please see me"on their papers, students view these as an indication that I am personally interested in their success. That I take the time to read and respond rather than grade and correct their work makes them feel they count. And, when I use their feedback to make changes in my teaching and tell them why I am doing so, they begin to feel some ownership of the class. No longer does the class belong solely to the teacher. It is also theirs, and what they do can make a difference. Most choose to make it a more comfortable and less stressful place for all of us. I can honestly say that, with very few exceptions, conflicts about grading are a thing of the past. The students and I collaborate as learners. As they learn the content, I am still the expert. But, they are also my teachers. Through their informal writings, I am constantly learning better ways to teach. My only regret is that no one told me when I was a failing and floundering first-year teacher how powerful the simple idea of informal writing could be.

Chapter 8

Using Vignettes in a Sophomore Math Classroom

Sharon B. Walen and Kathleen L. Ayers

The popular press often views those who study mathematics as different from the average person, somehow brighter, while students talk of mathematics teachers whose classes they fail as "too smart to explain math to me." Math teachers may have only themselves to blame for these views, not because of any intentional move to become an elite group, but simply because of the abstract way mathematics has traditionally been presented to students. When students ask, "When are we ever going to use this," teachers have customarily answered, "You'll need it later—in algebra, in geometry, or in calculus." In the past, it was common for high school mathematics teachers to expect all *non-mathematics oriented* students to take only the minimum number of classes required for graduation and to expect to lose half their *mathematics oriented* students each year after the eighth grade (National Research Council 1989, 1990). However, many teachers are currently attempting to change these trends by reforming their classrooms to reflect the goals outlined by the National Council of Teachers of Mathematics in the *Standards* documents: *Curriculum and Evaluation Standards for School Mathematics* (1989), *Professional Standards for Teaching Mathematics* (1991), *Assessment Standards for School Mathematics* (1995), and *Principles and Standards for School Mathematics-Draft* (1998).

Reflecting the general tone of these reform documents, teachers, such as those participating in the Systemic Initiative for Montana Mathematics and Science (SIMMS) Project, are currently attempting to provide students with sense-making experiences through which they may construct mathematical knowledge through meaningful engagement with concepts in real world settings. Ms. Kay, the teacher who shares her classroom experiences in this story, is one such teacher. Following this new philosophy of mathematics teaching and learning, Ms. Kay commonly incorporates the use of technology, writing assignments, alternative assessment techniques, and small-group structures into her secondary mathematics classroom. Her intent is to have mathematics become a subject for all, not just the elite. Although this chapter reflects the views of many teachers working to reform mathematics education, the voice of this particular teacher and the voices of her students provide a discussion of what it is like to experience small-group structures in reform classrooms.

Research on small-group structures is not new. Several excellent summary reviews are provided by Johnson et al. (1983), Slavin (1989), and, most recently,

Good, Mulryan, and McCaslin (1992). In addition, there is a growing body of research examining the social climate of the mathematics classroom (Lo & Wheately 1994; Cobb, Wood, Yackel, & McNeal 1992; Mehan, 1979). Supporting these efforts, detailed analysis of interactions between individuals (Mulryan 1995; Williams & Ivey 1994; Lo & Wheately 1994; Voigt 1994, King 1993) and whole groups (Frid & Malone 1994) have provided us with a rich picture of the effect of classroom social interactions on individuals. However, in their comprehensive review of grouping for instruction in mathematics, Good, Mulryan, and McCaslin (1992) state research on small groups is incomplete, particularly on students' reactions to working in groups and on instructional activities:

> Information is needed, however, about how groups can facilitate certain student attitudes and problem-solving abilities, including the knowledge of when to work with others, when to work alone, and how to vary these two approaches. We believe that programmatic research on small-group instructional processes could yield information that is extremely helpful to practitioners by providing them with concepts, findings and theories that could lead them to design better small-group instructional activities (p. 193).

In meeting this challenge, this chapter documents the contrasting classroom views of a teacher and her students regarding the nature and effectiveness of student groups. This work is framed broadly within a constructivist view of knowledge and learning; that is, individuals are believed to frame their knowing by reflecting within their world. Because students construct their knowledge in the social and cultural environment of the classroom (Gillespie 1992), this work places primary importance on the social setting. In particular, we will show how Ms. Kay was able to use vignettes and her students' written reactions to discover hidden problems and to help her students resolve problems present in the small groups in her classroom.

The students and teacher described in this chapter were part of a two-year project that took place in Montana in a mid-sized high school. The larger project was designed to examine the use of journals in secondary mathematics classrooms. Data referred to in this chapter are part of that project and include field notes, brief student interviews, in-depth student interviews, in-depth teacher interviews, and classroom artifacts. In particular, three distinct sources of information combine to tell this story of Ms. Kay and her students: the teacher's reported views of her classroom, students' reported views of that same classroom, and the teacher's and students' responses to a vignette activity designed to encourage students to talk and write about small-group problems.

Teacher's Views of Classroom Groups

As Ms. Kay discussed her philosophy of education and the changes she had made to her classroom, she expressed confidence that the changes she had made to the classroom's social setting would not produce negative emotions or otherwise hamper her students' abilities to gain knowledge. Ms. Kay indicated that she saw small-group interaction as promoting an individual's ability to learn and considered groups a vehicle to support students' construction of meaningful mathematics. Although the integrated materials used by Ms. Kay were designed for group work, teachers in this project were autonomous in their classrooms. Ms. Kay did not adopt a pedagogical policy dictated by others but independently determined how she would teach. She began her efforts with little or no classroom experience in teaching students in a collaborative group setting. However, she was a master teacher with many years of experience in teaching mathematics at the secondary level and approached learning new classroom routines with confidence gained through experience.

Ms. Kay thought that her students needed help in getting started working in groups and reserved the first week of the school year for that purpose. During that week, she designed opportunities for students to "get to know each other." She used activities gleaned from conversations with other teachers, texts on cooperative groups such as those authored by Johnson and Johnson (1991), Artz and Newman (1990) and Kagan (1992), and teacher journals such as the *Mathematics Teacher*. Some of the activities were similar to scavenger hunts, in which she gave students a list of criteria such as "find someone in the class who likes horses." Other activities included variations on a theme where students were required to *find out* about a classmate and introduce them. Ms. Kay said that these activities "build a sense of community" and "help get the year off to a good start." Yet, she did not describe any activities or mention a need for teaching small-group skills after the students had been working together for a period. These activities were introductions, allowing students to meet their classmates, but did not provide a picture of students in work settings. Interestingly, these activities did not make an impression on the students who were interviewed. When asked later in the year, none of the students participating in these activities remembered these lessons on cooperative learning.

Initially, Ms. Kay also provided her students with a formal structure to use as they began to work in groups. This formal structure commonly involved assigning roles to the group members such as those advocated by Johnson and Johnson (1991) for establishing interdependence. Ms. Kay talked about establishing formal turn-taking rules and commented that these strategies had merit in placing structure on the groups to guarantee that all students participated. Although well intentioned, Ms. Kay later commented that these structures were placed on the small group by teacher directive. She stated that mandated roles did not show students how to make collaborative decisions or learn to determine if individuals had something to add to the discussion. Ms. Kay also commented that mandated roles also did not guarantee the appearance of talents, emergence of ideas, or sharing of knowledge. Although she began by assigning roles, Ms. Kay came to feel that the entire notion of *telling* students to work together was counterproductive for students learning to negotiate their own group roles, to add to the group in the best way that they might, and to be proud of their contributions. Ms. Kay ultimately argued that assigned roles actually inhibited some small groups from functioning. She commented, "Students with a set of 35 factoring problems just divide up the work and then combine their answers. They don't work collaboratively. Group roles do that—just divide up the work."

Ms. Kay reported that, in the beginning, the novelty of the small-group setting motivated students. As time passed, she and her students began to view small groups as common classroom practice. It was only then that she noticed some groups were not working as efficiently as she thought that they might. Even with this information, she found that she could do little to diagnose or to correct the problems; before using vignettes, her only tried and true solution was to re-form the groups in her classroom on a regular basis.

Students' Views of Classroom Groups

Ms. Kay's students began studying mathematics using the integrated materials in their Grade 9 year. Occasionally, one of the students transferred or another joined the class, but the group of students remained primarily intact for the two years they worked with us. This group of students had similar backgrounds and came from relatively stable middle class families. Many of the students had known each other for several years before working together in this mathematics class. On the surface, the class appeared to be a model classroom for reform teaching and learning of secondary mathematics.

As part of the project, individual students in this class were interviewed and asked to reflect on working together. One of the questions asked them to contrast what they felt were problems in first learning to work with a group to current problems. Although all students' interviews contained themes similar to Jan's, a Grade 10 girl, she tells the story best. In the following transcription, Jan describes what it was like when she first started working in small groups:

J: I don't think it was really hard. I mean, well, it was hard in the sense that people have different answers than you. And it was hard to know who was right. You have to go through and see who was right. That was kind of hard. But then you can check *some* of it and see. You get that option to see if you're wrong or not. That was kind of hard.

I: Is it still hard when you have different answers?

J: No, because that was before, when we just started and we really didn't know—I don't know—we didn't really know how to work with each other. And so, then, when we got used to working with each other, it got easier that way. You can work on the problem together, and, like, some people wouldn't rush ahead. That was kind of a real problem in some groups. Some people always did everything first, and then you never got a chance to do it. Then they just tell you the answers instead of helping you out. That was kind of a downfall because you didn't learn anything that way, because they wouldn't help you. They'd just tell you what it is.

I: Did your teacher do anything to get that evened out? Or did the group work it out?

J: Sometimes we just left the person who did it on their own because he wouldn't help us at all. We'd ask him how he got it, and he wouldn't tell us anyway. So, we just tried to take care of it ourselves.

I: How did you come to that agreement that *that* person was really not doing anything for the group and you were going to just let him go his own way?

J: I don't know, we all just kind of—I guess it just kind of happened. We didn't really talk about it or anything.

I: The teacher didn't do anything?
J: She didn't know.
I: Would you have liked it if she knew?
J: Yes.

Notice that during this segment of the interview, Jan began describing problems that addressed the surface structure of the small group. She was busy describing getting the work done and describing what it was like to deal with problems with multiple solutions when she suddenly changed themes to reflect the social nature of small-group work. As she began the discussion, she talked of *some people* rushing ahead. She described a setting in which her learning depended on working with people who did not work with her. For Jan, helping was not telling an answer. As Jan continued the discussion of some people, she allowed us to see that some people was a *he*. Although almost two years had passed since she first encountered this particular problem, Jan talked about it as though it had occurred last week. As she continued, she stated that yesterday's problem is still a problem. Her perception of how one member of the small group failed to contribute is powerful, but what follows is even more insightful and brings the social issue of working in small groups to the surface.

I: What could you do so that the teacher could help you with that kind of situation?
J: I don't know. I don't know. I just wanted to say, "Stop being a jerk." But, something stops me from saying that 'cause maybe it would be worse.
I: I would really like to help teachers help students, but I don't know how to tell teachers how to know what's going on.
J: Well, yeah, because she wouldn't have had a clue that he didn't tell us how to do it or even *help* us. She wouldn't of known because we didn't ever say anything to her about it. I don't know, we just kind of went along with him for a while. There was nothing ever said about it.
I: What can we do? You get in a group and it's hard to get all that stuff ironed out. I don't have an answer, do you?
J: Well, when we ended with that module, we moved to a different group. You just wait until groups change and you move to another group. You just hope that you don't get in the same group again. But that's not really good because you dread being in another group with him. I don't know.

Jan's perception of the teacher was accurate. Ms. Kay did nothing to help Jan work with this particular *he* because she did not know that there *was* a problem. In stark contrast to Jan's perspective, Ms. Kay thought that the boy in Jan's discussion was an *asset* to the group. The teacher saw the boy as a leader with excellent mathematical insight and problem solving skills. To the teacher, the boy appeared to help his group. To Jan, he *told answers* and this did not help her to understand. Jan could not say anything to the student causing the problem because adolescent social rules prevented her from confronting another student who was not pulling his weight. Jan would have liked the teacher to know about the problem but did not have a way to talk to her teacher. Jan's response to the problem was to wait until the groups changed and hope never to be in that group again. Of course, she often found herself in the same group as the boy. The boy never knew that he was a problem and Jan did not find a way to tell the teacher or confront the boy. As Jan continues, she describes another situation that has the outward appearance of a working group.

I: I agree, waiting until the groups change is one way to solve the problem.

J: Now, for me there's this other group that I really don't want to be in. Because I feel, well, [pauses and searches for a word] what word would you use for it? I can't think of the word. I feel like I don't want to say anything because I'm like scared, *but not scared*, but what's the word for that?

I: Are you afraid of what they are going to say to your ideas?

J: No, not really. It's just that the people are, I don't know, I never got along with them. I haven't gotten along with them. I don't communicate normally with them. I mean everyday in the rest of the school, I never talk to them. Then you just feel kind of weird being in the group with them because you don't know if they're—It's like I don't belong with them. It's hard for me to work with them. Like, I can work easier with some of the people in the class because I know them, sure, they are my friends. Then there's some that—I don't mind them. I don't hate them or anything, it's just hard to work with them because I don't know if they hate me or not. I mean, I just have the feeling that if they don't like you enough to talk to you outside of class, then they probably don't want to talk to you in a group.

I: I know what you mean.

J: I feel like I just don't fit with them. Well, in this one group, I had a friend that I talked to, so it was easier. But it wasn't really group work. There was four of us. The two of them, the two talk all the time, you know, they communicate. We don't communicate with them. So, us two work together and those two work together, and we didn't really work as a group. The only time we ever talked to each other was when we had to ask a question to see if they knew the answer. It just wasn't really group work.

I: What would you have liked to say to those people? Did you ever just sit there and think, "Gee, I wish I could just tell them something"?

J: No, I never did have anything that I really wanted to say to them. I mean, they weren't doing anything that was *wrong*. It was just that we—the four of us couldn't communicate with each other in class because we don't outside of class. I don't know. It was just a keep-it-that-way kind of thing. You know, *not try*.

From the teacher's view, the students were working. They were working together and talking about the task. Of course, since the teacher was not in the group, she did not know that only pairs of students were working together and the only *whole* group talk was to check answers. The point that Jan makes so eloquently about the difficulty communicating *in class* with people she did not talk to *out of class* was crucial. This teacher made the erroneous assumption that regardless of roles, students *can* talk to each other and will work together if she put them in a group.

I: What does a teacher need to know to help you through that kind of situation?

J: I'd like to group myself. I mean I would like to group ourselves because I think it would be easier. You don't have to deal with any of that stuff then. I don't think the teacher is going to know that we don't communicate like that. You know, I don't expect her to know that about us. It's hard. I think it would be easier if we could do our own—pick our own groups.

I: If teachers do decide to assign groups, what should they ideally know about before they assign students group work?

J: If they had all the information about us, I don't know. It would be hard. If I was the teacher, and I knew all of this, well, I can see that you would have to worry about the *people*. If I put all the friends together, they might not get work done because they're talking. You know, just sitting there and talking and not getting anything done. *That* you might worry about, but I don't know how I would choose groups. I would probably—I don't know. It's too hard.

I: If you were a teacher, how would you let your students know what you expected?

J: Well, I don't know. You just kind of think that if she puts you in a group of four, you gotta work together. You *just know*. It's hard. I wouldn't like to have to put the groups together. I think it would just be easier if you could work with people you wanted to work with. Then you need to make sure you get the work done. If they are not doing the work, then she could always separate you.

I: Finally, after all this, I would like to have you tell me about how groups influence your understanding about mathematics. Is there anything about mathematics that you can say, "I learned this in mathematics class because I was in a group. I would have never learned it on my own"?

J: Yeah, I think I have. I think a lot of it I wouldn't have learned. Groups help give a second opinion.

Jan was quite certain that working in groups helped her learn. Throughout the interview Jan did not suggest that working in groups was ever something she regretted. She enjoyed group work. However, some of the groups she participated in just did not meet her expectations or her needs. She thought that if you were in a group of four, then four people should be working together. These problems were too subtle to be noticed by her teacher. Perhaps the only reason that Jan mentioned the hidden problems was that her teacher had handled the obvious problems. Even so, Jan was troubled by what was hidden. She did not have a simple answer to grouping students. She simply said that it was hard.

Unlike the healthy view of classroom conflict reported by Lo and Wheatley (1994), Jan wanted to avoid conflict that might end up "making things worse." Remember that Jan felt that if she waited just a few weeks, things would change. The teacher also found changing groups a generic solution to group problems. However, as things got better for Jan, they became worse for others; the offending male's behavior frustrated another group. In any case, waiting for the group to change did not allow Jan, and others like her, to learn mathematics in the best possible setting nor did it help her learn to deal with similar situations that she would encounter as an adult. What can teachers do to become more aware of difficult group settings? How can one student be made aware that he or she is doing something that the other group members hate? Vignettes provide one method teachers may employ both to gain information from their students about group problems and to provide an opportunity for students to communicate with their peers.

The Role of Vignettes in Merging Teachers' and Students' Views of Group Work

Vignettes are not complete *stories* (Whyte 1981) with a well- defined beginning, middle, and end. They are story fragments designed to be vague. With this design, the reader provides information necessary to complete the story. This additional information comes from personal experiences working in the classroom. Through this interaction between the text and their personal experiences, readers illuminate the meaning of the text and bring about understanding through reflection. As students flesh out a story and make connections between their experiences and the vignette students, the story becomes real. The vignette students also become real and are given gender and personalities. The students themselves create stories that open up the texts and uncover what lies hidden (Gadamer [1960] 1989). What does lie hidden? For these students, problems they experience, but cannot alter, lie hidden within the text. Vignettes provide ways to talk to other students about problems and, in one student's opinion, ways to "say what needs to be said when you don't have the words."

Implementing a Vignette in the Classroom

Ms. Kay's students expected their daily activities to include group work and individual reflection and writing assignments on mathematically related topics. Therefore, the following sequence did not seem out of place.

Figure 1
Working in a Group Vignette

Working in a Group

Four students in math class have the following discussion as they work on a group problem.

Kelly: I think I remember how to do it, but I'm not sure. We can figure this out.
Chris: Kelly, can I borrow your English paper?
Kelly: Here you go.

Figure 1 (cont.)
Working in a Group Vignette

Pat: Sure we can figure it out...but how will we know if we get it right.
Gerry: Let's just ask the teacher what the rule is. Math has a lot of rules and you have to use the right rule.
Kelly: No, don't ask for help yet, we can figure this out.
Pat: I get sick of spending so much time listening to you try to figure things out and I really want to know how to do it right.
Chris: Kelly, didn't we have to go to number 20 on the English assignment?
Kelly: No, just number 15.
Gerry: This takes too long, let's just ask for the rule. If we do it wrong, we'll just get all messed up.
Kelly: But to really understand you have to figure it out yourself. That's what math is all about, figuring things out.
Pat: Yeah, but we only have ten minutes of class left and I don't want to take this home.
Gerry: I still want to ask.
Chris: Thanks, Kelly, here's your English paper back.

What's the problem that the students are having?
What should they do next?
Give your reasons for why you would or wouldn't like to be part of this group?
How would you describe the students?
If these students were part of your class, which one would you like to have as your math partner? Tell why you choose that student.

First, Ms. Kay provided her students with the vignette in Figure 1 and asked them to individually read and respond to the assignment. Second, she collected individuals' responses. Third, Ms. Kay asked her students to form their working groups and come to consensus on the same vignette and set of questions. Fourth, she collected the group consensus response to the vignette activity and provided the students with a mathematical task to work on in their groups for the remainder of the class period. For homework, Ms. Kay assigned an individual journal assignment directing students to compare their own group with the group represented by the vignette students.

Through this sequence of tasks, Ms. Kay hoped that she would be able to see if an individual's ideas were incorporated in the group response. If one of the students expressed opinions radically different from the group, she felt she would have an insider's view of that group's ability to interact. This valuable diagnostic measure of the group's collaborative skills would not tell Ms. Kay what the problem was, but it would tell her that a student was isolated from the group or by the group. Before this activity, Ms. Kay suspected that there might be occasional problems in some groups, but she felt that the students in her class were generally working well together. Ms. Kay was surprised and pleased by the extent and depth of the information that she obtained from the vignette activity and was even more pleased by her students' reactions.

Students Talking to Others by Talking About the Vignette Students

Although teachers may obtain inside information about student groups by interviewing individuals, in-depth interviews are almost impossible to orchestrate with large numbers of students. Even if a teacher is able to arrange her schedule so that she may talk to her students in semi-private settings, interviews do not provide students with opportunities to mediate their own problems. On the other hand, the use of classroom vignettes allows students to reflect on particular problems by interpreting the written dialogs from their past experiences and provides an opportunity to communicate their feelings and to talk safely to their peers by talking about the vignette students.

The group of four students selected from Ms. Kay's class used to illustrate a vignette activity consisted of two girls and two boys. Although the boys' responses were important, the following discussion centers on the girls' reactions to the assignment. The written responses from two of the girls, Amanda and Nicki, provided clear evidence of the effective nature of this activity.

Figure 2
Amanda's Response to the Vignette

Please respond to each question. Use additional paper if you need more room to tell us what you think.

What's the problem that the students are having?

There are not concentrating at all, Chris is doing his English paper and the other three are just arguing about what to do.

What should they do next?

I think one of them should read it outloud while the other three listen. Then they should all spend sometime seeing if they can get it right. If after a couple of minutes they still don't understand ask the teacher.

Give your reasons for why you would or wouldn't like to be part of this group.

I would like to be in this group because I would get along with Kelly, since we both think the same thing. But I would get mad at the kids who wouldn't even try to do the problem.

How would you describe each of the students?

Kelly: works well in a group. wants to learn. and get things done.

Chris: a little disorganized, probably doesn't care that much about math.

Figure 2 (cont.)
Amanda's Response to the Vignette

Pat: only concerned about it it done and getting it right, doesn't really care if he learns anything.

Gerry: likes to argue, hard to work with in a group

If these students were part of your class, which **one** would you like to have as your math partner? Tell why you choose that answer.

Kelly, wants to do his work, learn something and do it right

Figure 2 gives Amanda's individual response to reading the vignette. Amanda's general reaction to the vignette was that the vignette students were just arguing. Amanda did not see their argument as productive; rather, the tone of her response indicates that the lack of productive work was annoying. As Amanda considered being part of the vignette group, she decided that she would like to be in the group because of Kelly. She saw herself as Kelly. She thought that they were students who both worked well in a group, wanted to learn, and wanted to get things done. However, Amanda knew that unlike Kelly, she "would get mad at the kids who wouldn't even try to do the problem."

Figure 3
Nicki's Response to the Vignette

Please respond to each question. Use additional paper if you need more room to tell us what you think.

What's the problem that the students are having?

They aren't all working together as a group. Most of them are arguing on what to do with the problem and they aren't getting anywhere 2 of them are talking about English assinement they are all off task.

What should they do next?

They should come to an agreement, and Chris and Kelley need to pay attention to the math.

Give your reasons for why you would or wouldn't like to be part of this group.

I would like to be part of the group because they like to argue and get off task. That is what i do.

Figure 3 (cont.)
Nicki's Response to the Vignette

How would you describe each of the students?

Kelly: Kelly most likely is a smart alick

Chris: most likely a smart alick

Pat: The type that likes to argue

Gerry: The type that likes to do the stuff the hardway and likes to argue.

If these students were part of your class, which **one** would you like to have as your math partner? Tell why you choose that answer.

Chris and Kelly because i'm a smart alick myself at times and I do the same thing they do

Ms. Kay found Nicki's interpretation of the vignette dialog in stark contrast to Amanda's. Nicki's response, in Figure 3, generally indicated that she saw the students having fun being smart-alecks. Like Amanda, Nicki also wanted to be part of the vignette group. Nicki's reason for that selection was the same as Amanda's—they both saw themselves as Kelly. However, Amanda saw Kelly as hard working and serious, while Nicki saw Kelly as a smart aleck. Each girl read the vignette and, from her experience, saw herself fitting into the group, but for very different reasons. As Ms. Kay looked at Amanda's and Nicki's responses, she noticed that both girls chose Kelly as a student that they would like to have for a partner.

Figure 4
Group Consensus Response to the Vignette

Discuss the following questions in your group. Write down a short response to each question.

What's the problem that the students are having?

they are too busy arguing to get a thing done. they don't know how to work as a group. They don't really understand what they are doing and are getting off task

Figure 4 (cont.)
Group Consensus Response to the Vignette

What should they do next?

they should all quit arguing, and to figure out the problem. and if they don't figure it out. ask the teacher

How would you evaluate each student's contribution to the group?

Kelly: he is the one trying to figure out the problem without the teachers help

Chris: he is not helping at all and is copying an English assignment

Pat: he basically just wants to get it done, he don't really care if he learns anything

Gerry: he doesn't want to figure things out by himself, he just wants to ask the teacher

If these students were part of your class, which **one** would you like to have join your group? Tell why you choose that student.

Kelly—he seems like he konws what he is doing. but he also wants to learn while he is doing his work

Amanda's reasoning was interesting to Ms. Kay as it confirmed her opinion of Amanda as a hard working student. However, Nicki's response to the vignette began to inform Ms. Kay more about the girls' working relationship.

Figure 4 shows the results of the group's discussion and illustrates that during the discussion the two girls came to consensus. They chose Kelly. However, the group's justification for making this selection appears to be influenced strongly by Amanda's criteria. During their discussion, Amanda made the point that although the group needed to discuss the issues, arguing prevented work from being finished and gave evidence that the vignette students did not really know how to work as a group. Nicki *heard* what Amanda said about the *smart-aleck* vignette students and learned that, unlike her, Amanda did not like to argue and get off task. In this safe setting, Amanda was able to talk about her *frustration* with the vignette students. Before this, Nicki had not known that her behavior was irritating to Amanda. She considered it *fun*. Amanda's talking about the vignettes had the result of talking to Nicki. Nicki later stated that it was in this discussion that she first started to realize that Amanda's occasional moodiness was a consequence of her behavior—behavior that she later stated she was going to change.

This dialog between the two girls did not have the negative consequences that Jan described could happen when confronting a peer. Through the vignette activity, these students were able to talk safely about a problem without placing blame on a peer. They were not like Jan who had no solution other than to wait for the teacher to change the groups.

What the Teacher Heard while Reading the Vignette Activity

This teacher found that although this particular group of four students appeared to be successful in working together, they were experiencing conflict. When Ms. Kay examined the set of individual and group responses from the vignette activity, she found incompatible expectations for group work. Only three students thought that all members of their group were working. Ms. Kay was excited to examine the individual journal responses that she had assigned for homework. When she read Nicki's journal response in Figure 5 she saw that Nicki had realized that there might be a problem. Nicki said that "... all four of them were like one of us, but we all work together." She emphasized the point that Amanda made so clear in the discussion of the vignette students—working together was important, more important than having fun.

Figure 5
Nicki's Journal Response to Reflecting on Classroom Activities

Please respond to the following questions about your experience as you worked on a solution of the "Ice Cream" problem.

How would you evaluate your contribution? (You might include your part in the selection and carrying out of a plan for solving the problem.) How would you evaluate all your group members contributions to the "Ice Cream" problem? Was anyone in your group like Gerry, Pat, Kelly, or Chris in the vignette? Why?

```
I say i contributed pretty good. They all contributed to the
problems, so our group works good together. Yes there is because
all 4 of them is like one of us but we all work together.
```

When the teacher read Amanda's response in Figure 6, she saw the real frustration that Amanda had hidden from the teacher. This was important; now, Ms. Kay knew that there was a problem.

Figure 6
Amanda's Journal Response to Reflecting on Classroom Activities

Please respond to the following questions about your experience as you worked on a solution of the "Ice Cream" problem.

How would you evaluate your contribution? (You might include your part in the selection and carrying out of a plan for solving the problem.) How would you evaluate all your group members' contributions to the "Ice Cream" problem? Was anyone in your group like Gerry, Pat, Kelly, or Chris in the vignette? Why?

In my group, I feel like I'm the only one who ever does anything. I like the people but I think it is really unfair that I do all the work and they just copy me It's hard to spend the whole period trying to get your group to understand when you know they don't care anyway. All three of the other kids in my group have had F's since the beginning of the year. And I have been getting A's, it gets really hard to deal with them. I feel that I should of been placed in a group that was easier to work with.

As a result of reading these responses, Ms. Kay said that she had all the information she needed and that she knew just what to say and how to help this particular group. Ms. Kay talked privately to Amanda and Nicki and spent the next several class periods focusing her attention on their troubled group. With this increased teacher attention, the students in the group "got down to business."

Nicki responded to the vignette activity discussion and talking to the teacher almost immediately. She wanted to learn and noticed that working in the group was a lot of fun when Amanda was not quite so curt with her. Amanda remained frustrated for a few days, until she saw that Nicki became more serious. With the help of the teacher and the vignette experience, the girls worked out their problems. As the teacher described by Cobb, Yackel, and Wood (1989), Ms. Kay minimized the negative student response by helping the students to establish the appropriate social norm in the group. However, in this case it took the vignette activity to inform Ms. Kay of the problem.

Ms. Kay felt empowered. This strategy did not embarrass, frighten, alienate, or offend. The use of a vignette allowed her to obtain insider knowledge about how the groups were working. By combining this information with what she knew about students and her previous experience with managing visible problems, she could assist her students to negotiate appropriate group norms. Rather than changing the groups, providing them with rules to follow, or expecting the students in the groups to work out their own problems, she assisted her students by working with them in the context of their small group. This interaction in the context of group work between the students and their teacher allowed for a meaningful resolution of hidden problems and an establishment of appropriate social expectations for small-group collaboration.

Conclusion

A major part of the value of vignettes in this classroom was to provide opportunities for students to say safely what they wanted to the teacher and to the other members of their small group. They were able to say what they needed to say to their teacher by reacting in writing to the vignette. Amanda said that "Just being able to talk about it and letting the teacher know helps." In their groups, as they discussed the vignette students, they became less emotional about their own group and were better able to think about their problem as they resolved the vignette students' problems. Although teachers may wish for high school students to talk directly and honestly to their peers, society and experience have convinced adolescents that direct confrontation is not possible without disastrous results. As Jan said in her interview, "I just wanted to say, Stop being a jerk, but something stops me from saying that 'cause maybe it would be worse." Most likely, it would have been worse. However, students say that they can talk *about* a third party, especially a not-real vignette student, much easier than talking *to* someone. In this *talking about*, Amanda thought that "hearing others in the group express the same feelings I had somehow made feeling that way OK." Nicki said, "I didn't really know what I did bothered Amanda so much." This teacher-directed experience assisted the students in establishing social norms for group work. Lo and Wheatley (1994) support this format by stating, "...the responsibility of negotiating meaning and social norms lies with everyone" (p. 159).

Vignettes are not a panacea nor are they new to education. Researchers have long supported the essential placement of narrative or stories as tools for teaching and reflection from views within the educational system and the general culture (Jackson 1995; Egan 1988; Kuhns 1974). Narratives have grown in popularity in mathematics education since introduced by NCTM in the *Professional Standards for Teaching Mathematics* (1991). However, they are not commonly used to stimulate high school students' reflections on *their* classroom practice nor are they typically used to gain insight into group processes in high school classrooms.

Although interviews do not have the potential that vignettes have for motivating student reflection, interviews are more commonly used for that purpose. Consider Jan. The abstract nature of her reflections resulted from physically taking her out of her everyday setting and classroom activity. At best, Jan's abstract reflections during the interview process allowed her to define her particular problems. Jan's interview did not provide her with immediate access to other students' opinions, nor did her interview provide a structure through which her group could discuss and negotiate changes in current practices. Unfortunately, the vignette activity did not provide Jan with this opportunity either. When her class participated in the vignette activity, Jan responded to the vignette with respect to her current group, and neither the boy nor the two girls that she described in her interview were in that group. The success reported in using vignettes is a matter of timing. To be most effective, vignettes need to be used on a regular basis.

Teachers who liked using vignettes commented that they were easier to use in their classrooms than interviews. Juggling individual interviews in secondary classroom settings was viewed as an impossible task. During the past several years, teachers who used vignettes have asked an important question. "Where do we get more of these stories?" When suggested that they might write customized vignettes for their classrooms, they said, "That's impossible." However, during an inservice session, teachers working in groups created excellent vignettes. Their vignette topics focused on mathematical content or social skills that they had previously found difficult to teach. The vignettes or story segments the teachers created were not designed to either *transform* or *inform* (Egan 1988), but rather to frame a classroom discussion. Once teachers wrote a vignette with a team of teachers, they gained confidence in their abilities to create their own classroom stories.

References

Artz, A. F., and C.M. Newman. 1990. *How to use cooperative learning in the mathematics class.* Reston, VA: National Council of Teachers of Mathematics.

Cobb, P., E. Yackel, and B. McNeal. 1989. Young children's emotional acts while engaged in mathematical problem solving. In *Affect and mathematical problem solving: A new perspective,* ed. D.B. McLeod and V.M. Adams, 117-148. New York: Springer-Verlag.

Cobb, P., T. Wood, E. Yackel, and B. McNeal. 1992. Characteristics of classroom mathematics traditions: An interactional analysis. *American Educational Research Journal* 29: 573-604.

Egan, K. 1988. *Teaching as storytelling: An alternative approach to teaching and curriculum in the elementary school.* London: Althouse Press.

Frid, S., and J. Malone. 1994. *Negotiation of meaning in mathematics classrooms: A study of two year 5 classes.* Paper presented at the Annual Meeting of the American Educational Research Association, New Orleans, LA. (ERIC Document Reproduction Service No. ED 335 238)

Gadamer, H-G. [1960] 1989. *Truth and method.* 2d ed. Translated by J. Weinsheimer and D. B. Marshall. New York: Crossroad.

Gillespie, D. 1992. *The mind's we: Contextualism in cognitive psychology.* Carbondale, IL: Southern Illinois University Press.

Good, T.L., C. Mulryan, and M. McCaslin. 1992. Grouping for instruction in mathematics: A call for programmatic research on small-group processes. In *Handbook of research on mathematics teaching and learning,* ed. D. A. Grouws, 165-196. New York: Macmillan.

Jackson, P.W. 1995. On the place of narrative in teaching. In *Narrative in teaching, learning, and research,* ed. H. McEwan and K. Egan, 3-23. New York: Teachers College Press.

Johnson, D.W., and R. T. Johnson. 1991. *Learning together and alone: Cooperative, competitive, and individualistic learning.* Boston: Allyn and Bacon.

Johnson, D.W., R.T. Johnson, and G. Maruyame. 1983. Interdependence and interpersonal attraction among heterogeneous and homogeneous individuals: A theoretical formulation and a meta-analysis of the research. *Review of Educational Research* 53: 5-54.

Kagan, S.P. 1992. *Cooperative learning.* San Juan Capistrano, CA: Kagan Cooperative Learning.

King, L. H. 1993. High and low achievers' perceptions and cooperative learning in two small groups. *Elementary School Journal*: 399-416.

Kuhns, R. 1974. *Structures of experience.* New York: Harper and Row.

Lo, J., and G.H. Wheatley. 1994. Learning opportunities and negotiating social norms in mathematics class discussion. *Educational Studies in Mathematics* 26: 145-164.

Mehan, H. 1979. *Learning lessons: Social organization in the classroom.* Cambridge, MA: Harvard University Press.

Mulryan, C. M. 1995. Fifth and sixth graders' involvement and participation in cooperative small groups in mathematics. *Elementary School Journal*: 297-310.

National Council of Teachers of Mathematics (NCTM). 1989. *Curriculum and Evaluation Standards for School Mathematics*. Reston, VA: Author.

______. 1991. *Professional Standards for Teaching Mathematics*. Reston, VA: Author.

______. 1995. *Assessment Standards for School Mathematics*. Reston, VA: Author.

______. 1998. *Principles and Standards for School Mathematics-Draft.*. Reston, VA: Author.

National Research Council. 1989. *Everybody counts: A report to the nation on the future of mathematics education*. Washington, DC: National Academy Press.

______. 1990. *Reshaping school mathematics: A philosophy and framework for curriculum*. Washington, DC: National Academy Press.

Slavin, R. 1989. Cooperative learning and student achievement. In *School and classroom organization,* ed. R. Slavin, 129-156. Hillsdale, NJ: Lawrence Erlbaum.

Voigt, J. 1994. Negotiation of mathematical meaning and learning mathematics. *Educational Studies in Mathematics*: 275-298.

Williams, S. R., and K.M.C. Ivey. 1994. Exploring the social in social construction. In *Proceedings of the Sixteenth Annual Meeting of the North American Chapter of the International Group for the Psychology of Mathematics Education,* ed. D. Kirshner, 2: 105-111.

Chapter 9

Using Journals for a Variety of Assessments

Rebecca Sanchez

When I talk about journals in my English classroom the first day of school, students ask, "You mean we're actually going to do something with these journals? You mean you're actually going to read them sometimes?" When I answer yes, we are going to do something with these journals, I definitely mean "we." And when I say yes, I will be reading their journals, I sincerely mean it.

Much of what can go wrong with journals in the classroom boils down to the teacher failing to plan thoughtfully for their use. If a teacher fails to use journals regularly and respond to them consistently, the students chalk that up to yet another typical year for journals, kicked off by the teacher speech about their effectiveness with little follow-through until they sit in silent stacks, gathering dust on the shelves.

So why do journals work for me and my students? How do I set up and maintain journals so that everyone writes every time we use journals? Why are my journals still in full gear the last week of school? Why don't I tire of reading and responding to them?

I explain to my students on the first day of school that we will use an in-class journal as a vehicle to respond to our reading, to connect other classes to our English classroom, to try out different modes of writing, to play with language, and to reflect upon our work and our learning. I call the journal an in-class one because the writing will be done in the classroom and because the journal will not leave my classroom. What if the muse strikes in the evening when the journal is locked in my classroom? That's why paper, writers' notebooks, and school tablets exist. The clear advantage is that day after day in the classroom all the students have their in-class journals at the same time. So reliable is the system that I often take roll by glancing at the names on the journals left on the shelf after we have begun to write.

Most students tell me I am the first teacher they ever saw write in a journal while they do. All my students tell me I am the first teacher to share her journal entries with them. By keeping a journal and reading my entries aloud, I validate using journals. If I take the time to write in my journals with my students, then I am communicating to them that journal writing is worthwhile. Reading my entries aloud provides yet another voice in the classroom, a voice that students don't often hear. I tell my students that if I read all of their entries and hear their voices, then it is only fair they hear mine. When I play with language or try new words out on paper, my students hear that. Soon they begin to experiment with language. Missy, a tenth grader, wrote to me, "Several things brought out the words in me. I trust you, the teacher and my reader, and I like to read powerful stuff. Since I trust you, I try to write powerful stuff for you to read. I have also learned from listening to you read your writing to us. I like your images."

Images and trust—the stuff of which journal entries are made. Student after student embraces the language while accepting that yes, I, the teacher, am the audience. No, I don't show their journals to other teachers; no, I don't let students read other students' journals without permission. The audience for the entries is me unless I clearly state otherwise. Journals nurture an atmosphere of trust between the teacher and students, making it possible for students to transfer that trust to sharing ideas, drafts, and projects with others. Amy, who had never used journals before my class, wrote to me, "I found the language within when I realized that only you were going to read my journal."

How does a teacher keep up with reading and responding to journals? Most teachers are quick to recognize the value of journals and are reluctant to surrender their success. Yet how can teachers keep up with reading journals when class sizes look more like industrial quantities than the class rosters of our dreams? First of all, teachers, before introducing journals, need to think about what they can reasonably accomplish given their daily schedule and time outside of school. Students' past experiences often have been that teachers read journals at the beginning of school and then gradually give up. In order to make journals work and to reinforce that sense of audience, some kind of teacher response is necessary, but it must be efficient for the teacher and consistent enough that the student maintains a sense of teacher as audience.

When my students turn in their journals after writing, I ask them to pass the journals in open to the day's entry. Having a stack of journals before me already open to what I must read speeds things along. I work with a fine-tipped colored marker so that responses jump out at the students. Sometimes I tell students I will only underline a promising idea or colorful language. For example, after responding to Sassoon's World War I poem "Suicide in the Trenches," Colleen opened her journal upon its return to find *tumbling, thick with hope,* and *fear like grit under their nails* circled in color. A written response could not have been more effective in encouraging her to use striking language in her journal.

I also make clear to students that although they have written perhaps half a page, given my student load, I often will reply only with a phrase or a line. When Jonathan sketched out three ideas for a historical fiction assignment, for instance, he wrote one page front and back. I responded by focusing on the idea with the most potential: "Jonathan, the runaway slave writing down his adventures along the underground railroad would make a great piece, especially since he wants to preserve the stories for his own children." In Jessica's journal, she also sketched out three ideas but indicated her heart was with the first one. I responded, "Go for it." The alternative—not having any response at all—makes even the briefest of responses very desirable to my students. Logically, teachers do not have to use journals in every class on the same day. Staggering the use of journals so that each class writes at least twice a week can also provide freedom for the teacher to read and respond.

An alternative to the teacher response is to announce to students before they begin writing that they will exchange journals with a peer who will write a response to the entry. When students know this beforehand, they are comfortable responding and later exchanging. Asking them to exchange journals yet again, read, and respond to another peer gives the writer two responses to an entry. Actually, we often exchange three or four times, with my journal circulating as well. When the class ends, I have responded to four students as part of the activity and my journal contains some student responses as well. For example, peppered among my own journal entries might be my students' comments concerning my view of Richard's work hours in the novel *The Christmas Box;* from Bobby, "I don't know, Mrs. Sanchez, a guy feels an incredible need to provide. Maybe bedtime stories can wait for another night. Putting bread on the table is more important." Ryan followed with "Come on, Bobby, she has a valid point. Any dad can see his child is growing older. Mrs. S. and Mary in the novel are right. Jenna needs her dad more than the business needs him." Jennifer added the last response: "I took Richard's attitude to be one of making up for lost time when his shop did poorly. He almost has to work harder in December. All clothing businesses do." On such a day, I will pull several journals after class, read the dialogues, and leave my "trail"—a response in colored marker—so that the students sense that although they exchanged peer responses by dialoguing, I am still part of the audience and what they write must be appropriate.

As their audience, I don't always have to write something in the journals for students to know that I have read their entries. Perhaps I have finished the class period by asking students to predict what will happen eventually to Ralph in Golding's *Lord of the Flies.* As an alternative to my responding in their journals, I simply write the students' predictions on an overhead transparency to use in class the next day. Although I do not list students' names beside their ideas, students recognize their own and often claim them during discussion. From the standpoint of teacher efficiency, the students know that I have read their entries even though on such occasions I do not write back to them. Most importantly, making the students' ideas a part of the lesson the next day once again validates journal writing as a learning tool for them and an assessment tool for me.

Just what sparks students to write in their in-class journals? The catalyst for all their responses is the prompt, a question or statement of task that focuses them on some aspect of their learning. My prompts do not come from a book nor do they exist in a data bank. I design them to connect to the current learning and progress of students. Some prompts pave the way for reading. For example, before students read Sandra Cisneros' story "Eleven," they write to this prompt: "Just what does 'acting your age' mean? In what circumstances do you feel younger than you are? Why do you think that happens?" I share my response aloud and so do several students. We then read the story where being eleven is also being ten, nine, eight, seven, and so on. Students refer to their journal entries repeatedly during the discussion, instantly connecting their reading to their writing. As I encourage them to interweave their journal responses into our discussion, I assess how on target their perceptions of age are and to what extent Rachel's humiliation in the story is their humiliation. Most importantly, though, students find a way through their journals to get inside a story even before they read it.

When I assign out-of-class reading, the journal becomes a true work horse. In the case of wanting to know if my students have read the assignment, this prompt can serve as a pop quiz: "Prove to me you read last night's assignment." Students are free to tackle their responses from whatever angle they choose, even emphasizing what intrigued or puzzled them. The details of events covered—not the amount and their order—clearly indicate if the student has read the assignment. Reluctant readers as well as grade-conscious students are comfortable with this prompt because they can discuss how they read the assignment instead of guessing, sometimes even correctly, at a set of five specific reading questions in the traditional quiz format.

Sometimes journal prompts can get at the essence of the reading. "Just what is this selection about so far?" I ask. "What is the author trying to do here?" The product of this prompt is too good to leave for reading after class. A teacher can do a round robin, asking each student to offer an idea from his or her journal while another student jots the ideas on the chalkboard. By having something written in their journals, students tend to be more comfortable in offering an idea as opposed to trying to come up with one on the spot in a discussion. Once the ideas are on the board, we have fuel for many discussions. And since the ideas are on the board and because everyone contributed, I do not have to write responses in the journals, but I have a quick assessment of where students are in their understanding of material and I can make adjustments for the next day's lesson, if necessary.

Journal prompts do not have to focus students on only what they have experienced or on what they know: prompts also can focus students on what they do not know. For example, sometimes I ask, "What puzzled you in the reading?" Other times I am more blunt: "What didn't you understand in the reading?" Imagine what goes on in students' minds as they see their peers and teacher writing down things they had trouble with in the reading. Suddenly everyone feels comfortable about not understanding everything in the assignment. After this type of prompt, a teacher has several options for discussion: a round robin to list items on the board, asking a few volunteers to share entries, or saving entries to read after class while planning tomorrow's discussion. Once again, the teacher has a quick means of assessing students' comprehension. Many of my colleagues across the curriculum have incorporated these techniques into their students' journals, since these teachers also assign reading to be done outside of class.

This business of linking disciplines is a two-way street. When my students are reading Harper Lee's *To Kill a Mockingbird,* my history colleague asks the students to write a response to this prompt: "Explain the purpose of the WPA (Works of Public Administration) during the Depression and tell why Walter Cunningham's daddy refused a WPA job." An equally effective prompt in this case that emphasizes the historical connection is "In the voice of little Walter Cunningham, explain why the WPA is a good idea for some people, but not for your daddy."

Clearly, if journals are to survive the school year as the work horses of the curriculum, teachers must:

- set up a system that permits frequent student use of journals
- communicate to students who is the audience for the journal writing
- read the journals frequently, leaving their "trail" for students to see
- vary uses of journals so that response doesn't become just another task
- consider ways of responding other than writing back to students

In addition to maintaining an in-class journal, my students often keep a split entry journal when we are reading literature. I first encountered the split entry journal in Barbara Page's article "From Passive Receivers to Active Learners in English" (1987). At the time I was frustrated with end-of-the-story homework questions and worksheets. More importantly, I was even more tired of using the same questions with every class and ensuring that everyone had a set of "correct" answers when class ended. In an effort to find other ways to teach literature while placing more responsibility on students for their learning, I embraced split entry journals.

Essentially, a split entry journal features a vertical line splitting the paper in two. The left side should be somewhat narrower than the right, for the students will write far more on the right side. The left side is labeled "Observations" while the right side is labeled "Responses." Horizontal lines then separate the front of the page into three strips. The same set-up continues on the back of the page with three more strips. As the split entry journal evolved in my classroom, I customized it for my students by featuring a block in the lower left portion of the back page for the students to write in vocabulary words or to collect samples of dialect found in the reading. In the lower right hand portion of the page, I labeled a block for questions students have on the reading. In this way, the split entry worked as a place for students to record their observations as they read, to respond to those observations, to collect vocabulary words from the reading, and to jot down their questions as readers.

In Edmund Rostand's play *Cyrano de Bergerac,* students meet Cyrano, a poet who feels unworthy of any woman's love because he considers himself too ugly, and Christian, a handsome soldier who is tongue-tied around women. Brian, a student of mine, recorded his entry about events at the end of Act II when Cyrano and Christian have agreed to join forces to woo Roxanne, a woman they both love. Figure 1 provides a sample of Brian's split entry.

Figure 1

Split Entry Journal	
Observations	**Responses**
Roxane: "Here it is. I am in love with someone. He is noble, proud, fearless, handsome..." Cyrano: "Handsome!"	Cyrano must be crushed when he learns that Roxane doesn't love him. Maybe that's what pushes him to make up that foolish plan.
Christian, not wanting to be laughed at, begins to make fun of Cyrano's nose. This is a definite change in character.	First, I think Christian wouldn't have taunted Cyrano if he wasn't pushed by the other cadets. Second, Cyrano controls his anger. From earlier incidents, you wouldn't think this would be possible.

Figure 1 (cont.)

Christian: "Beyond the end of your nose." "Resent your nosiness." "Nosed you out in the darkness." Cyrano strikes an agreement with Christian that if Christian will be the face, he will be the voice.	It lightens me to see such humor. I'm glad the play has light moments even though it is exploring some serious ideas such as inner beauty and physical looks. If I was Christian, I would tell Cyrano to get lost. Christian has a better chance of winning Roxane alone. Roxane could discover the deal and get mad at both of them and then Christian will never win her.
Christian has now caved in under peer pressure twice. The cadets convinced him to make fun of Cyrano's nose and now he says yes to the plan.	This looks like the start of a bad habit for Christian. He better straighten up or people will have him doing anything they want. If he woos Roxane with Cyrano, he will still want to have some say in the wooing.
My impression of Roxane so far	She seems nice enough but she is a little materialistic. I think Cyrano may be a little too good for her since he has ideals beyond materialism. She could change her opinion of him and learn to love him. But that wouldn't be love at all, would it?
Vocabulary	**Questions I Have on the Reading**
Feint—a movement meant to deceive Patron—a wealthy person who supports an artist	Does Cyrano think his plan will really work? If Cyrano thinks he may gain Roxane's love, what does Christian stand to gain? How can Cyrano be so honest that he offends everyone, and how can I still admire him?

Clearly superior to traditional homework questions, the split entry gives students the responsibility of identifying important features in the reading while putting the pieces of meaning together themselves. By glancing at the questions the students list, I assess how well they understand the reading. Conveniently, I have a ready-made list of the students' questions for discussion. As a spin-off activity, students "cluster" in small groups and combine their vocabulary banks to form the basis for a class generated vocabulary list from the reading. Students can also share their split entries with a partner or in small groups or present one observation and one response to the whole class.

Observations	Responses
Calendars based on the moon and sun were used in Egypt long before 2500 B.C.	Wow. I thought modern people were the first to study the sun. I just never thought it'd been going on for a long time. A real long time.
People once believed that the earth was the center of the universe.	Just because I know something is true doesn't mean that people have always believed it. Did people still worship the sun as much since they did not think it was the center of the universe?

Elizabeth, in the example above, has just realized that the study of the heavens has not been confined to the twentieth century. She also has posed an interesting question about ancient people's worship of sun gods. My history colleague has her students keep a split entry journal for each new chapter of reading in place of the chapter questions as homework.

My assessment of the split entry journal evolved out of the need for a kind of evaluation which would differentiate among levels of effectiveness while also providing a specific grade for my grade book. By putting students in groups to review split entries and coming together for several large group discussions about the characteristics of top entries, the following system emerged to rate one page of six entries, a typical assignment for one out-of-class reading. See Figure 2 below:

Figure 2
Scoring Rubric for Split-Entry Journals

Strong

- completes six entries for the assignment
- provides variety in observations and responses
- includes observations which reflect entire reading assignment
- offers well developed responses with ample details/explanations
- gives a sense of time invested

Good

- completes six entries for the assignment
- tends to provide variety in observations and responses
- includes observations which reflect entire reading assignment
- offers responses which include details and examples
- a sense of time invested

Figure 2 (cont.)
Scoring Rubric for Split-Entry Journals

Average

- tends not to complete all six entries for the assignment
- tends not to vary the type of observation or response
- includes observations which reflect only part of the assignment
- offers responses lacking in details and examples
- gives a sense of limited time invested

Weak

- does not complete six entries for the assignment
- makes little or no effort to vary observations or responses
- includes observations which reflect only partial reading of assignment
- offers responses with little or no details/examples
- gives a sense of a rush job; probably done on bus or in cafeteria

After these criteria are refined, they are placed on poster board and displayed in the classroom. Students also receive their own copies. By reading others' split entries, the students become adept at rating their own and others' journals. When I review their assessments, I usually have to change only two or three ratings—not bad when I am working with 110 students, the whole tenth grade.

As far as managing the grade book for a set of split entry journals, I record the individual ratings, which range anywhere from five for a play like *Cyrano de Bergerac* to twelve for a novel such as *Lord of the Flies*. Then I convert the scores into a set of 100 points for the grade book by using a conversion tool like the following, which is based on five ratings. See Figure 3. Teachers can tighten or expand the conversion tool to accommodate their grading systems. My history colleague, for example, calls a strong split entry an A, a good one a B and so on. She then takes these letter ratings and converts them into points for the grade book. Before my present system evolved, I used the ratings of ++, +, and – to stand for a top, middle, and weak journal. Over time I found that I needed another category between top and middle in order to evaluate more precisely.

Figure 3
Split Entry Rating Conversion Chart*

Split Entry Rating Conversion Chart		
Ratings	**Points**	**Grade**
SSSSS	100	
SSSSG	97	A
SSSGG	95	
SSGGG	93	

Figure 3 (cont.)
Split Entry Rating Conversion Chart*

Ratings	Points	Grade
SGGGG	92	
GGGGG	90	
GGGGA	89	B
GGGAA	87	
GGAAA	85	
GAAAA	84	
AAAAA	83	
AAAAW	81	C
AAAWW	79	
AAWWW	77	
AWWWW	76	
WWWWW	74	D
WWWW	72	
WWW	70	
WW	68	F
W	66	

* This conversion table is based upon the following school grading scale:
A 100–93; B 92–85; C 84–77; D 76–70; F 69 and below.

I do not use split entry journals for every reading assignment, but when I assign them, I reduce the use of the in-class journal or perhaps forego using it at all for a time so that students will be receptive to the in-class ones when we return to them. For the teacher, the message with any journal use is to incorporate variety in prompts in order to assess a range of performances: comprehension of the reading assignment; explanation of trouble spots; links from one discipline to another; predictions; reveling in language; and connecting personal responses and opinions to reading. These assessments can benefit the teacher by indicating how tomorrow's lesson plan can better target where the students are in their understanding or can provide, as the split entry journal does, a concrete assessment for the grade book. Students appreciate variety in their learning and assessment. Journals can provide it.

Works Cited

Page, Barbara. 1987. From passive receivers to active learners in English. In *Plain Talk: About Learning and Writing Across the Curriculum*, ed. Judy Self, 37–50. Richmond, VA: Virginia Department of Education.

Chapter 10

Whose Essay Is It Anyway? Students Choose Essay Prompts to Assess Learning in Biology

Michael Lowry and Pamela Childers

During the 1996-97 school year, Michael Lowry and I began experimenting with some essay writing activities with three biology classes. Michael was frustrated with the typical paradigm "teach, test, hope for the best." He was hoping to move beyond the traditional modes of assessment that his colleagues favored (multiple choice, true-false objective tests). Essay tests are a better gauge of student learning. He also thought it important to offer a variety of options—if for no other reason than it would break up the monotony of reading the same essay repeatedly. However, we had no documentation of the specific success or failure of those writing assignments other than the students' positive responses to the choices.

In February 1997 Michael completed a biology unit entitled "Continuity Through Development." We decided to give students the option of five essay topics, including a typical science essay question. The purposes of these essay questions were (a) to encourage students to think evaluatively, creatively and critically about the content they had learned; (b) to provide students with an opportunity to demonstrate their knowledge in another genre other than a strictly scientific essay; (c) to offer interesting options for students with various learning styles; and (d) to allow students to have fun learning (see Figure 1).

Figure 1
Biology Essay Test: Continuity Through Development

Choose ONE of the topics below and write a concise essay not to exceed two and one half pages, typed and double-spaced (12 pt. font). Be sure that you have answered the assignment posed in the topic.

1. Using your knowledge of developmental biology, cellular differentiation, and regulatory molecules, explain how you might create creatures similar to those found on the Island of Doctor Moreau (an island inhabited by half-human, half-animal monsters!). Imagine which creature you might want to merge with and describe the positive and negative characteristics of that merger. Include sketches of your creature.

Figure 1 (cont.)
Biology Essay Test: Continuity Through Development

2. A classic statement in biology is: ontogeny recapitulates phylogeny. Research the meaning of this statement and apply it to the development of a human embryo and frog embryo. Include specific similarities and differences in these developmental processes.
3. Write a dialogue for a one-act play in which two "Progenitors" (god-like beings that can create life forms) are in the midst of a heated debate. The two major characters are:
   a. Merlin: He believes that the cells of life forms should contain only the information necessary for that individual cell (e.g., a skin cell contains only information for making skin cells);
   b. Gandalf: he believes that each cell in a living thing should contain the information for all other cells (e.g., a skin cell contains information for skin cells and any other cell in the body).

   Your dialogue should include the merits and weaknesses of each position. You may include other characters as you see fit. Remember that a play has a setting, so you may create where this debate takes place.
4. Write a poem, short story or song that reflects your understanding of this unit. It may take any literary form but should demonstrate your knowledge.
5. The typical hospital often contains green walls, sterile hallways, dark corridors, and silent rooms. You have been hired as a consultant for a new building project at Erlanger Hospital. You will be responsible for submitting a proposal for a new obstetrics, gynecology and pediatrics wing of the hospital. Using your knowledge of the developmental needs of pregnant mothers and new-born babies, create a floor plan (OR 3D model) for this new wing of the hospital. Your written component should explain your choices in your floor plan or model as well as decisions for atmosphere (visual, sound, space utilization).

After the essays were completed and grades given, Pamela visited each class and asked students to complete the following questions: (1) Which essay question did you choose to answer? (2) Why did you make this choice? (3) What was your reaction to getting the choices on this assignment? Please explain. (4) Please give any further comments or recommendations for future essay assignments.

Out of 51 students in the three sections, only three answered question 2, the typical science essay. Surprisingly 35% of the students chose to write a poem, short story or song that reflected their understanding of the unit, while 22% chose to do question 1 and the same percent selected question 3. Although some people thought that question 5 was an "easy and inappropriate" question on this test, eight students spent a great deal of time writing lengthy explanations and giving detailed floor plans (one student had six floors). Perhaps we had tapped into some future architects of health care facilities! On the questionnaire, students indicated that they did not mind taking more time on something in which they had some choice, and with which they had an opportunity to create something interesting.

But what of the relative merit of the essay questions themselves? In question 1, students were asked to apply knowledge of developmental biology, cellular differentiation, and regulatory molecules to ponder the possibility of half-human creatures, evaluate their positive and negative characteristics, and create visual images. As difficult as this question might have been, eleven students took on the challenge of responding. In some ways this question gave students the freedom to create half-human creatures with no right or wrong answer, but they had to apply accurate scientific information to justify their creations. In quite a different way, question 2 led students directly through the prompt, giving them a scientific statement, telling them to research it, and apply the information to a comparison and contrast of human and frog embryos. The three students who seemed to want to be told every move to make without having to think on their own made such a choice. In question 3 students must create a fictional debate in the form of a play and apply their knowledge of the merits and weaknesses of each side of the debate on individual cells. Since the two characters are Merlin and Gandalf, students have an opportunity to call upon their reading experience of the *Legend of King Arthur* and *Lord of the Rings*. Question 4 was more open-ended than we wanted, but we gave it a try anyway. More students chose this question, perhaps, because they had the freedom to create poetry, fiction or song lyrics as a means of demonstrating their knowledge of the biology unit. By making this choice, students suggested their need to express and process their knowledge of subject matter in a different written format. Finally, we were worried that students who tended to be visual learners might be short-changed by our choices. We were also aware that we had not offered any real-world options for students; therefore, we thought that this creation of a visual structure with written justification for its layout and design might offer special students an opportunity to show their expertise. We were right because those who chose this option tended to be students who were loners, frequently late with other assignments yet early with this one!

At the end of April after students had completed the unit on "Ecosystems," we again created a choice of essay questions for their test (see Figure 2 below). This time we gave students six options, including a typical science essay question. We knew we might be pushing students farther than they could go with some of the essay questions, but with options we wanted to give capable students the opportunity to try something more difficult.

Figure 2
Biology Essay Test: Ecosystems of the Past

Choose one of the essay topics below. Your essay should not exceed two pages (written material) in length. It should be typed, double-spaced, 12 pt. font.

1. A deadly virus has wiped out most of humanity. Except for you and the 200 others that live on an island in the Pacific, no other humans have survived this disaster. Write a letter to a follow scientist explaining your views of how humans may change over time. Use your knowledge of evolution, natural selection, and adaptive radiation to support your predictions.

Figure 2 (cont.)
Biology Essay Test: Ecosystems of the Past

2. Critique Ann Gibbons' article "Did Cooler Heads Prevail." To critique the article, write a laboratory report in which you use the following headings:
   a. Question of Interest—a question that clearly defines the system and variables being tested;
   b. Hypothesis—a specific cause-and-effect prediction which answers the question of interest with supporting reasons;
   c. Data and Observations—the actual data (e.g., evidence) being discussed;
   d. Limitations—explores the limitations of the hypothesis.
3. You board a time travel device. As you enter, a coolly rational computer voice says, "Specify desired time period." The following options flash before your eyes: Cambrian, Silurian, Devonian, Permian, and Pleistocene. Choose one of the time periods. Keep a journal of your travels. For each entry (5-9 entries), specify the time and location. Describe the flora and fauna you see as well as any major geological events. Collect samples to bring back with you and describe how you might determine their age. Include visuals where appropriate.
4. While vacationing in Alaska, you visit the Mendenhall glacier. While exploring the upper reaches of the glacier, you notice an unusual object sticking out of the ice. On closer inspection, it appears to be a spear tip. To your utter amazement, you have discovered a hominid frozen in ice! In addition to his spear, you notice the following: many layers of animal (of unknown type) skin clothing, some kind of sack containing dried plants and other objects; curious red clay (ochre) scattered about the perimeter, and a small bone fragment with unusual carvings. Write a short story in which you explain how the hominids arrived at this site. Your story should incorporate your understanding of human evolution and archaeological methods.
5. Write a poem that reflects your understanding of this unit. It may take any poetic form.
6. Palentologists often say, "The key to the past is found in the present." Write an essay in which you use this statement to explain how we reconstruct the past.

Students were asked to respond to the following questions: (1) Which essay question did you choose? Why did you make this choice? (2) What grade did you get on your essay? (3) Now that you have had a variety of choices on several essay tests, would you recommend that we do this again next year? Why or why not? Please explain. (4) Do you have any other recommendations for improvement in writing, thinking, and learning in biology? The results, based on a follow-up questionnaire, are not surprising since this test occurred only one month prior to final exams.

This time 12% chose the typical science essay (#6), but they stated that they made this choice because they did not have time to work on the other essay options. The question was a clear cut explanatory essay where students were given a statement to explain in relation to what they had learned in the unit. Their honesty in facing the end-of-the-year crunch was refreshing, and led us to conclude that we should not offer as many options late in the school year. Only one student chose question 2, so we concluded that reading an article and writing a critique as a laboratory report might have been too confusing and time consuming. The article itself might have been difficult to understand, but then turning an article into a lab report critique was seemingly beyond all but one student's capability and interest. On the other hand, students were extremely fascinated by the idea of a deadly virus wiping out most of humanity, so 42% chose to write a letter to a fellow scientist explaining their views of how humans may change over time. In this response, they had to support their predictions with their knowledge of evolution, natural selection, and adaptive radiation. Using what they had learned did not seem to bother those who made this choice; the topic's interest outweighed any other difficulties.

The other choices were fairly evenly divided with 20% each selecting questions 3 and 4, 12% choosing question 6, and 8% choosing question 5. Question 3 involved detailed knowledge of a particular time period so that the student could write 5-9 journal entries that included time, location, descriptions of flora, fauna and major geological events, and explanations of how to determine the age of samples with appropriate visuals. In other words, this question involved an in-depth study of a particular time period as a scientist discovering it.

The next question (#4), which received the same number of responses, required students to create a short story based on a given plot (the discovery of a hominid frozen in Mendenhall glacier), inclusion of accurate scientific information based on given facts, and application of knowledge of human evolution and archeological methods. What a great lesson for students who would like to be fiction writers; accuracy of information within a fictional work is so important that authentic authors must do the necessary research in order to have a credible story. Question 5 was limited to poetry, asking for only one genre as opposed to the question on the previous test where students were given the option of poetry, short story or song lyrics. Having a plot with mystery and intrigue involved must have appealed more with the greater number of students answering the short story question (#4). Finally, question 6 required students to respond to a scientific statement by explaining their knowledge of how we reconstruct the past. This question required little thinking beyond a restating of the information studied in class and, based on the questionnaire responses, seems to have taken the least time to answer.

The final examination essay involved choice in the sense that the students had to come up with their own original creation, and follow specific scientific requirements to meet the criteria. Because there was still creativity involved, students seemed to react positively to this assignment as well (see Figure 3 below).

Figure 3
Biology Final Examination Project

Assignment: Complete #1, #2 or #3 below:

1. Create your own organism. Using the criteria below, describe the necessary characteristics and scientific data to submit your new organism to the Institute for Biological Inquiry (IBI) for their *Annual Catalogue of Living Organisms.*

Figure 3 (cont.)
Biology Final Examination Project

Criteria

Organism—Common name, scientific name (binomial nomenclature)
Habitat description—Where it lives and how it functions in that environment.
Niche—The role that organism plays and its connections to other organisms
Visual description—Verbal with drawing
Reproductive cycle
Life cycle
Food/Energy requirements
Defense mechanisms

The following criteria, if they apply:

Social interactions
Behavioral characteristics
Internal systems (digestive, circulatory, nervous, etc.)
Means of mobility
Evolutionary history (Phylogenic history)
Adaptability to its environment
Biochemical features

2. You are a member of a deep-space exploration crew. You are a xenobiologist in charge of cataloging any new organisms you find. In a scientific journal or report, describe a new organism you have discovered. Since this living organism will be functioning in its natural environment, you must describe that environment as well. You will need, however, to use diagrams or sketches of the environment as part of your description of both the planet and the organism.

3. Based upon the attached sketches of living organisms, determine scientific names, group into genera, and examine fossil records to create a phylogenic tree. For the living organisms, speculate function/role, habitat, and life cycle based on the visual information given in the sketches.

As the final summative assessment of their course, students were asked to submit a letter to Michael that was not read until grades were completed. They were asked to assess labs, oral presentations, homework, essay tests with choices of prompts, research papers, and journal-focused free writing (see Figure 4).

Figure 4
End of the Year Letter

After rereading the letter you wrote in the fall, please write a letter to me in which you include responses to the following:

1. What you liked and/or disliked about
   - labs
   - oral presentations
   - essay tests with choices of prompts
   - research papers
   - journal-focused freewriting
2. Recommendations for ways of improving the course next year.

   You may choose to divide your letter into subtopics for clarity. Just remember to give specific examples or suggestions when you answer.

   This letter has several purposes. First and foremost, it is an opportunity for you to reflect upon what we have done in biology this school year. Second, it will allow me to evaluate what did and did not work so that I may revise the course and my teaching to reflect your responses and recommendations. Hopefully, we will all learn from this experience.

The majority of the students said that the essay tests with choices were the best part of the class. Comments included: "The ideas were creative, and in turn gave the author the opportunity to think about the chapter and also be creative. At times biology can become boring when writing about genetic mutations, but when taking genetic mutations and asking the writer to discuss what the creature might look like combines the knowledge of genetics"; "The essay tests were great. They let me think and be as creative and complete as I needed to be"; "Essay tests were one of the best parts of the entire year. They were fun to write and would give you a good grade if you put some creativity into them"; "Essay tests were the best thing in the class. They were much better than regular tests"; "I have enjoyed the essay tests a lot, too. The room for creativity is a help for me, and I am sure that it is a great help to a lot of other students. Having to regurgitate material in an essay is not fun at all"; "The thing I liked most about this semester were the essay tests. They were easy because you had many topics that you could choose, and you could be creative and learn at the same time"; and "The essay test choices this year helped everyone a lot. Because different students excel in different areas, they could put out their best effort in a subject that suited them." However, not everyone liked these choices. One student said, "I didn't like the essay tests with a lot of different choices; I prefer the teacher making the choice. I don't know why, I guess it makes me feel like it's graded more fairly since everyone did the same thing."

What have we learned? First of all, you will never please all the students no matter what you do, but we discovered that students could actually enjoy writing and learning at the same time. Yes, we will continue to revise the essay questions to improve the quality and even ask students to create some prompts that would be appropriate as options. We will also continue to try to make these prompts as close to possible real-life writing experiences as possible.

Since this initial test, we have also used choices of essay prompts in physics and chemistry classes. In fact, this year we team taught a senior interdisciplinary science seminar course entitled *Oceans Past and Present.* A semester-long course, we tried allowing students to create essay prompts for their classmates (see Figure 5 below).

Figure 5
Oceans Past and Present—Semester 2
"Land of the Tiger" Writing Assignment

Background: Everyone in the room has watched this video and taken notes on what they have learned.

Assignment: Each student must create a writing activity for another student to do. This activity must help your fellow students apply what they have learned in some way.*

Due Date: Thursday, January 14, 1999.

PLEASE TAKE ADVANTAGE OF THIS OPPORTUNITY TO COME UP WITH YOUR OWN ORIGINAL IDEA.
THERE IS NOT AN "INCORRECT" ANSWER!!

* For instance, if you really enjoyed the narrator's use of metaphors, you might write the following assignment: Think of a way to write a metaphor for something you have learned about the ocean from this video. Be thorough and clear in your description. Another example might be that you discovered the immensity of a particular species of fish/mammal. Your writing assignment for a classmate might be to write a letter to a friend describing this fish/mammal as if you have seen it for the first time. Your assignment might be a diary/journal entry from the daily life of an Indian fisherman. Another assignment might be to create a scientific research study to be funded by the National Science Foundation.

Your writing assignments may be letters, journals, memos, scientific proposal, creative writing, short essay, etc. This assignment may be descriptive, persuasive, comparative, contrasting, analytic, figurative, or literal.

Each student received the essay prompt of another classmate and responded to the prompt. We used a peer response sheet so that students could make revisions before submitting their essays to the originators of the prompts. In the peer response, students were asked to respond to the following.

Read the writing assignment and the response.

1. Has the writer followed the directions and done what he/she was asked to do?

   Yes No

2. Now write a one paragraph summary of the response.
3. Write a letter to the writer. Explain the specific strengths in the content of the response, referring to lines or areas marked in the margins. Give the writer some specific recommendations for what might be done with the piece to improve, revise, or publish. Finally, if there were any glaring grammatical errors, you may wish to suggest improvements in mechanics.

Although this activity only affected a small group of students, their response to being invited to create an essay prompt proved beneficial. At the beginning of a new semester students felt empowered and trusted to make an appropriate writing assignment. In fact, the results were just as exciting for us as teachers. We had a chance to read letters written from the point of view of a fish, descriptions of a day in the life of an Indian fisherman, and other topics in which students demonstrated their knowledge of the segment focusing on life under sea around the Indian Ocean. Finally, the assignment enabled us to see what students did not understand and to determine how much they had actually learned from the use of this popular video whose narrator uses beautiful metaphoric language to describe marine life around India. Some students who had literary interests picked up on the use of language and created essay prompts that required their classmates to focus on this aspect as well.

Figure 6
Reading and Writing Assignment

- Read the essay at *http://wwvw.pbs.or~/wgbh/nova/longitude/secrets.html*
- Respond on email by summarizing the key points
  - major contributions and innovations by different cultures
  - instrumentation
  - the impact on life at the time of the contribution/innovation (how did it change the way people interacted, economic factors, political factors, etc.) the effect on contemporary times
- Choose one of the following audiences, indicating who your audience is at the top of your email message.
  - Queen Elizabeth
  - An admiral on the Joint Chiefs of Staff
  - A fourth grade science class
  - National Science Foundation Committee on Navigation
  - Historian for the Museum of Nautical Archives
  - Hasbro Toy Manufacturers who are designing a new board game on navigation

Figure 7
Test on *The Perfect Storm*

The test of *The Perfect Storm* must be completed no later than April 22. Select one of the options below. Submit your paper printed from a word processor, using 12-point font, one-inch margins, and double spaced. Be sure to put your name and the number of your choice in the upper right-hand side of your paper. You may assume any of the following positions to fulfill your goal to test your reading and comprehension of this book:

1. You are an oceanographer. Write a report or letter to a new member of your team. In the letter, refer to specific sections of the book to help them understand (a) ocean conditions, (b) predictions of conditions in the Atlantic Ocean based on the past and present, (c) suggested research methods based on Junger's methods and methods developed in class discussions.

2. You are a meteorologist. In an article for *Meteorological Times,* a monthly magazine, describe the background reading necessary to describe a meteorological event. Be sure to include specific references from Junger (put page numbers in parentheses).

3. You are a nautical scientist. For the conference of the National Nautical Association, write a report describing how a swordfishing boat, or other boat of comparable size, should perform in extreme conditions. Give examples of your points from *The Perfect Storm* (put page numbers in parentheses).

4. You are a naval architect. Write a proposal for the design of a more efficient and seaworthy swordfishing vessel. Refer to specific points from Junger's book that describe real situations and put page numbers in parentheses. Include a visual model large enough for your audience to see.

5. You are a marine biologist. Describe habits, ecological factors, migration, etc., of swordfish. Document your information with information from Junger's book (put page numbers in parentheses).

6. You are the Commissioner for Conservation of Swordfish. Do a case study of swordfish, giving information on overharvesting, laws, economic considerations, and recommendations for conservation.

7. You are an anthropologist. You are doing a study of the culture of life at sea. Use a few real people from the book as the basis of your study. Describe how they live, how they behave, how they interact with others, their quality of life, etc., based on documentation from Junger's book (put page numbers in parentheses).

8. You are a historian. Create a record of ocean disasters and storms based only on information from Junger's book (put page numbers in parentheses). You may choose to do this in the form of a time line.

Figure 7 (cont.)
Test on *The Perfect Storm*

Evaluation Criteria
The Perfect Storm Test

_____ **Knowledge—45%**

Stays on topic
Meets requirements of the option
Demonstrates an understanding of the subject
Covers material thoroughly

_____ **Creativity—20%**

Interesting coverage of the option
Descriptive

_____ **Mechanics—20%**

Grammar
Spelling
Format required by option

_____ **Documentation—15%**

_____ **Total Points**

Comments ____

We have used other assignments (see Figures 6 and 7 above) that require students to have done their work thoroughly in order to select the "fun" topics and respond appropriately.

Using *The Perfect Storm* test, for instance, we received an original anthropological study of man from the point of view of a swordfish, the life of a fisherman, formal proposals for boat designs with sketches, historical records of boat disasters in the Atlantic, and a variety of other unique responses that demonstrated their comprehension of the book and use of citations from it. Like most classroom teachers, we have little time to analyze each assignment but through formative assessments throughout the semester, we discover what worked well and what didn't. Without a doubt, allowing students to choose their essay prompts to assess learning may be used across the disciplines, not just in science classes.

What can we conclude from these activities? Perhaps the most relevant and obvious point is that students learn in many different ways. Likewise, the ways in which we assess that learning should be varied to meet the needs of different learners. Questions that stimulate the readers' curiosity evoke powerful results. Guiding a student's learning is difficult but holds great rewards for those educators who "step up to the plate." We must never absolve ourselves from the important task we have as educators to pragmatically and systematically improve learning.

Chapter 11

Did They Get It? Assessing Student Learning Through the Lab Report

John Fredericks

If you asked science teachers, "Do your students write across the curriculum?" most of us would say, "Yes, they write lab reports." We might say that we do this to prepare students to write the types of reports that will be expected in college science courses. However, that is not the only reason most teachers assign lab reports. Lab reports are one means to assess whether students just measured and manipulated some numbers or whether they gained insight into a physical process.

Assessing lab reports in a fair manner is tricky. One approach is the "pile" method: read your students' papers, then stack them into piles for A, B, C, D and F. I'm sure most of us had lab reports returned to us with only a letter grade and a few brief comments on the last page. Students can see this grading scheme as arbitrary, and often it does not help them improve on specific problems in their writing or understanding. In an effort to be fairer, many instructors use an itemized scoring guide that looks at each section of a report individually. An itemized scoring guide also provides useful feedback for students to consider when writing their next report.

One trap in using an itemized scoring guide is that it becomes merely punitive, a way to subtract points based on what was omitted. A scoring guide must serve this function, but it also should provide the instructor a way to assess what students know, whether they "got it." In this article, I will describe how I use my scoring guide to see if students "got it." Secondly, I will provide examples of student writing and how I would score that writing in terms of understanding. The third topic that I will discuss is how to get students actively involved in the assessment process. The fourth section will give you the opportunity to read some actual student writing samples and assess them using this scoring guide.

Lab Report Format and Scoring Guide

High school students need a format to guide them in writing their lab reports. The lab report format that I use in my high school chemistry classes is shown in Figure 1. The format provides the students with suggestions and point totals for each section. This allows students to know how they will be graded when writing their reports. They are directed to write for someone who knows a little about science, not to write for their teacher.

Of course, all instructors will individualize their lab report formats based on what they think is important. Many teachers require that students write the procedure that they used; some require statistical calculations such as standard deviation and statistical range. Some instructors prefer that students write in a paragraph format like that of a journal article (Licata 1999). Despite variations in content and style, most lab reports will contain at minimum the components listed in Figure 1. For now, it can serve as a model for our discussion of assessing student writing.

Figure 1

Lab Report Format

Name: Title of Lab

Partner Date

1. **Purpose—Why did you do the experiment? (2 points)**

   Example of a good purpose: "To measure the heat capacity of different metals and compare them to the accepted values"

   Example of poor purpose: "To learn about heat"

2. **Observations** (Written in sentences) **(2 points)**

   Example—"When copper and sulfur were heated, a blue flame was seen at the top of the crucible. Towards the end of the heating, the flame disappeared."

3. **Data Tables** (may need more than one) **(2 points)**

	Trial 1	Trial 2	Trial 3	Trial 4
Measurement				
Measurement				
Measurement				
Calculated Value				

   Average Calculated Value

   Accepted Value (from book or instructor)

4. **Sample Calculations (2 points)**

5. **Error Analysis (2 points)**

$$\% \text{ Error} = \left| \frac{\textit{Experimental} - \textit{Accepted}}{\text{Accepted}} \right| \times 100$$

6. **Conclusions**

   a. How well did your experimental values compare with the accepted value? Was your percent error low enough for the lab to be considered accurate? Is this a good way to do this experiment? **(2 points)**

Figure 1 (cont.)

b. How precise were your measurements? Is this an effective way to take these measurements? **(2 points)**
c. List *at least* three things that should be changed in the procedure if you were to repeat the lab. Explain why each change should be made. **(2 points each)**
d. Additional Questions—These are provided with some labs and should be answered here.

Notice that each section and each item in the "Conclusions" section is worth two points. Many of the rubrics for assessing student writing suggest a 1 through 5 ranking of student writing. This system is very effective when looking at a student paper as a whole. However, it is cumbersome when evaluating each of the components in a stack of a hundred or more lab reports. A simpler method is to look at each component of the lab report and assign it a 0, 1, or a 2. This allows teachers to assess whether the student understood and explained his or her understanding clearly.

How do we decide if a section receives a 0, 1, or a 2? A student would receive a zero on a section if it was left blank or provided a blatantly wrong answer. A score of 1 indicates that the student did show some understanding, but did not explain the answer in sufficient detail or clarity. A score of 2 indicates comprehension of the concepts and a clearly written explanation. Let's look at some examples of student writing and how they would be scored using this rubric. We'll focus on the areas of the purpose, observations and conclusions since those areas give us the best indicator of whether a student "got it."

How to Use the Scoring Guide to Assess Student Papers

As teachers, we are not merely statisticians, checking only that the format was followed to the letter. While the format is important, we also want the students to show that they gained insight from the experiment. We look for depth of explanation, quality of the explanation, and writing that reveals understanding, not misconceptions. What do I mean by "depth of explanation?" When a student loses a point on a written explanation, the student often will complain, "But you knew what I meant!" Let's face it, that's true. We usually do know what students mean because we spend a great deal of time with them, and know how they think and speak. In assessing writing, that must be put aside. We have to ask what a stranger could learn about the lab from their writing. The lab report is one vehicle to train students to write for a larger audience than just their teachers.

In one lab that my students performed, students had to determine the concentration of a base and an acid. Here is how two different students wrote their purpose:

Student A: "The purpose of this lab was to standardize solutions by adding a base to them."

Student B: "The purpose of this lab was to determine the molarity of NaOH by titration with HCl, and vinegar by titration with the NaOH. Those molarities were then compared to the accepted values."

Student A's purpose was scored a one, and Student B's a two. While Student A did use the proper term "standardize," the student did not detail which solutions he was standardizing. The teacher would "know what he meant," but an outsider would not. Student B's detailed explanation would allow anyone with a little chemistry background to understand why the experiment had been conducted.

Other examples of depth of explanation can be seen in how students describe their observations. The first example below received a one, and the second a two. The first is sufficient, but the second shows a keen, careful eye:

"When the filter paper was allowed to dry, white crystals formed."
"The substance was white, in paper-thin slices, and cracked very easily."

Along with depth of explanation, teachers are concerned with the quality of explanation. We can illustrate that by examining students' suggestions for improving experiments. As science teachers, we want students always to consider the limitations of any experiment, and to consider how an experiment might be improved. Often students will write suggestions such as:

"We needed more time to do this. We rushed through to get it done."
"We shouldn't break the beaker next time like we did in Trial 3."
"Use someone that is not so clumsy to pour the NaOH so nothing gets spilled all over the table next time."

All of these suggestions have some merit, but they would receive a one on the scoring guide. They reflect problems that the particular students encountered, but don't suggest ways to improve the lab procedure. Suggestions that would receive a two illustrate ways to improve the experimental procedure for any student. Some examples are:

"If we placed a watch glass on the beaker while heating, we might not lose the product which popped out of the beaker."
"If we added the NaOH slower, we might be able to get smaller drops and see a more accurate color change."

Grading the lab report can help the teacher know what students understand, and where their misconceptions lie. The "Observations" section often reveals gaps in understanding. For example, in a lab in which chloride ion (Cl-) was precipitated from a solution with silver ion (Ag+), one student wrote: "The equilibrium shifted to the reactants because we replaced the Cl- with Ag+." This response would receive a one. Although the student understood that there was some interaction between the chloride and silver ions, the student did not understand that it was a precipitation to form solid silver chloride.

Another example involves a lab in which iron metal reacts with copper(II)sulfate. This was a single replacement reaction that produces copper metal. Even though we had discussed the reaction before the lab, one student wrote "The iron rusted and turned into copper." This was scored as a one. The student understood that copper metal was formed, but his answer suggests that copper and rust are the same substance. To receive a two, the student should have written that the iron displaced the copper, or that they "switched places."

Here's one last example that shows how lab reports can reveal misconceptions. After doing a discovery-based lab on acids and bases, students were supposed to discover that bases end in the hydroxide ion, expressed in the formula as OH. However, some students wrote: "Bases end in H" and only received a one for that answer. To receive a two, the student would need to write that bases end in OH. However, the concept is so important that I did re-teach the topic at the beginning of the next class. This can happen when using discovery learning. Sometimes students don't discover what we wanted, and re-teaching for clarification is necessary. The lab report can point out those areas and help teachers prepare more effective lessons.

After grading a set of lab reports, a teacher sometimes feels discouraged. Using the scoring guide properly may only reveal that a number of students either didn't write clearly, or that they still have misconceptions about the science topic. One way to minimize vague writing and misconceptions is to encourage students to use the drafting process. I allow my students to show me their working drafts, and provide them with written and verbal feedback before they write their final draft. Word processing has made the drafting process simple. Students can quickly make corrections on labs and then print a final copy. I give students my e-mail address and encourage them to e-mail their drafts to me (Fredericks 1999). I am able to return the labs to them with my comments interspersed throughout the report. This is much easier than trying to cram comments into the margins. The student hopefully learns that the drafting process should be used for *all* writing, not just in English classes.

Below is part of a lab that I reviewed via e-mail. The student's writing is marked with a caret symbol (">") and my comments are bulleted. In the experiment, the students determined the amount of calcium carbonate (CaCO3) in an antacid tablet.

> I feel that the substance we are testing needs to be changed. I feel an alternative substance that would better react with the HCl would provide better results.

- You need to re-think this suggestion. We can't change the substance to be tested. That is the point of the lab. Suggest instead a way to change the method of testing this same substance.

> I think the substance should also be heavier. Much of the CaCO3 could have stuck to the paper or blown away.

- What do you mean by heavier? Should we have used more of the substance, or are you trying to get at something else? I'm confused here.

> I also believe some different types of equipment may be helpful. A scale that was not open to the environment may have helped to keep more CaCO3 on the paper.

- Good suggestion. Maybe some kind of air shield could be set up?

Getting Students Involved in the Assessment Process

One activity that I have my students do is to grade a sample lab. Early in the course, after students have completed one or two lab reports, I pass out a teacher-generated sample lab, complete with some built-in mistakes. I give the students a copy of the scoring guide and ask them to pretend that they are the teachers. They often ask, "What did you give it?" but I don't tell them until after they have graded the lab.

Students attack this assignment with relish, and they tend to be harsher graders than I am. In the discussion that follows, it should become clear that students are vague in their criticisms. They might say, "I thought the purpose was stupid." Even comments like that give us a springboard for further discussion. I ask follow-up questions such as, "What do you mean? Is there a better way to describe it than 'stupid'?" After this activity, students tell me that they have a better idea of what is expected of them in a lab report.

A second way that students can be involved in the assessment process is through peer review of labs (Berenson 1995). Several times during the term, I have students read and assess other student labs. To give them guidance, I provide a copy of my scoring guide and ask them to answer the following three questions in a short paragraph for each question:

1. If you were the teacher grading this lab, what grade would you assign? Explain your reasons.
2. What did the student explain/show particularly well in this lab report?
3. What specific suggestions can you give this student to help them improve this lab report?

The next day, the labs and the peer evaluation reports are returned to the original author. The students now have the chance to re-write any sections of the report that the peer evaluation indicated needed improvement. They then submit the revised labs to me with the understanding that while I will take the peer reviews into account, I have the final say on the grade. After a recent peer review activity, students were eager to share with the class the positive things they saw in other lab reports. Most students indicated that the peer comments were helpful when writing the final draft of their report. Here is an example of how one student wrote a peer review.

1. I would give this lab an 18 or 19. I thought the calculations were accurate, but there could have been more observations
2. The student's purpose and sample calculations were very clear and easy to follow.
3. I would tell the student to be more specific on the observation section, and to go into more detail there. I would also say to be clearer on what you mean in the conclusions.

In peer reviews, students often do not provide the specific feedback that a teacher would. In the above example, the student's comment, "be clearer on what you mean in the conclusions," would not be of great help in revising the report. Student peer reviews can be improved. One way is to show them examples before they write their first peer review. Put a few examples of clear and vague peer comments on an overhead and have a class discussion about what constructive criticism should look like. Another way is to have the student who wrote the lab comment on the helpfulness of the review. Ask students to tack a paragraph at the end of their reports detailing which comments were helpful and which were not. Another option is to grade each suggestion on the 0, 1, 2 scale. Knowing that their reviews will be worth points may motivate students to be more helpful in their reviews.

Examples for You to Score

Below are three examples of students' conclusions. This is a lab to determine how much of the active ingredient (CaCO3) is present in antacid tablets. Read through each conclusion section, and grade each item on the 0, 1, 2 scale. There are five items, for a total of 10 possible points. If you do not score an item as a 2, you should write a brief explanation suggesting how the student could have scored higher. After you have scored these three examples, I will discuss how I scored them. You may wish to read through all three conclusions before you begin scoring.

Student A's Conclusions

1. Our experimental value was off by 53.4% error to the accepted value. Based on our percent error, this was not a good method for doing this lab.
2. We were not as precise as we could have been in our trials.
3. If we were to repeat the lab I would:
   a. do more trials
   b. allow more time to let the antacid dissolve in the solution
   c. dissolve the antacid in more acid

Student B's Conclusions

1. We had a 64% error. There was a very large difference between our CaCO3 per tablet and what they say on the bottle. I don't see very much wrong with the method for doing the experiment, but our numbers were very off. We might have made a mistake somewhere, or they just exaggerated the amount of CaCO3 on the bottle.
2. Our trials were very precise. They ranged from 0.17 grams to 0.19 grams per tablet, a difference of only 0.01 grams.
3. If I were to repeat the lab, I would do the following:
   a. While doing the titration, it would have been helpful to know exactly what color pink we were looking for. In our first trial, we

were expecting it to be darker, and might have added too much NaOH.

b. When we added water and indicator to the antacid, some of the powder stuck to the sides of the beaker, so we might have lost some that way.

c. It is also very important to be exact as possible when reading your volumes from the buret.

Student C's Conclusions

The calculated values for the mass of CaCO3 per tablet were fairly precise. Even though the numbers were fairly precise, they were not accurate. This inaccuracy is exhibited by the 67% error.

Based on the large percent error, the method used for this lab was not very good and could be improved tremendously. To improve the lab procedure, several changes could be made. One necessary change would be to use only white tablets. The green color made it hard to see the color change. In our experiment, the trials with the white tablet were more accurate than the one with the green tablet. Because much of the tablet did not dissolve, using a smaller mass of the tablet for each trial would be a second change that could be made. Instead of using 0.20 grams of CaCO3, if 0.10 grams were used possibly more of the tablet would dissolve. Using a greater volume of HCl (increasing it to 20 mL) also would allow more of the tablet to dissolve.

How I Scored These Examples

Student A scored a six out of ten. The student did discuss both accuracy and precision, but did not give much detail about precision and only scored a one. The student only scored a one for each of the three suggestions for improvement. The suggestions made were valid, but were not explained. Also, the suggestion of "do more trials" should be discouraged. It needs to be explained to students that the advantage of more trials is a given for any experiment.

Student B scored an eight out of ten. The student gave two possibilities for the 64 % error, and gave a detailed explanation of the precision among the trials. The only two sections that scored a one instead of two were the last two suggestions for improvement. It was good to note that some of the powder stuck to the sides of the beaker, but no suggestion was made for getting that powder off the sides. A simple suggestion such as "wash the powder into the bottom with more water" would have bumped the score to a two. The last suggestion about "being as exact as possible" is another generic suggestion like "do more trials." It merited a one.

Student C scored a nine out of ten. This student chose to write in paragraph form, but all of the components are there. The only part that scored a one was the discussion of precision. Like Student A, Student C only said that the numbers were not precise. Student C's suggestions for improvement are exemplary. All of the suggestions are specific to the experiment (as compared to "do more trials"), and are fully explained.

There is not one perfect lab report format, nor one perfect scoring guide. Every teacher will personalize his or her format, and some qualitative labs may require an entirely different format. Nor are written lab reports the only types of writing that should occur in a science classroom. Posters, essay questions, warm-up questions, narrative labs, and creative writing assignments all help a teacher assess whether a student has mastered a concept (Kirkland 1999).

However, all science writing can be scored using the 0, 1, 2 scale or some variation. You may feel the need for more levels depending on the nature of an assignment (Jensen 1995). The exact method is not as important as the goal. No matter how you grade, you are trying to determine whether students have mastered a concept, or whether further teaching activities are needed to clarify or reinforce the concepts. Most importantly, let your students be a part of the process. Give them the chance to evaluate sample work and the work of other students. You'll see the results in the next batch of lab reports.

Works Cited

Berenson, Sarah. 1995. Changing assessment practices in science and mathematics. *School Science and Mathematics* 95, no. 4 (April):182–186.

Fredericks, John. 1999. The chemistry of e-mail. *The Science Teacher* 66, no. 3 (February): 62–63.

Jensen, Ken. 1995. Effective rubric design. *The Science Teacher* 62, no. 5 (May): 34–37.

Kirkland, Willis L. 1999. Teaching biology through creative writing. *The Journal of College Science Teaching* 26, no. 4 (February): 277–279.

Licata, Kenneth P. 1999. Narrative lab reports. *The Science Teacher* 66, no. 3 (March): 20–22.

Chapter 12

Science Fair Finesse: Guiding Clear Communicative Writing

Kay Berglund

In science class, writing is about communication. Scientists publish their results in scientific journals and in recaps in the *New York Times*. Writing should be used to inform the public about discoveries and to communicate with other people studying the same topic. Clear writing is essential. Unfortunately, many science students and professional scientists struggle to convey their ideas in written form.

Science fairs are a common opportunity for writing in the science classroom and these fairs pervade our schools in an attempt to model for students the real-life scientific process. Any successful science fair also needs to model for students the written component of real-life science communications as part of this process. Effective assessment of our students' science writing should guide them to learn how to construct clear, communicative writing, and measure their success at this learning.

Why Science Fairs?

School science fairs ask students to model scientific research and communications. Most science fair mentors ask students to write a description of their methods and results, including clearly establishing materials, variables, procedure, results and conclusions. Sometimes we ask that introductory background material be included. Our goals are to have students formulate their ideas clearly, and then share these ideas with others.

Science fairs are notoriously work intensive. Students labor for hours over growing plants and spreading mold. Parents supply days of nagging, scolding, and negotiating. Teachers grade reams of papers and struggle to keep up with individual students. We need to find a way to tackle this project without overtaxing students and burying ourselves under mounds of papers to grade.

Science fairs can also be one of a student's most memorable experiences in school. Most adults can relate the topic of their middle school science fair project immediately and can often expound upon the experience (favorably or not) years later. For a science fair to be a profitable venture, to keep more than just the smell of the experiment lingering with the students, skill development must be a process, rather than just a one-time use. Students must nurture their writing skills through practice and patience, with constructive, integral feedback helping them to form and assess their own ideas. The fortunate part of this deliberate writing practice is that it can end up making the science fair easier and more pleasant for all involved: students, parents, and teachers alike.

Use Their Writing to Monitor Students' Understanding of the Subject

As science fair deadlines loom, it is tempting to forego rigorous practice of the elements of writing up experiments. But our class time spent explaining and practicing setting up meaningful experiments is not a waste of time, even as the fair's deadlines loom; instead, it is a keystone to this whole process. We expect students to write up what they have done, but if they do not understand their experiments, or experiments in general, they cannot write about them clearly. Asking them to write along the way can help us to assess their understanding of the concepts we want them to learn as we go, instead of waiting until the final stages to discover misunderstandings.

It seems an obvious mantra: what I do not understand, I cannot communicate. Writing can help us keep our students' attention, and monitor what they do and do not understand. This type of writing is rarely graded per se; instead, it allows us to glimpse a student's evolving understanding. Responsive writing can be used for science fairs or for reflection in a multitude of other subjects. Ask students to reflect and respond in writing before tackling a new topic, midway into an explanation, or at the conclusion of a unit. Writing gives us a window into their thoughts. Sometimes a student nods and looks pleasant in class, but written responses betray hidden misconceptions.

As I introduce science fair concepts, I ask students to practice writing up the experiments I model, and I pay attention to what they write. If time is short in class, I read them after class. On the other hand, if I am overburdened with grading, I ask them to read aloud to each other in class. If their answers are incomplete, I ask them to clarify in writing. Five minutes at the end of the experiment for quiet individual writing can direct the whole course of the next lesson: perhaps they understand it beautifully, or perhaps they still don't understand why to control extraneous variables. From their writing, I can see the confusion laid out on paper. For example, a student puts up a red flag when she writes:

> "The independent variable is the thing you change in the experiment. Like when you grow plants, the plants change."

She has correctly quoted part of the discussion she heard for an independent variable, but she has not applied the definition correctly in her example, and in fact has come closer to describing the dependent variable in this experiment (the height of the plants). With a simpler assessment activity, such as a multiple choice or memorize-the-definition quiz, she probably could have escaped with this misconception unnoticed. I can see from her writing, however, that I need to go back over this concept with her, and possibly with the rest of the class as well. I do not grade these exercises, and often do not even comment on them; instead, I read them to assess how well students understand what I'm teaching. I use their writing to help me formulate my next lesson.

Try brief, quiet writing as a part of a class discussion, with a topic even as simple as "Explain the variables in the experiment we just discussed." Whether introduction or mid-way check, this intensely individual responding allows students to relate their conceptions without influence of their peers, and creates an individual focus for a large class. It also allows their teacher to hear and respond to them immediately, adjusting lessons accordingly.

Practice, Practice, Practice

The more practice students have with communicative writing, the more successful they will be at doing it. A runner of marathons would never expect to do her best if she did not train with shorter distances prior to the "real thing." Ask students to write up mini experiments along the way. Try writing up just the variables on this experiment, or just the conclusion on that one. Keep it simple; keep it clear. Just as a runner may practice fast sprints one day and train for long-distance endurance another, your science fair writers do not need to practice all their skills at once to learn how to do the parts.

For example, to begin our discussion of variables and constants, we usually do a simple experiment on how paper airplanes fly. I ask students to list the variables they think could influence a paper airplane's flight. Instead of keeping this open as a class discussion, I ask them first to brainstorm individually on paper. Then I open it up to a discussion aloud. Following the discussion, I allow them to add to their lists. A student's initial list might look something like this:

- more weight
- fold it different
- bend wings
- smash it
- different paper
- make it bigger
- use a launcher

After discussion of how to categorize variables and make measurable changes, the same list might look like this:

- weight
- where a paper clip is on it
- length
- width
- the way it's folded
- type of paper
- flaps
- how stiff it is
- wind
- angle you throw it
- how hard you throw it

We continue with this exercise by brainstorming things we could measure about a paper airplane's flight. In this way, we explore independent variables, constants, and dependent variables. The writing exercise keeps students on task and focuses our discussion. My job is to peek into their ideas as they are set on paper, not to correct their papers, but to learn from their writings.

Clarify Directions

To keep writing (or any assessment task) an accurate reflection of students' abilities and understanding, it is crucial that they understand what they are asked to do in the assignment. An extra twenty minutes spent refining clear, precise directions for science fair reports translates into hours of time saved correcting students who omit or misunderstand parts of the assignment. Keep directions clear and simple.

For younger students, I have found that smaller pieces tax their understanding less: why have them turn in the whole paper all at once, when they could list their materials weeks before they can tell you their conclusions in organized fashion? I keep the assignment most direct at times by dividing it down. Later, we can put the pieces together if we need to. I assign "materials" due one day, "procedure" another, "results" when the experiment is completed, and so on. Dividing the assignment up also makes it easier for me to keep up with the grading by making the chunks smaller.

Make Grading Transparent From the Start

One remarkably effective technique with transactional writing is to ask students to assess themselves before they turn their papers in to you. Decide ahead of time how a paper will be graded. Sometimes developing a rubric with the students helps them to be involved in the process. Other times, it can be as simple as presenting them with the rubric in class well before the assignment is due. This technique makes clear to students the relationship between directions and grading, and also prevents them from being surprised by their teacher's assessment of their writing.

For example, I tell my students that a certain number of points for this writing assignment is based on whether they list all their materials and include measurements for each. Students can easily assess for themselves whether they have done so. I ask them to complete a grading list for themselves before they turn in the project. If they have not included a complete list of materials, they can immediately see that they have omitted it.

I use a formal rubric like the following to assess the conclusions section of a science fair write up:

Conclusion

0 pts . . . . Omitted section
1 pt . . . . Conclusion recaps results without further reflection

2 pts . . . . Conclusion addresses original question, but results are inaccurately applied (too broad or in error)
3 pts . . . . Conclusion addresses original question; results are accurately applied to answer this question
4 pts . . . . Conclusion addresses original question; results are accurately applied to answer this question; explanation is clear and easy to understand.

I ask students to rate themselves before they turn in the paper. Most students are surprisingly accurate at assigning themselves points for each section. This self-assessment also tends to keep them more focused on the requirements for the section, and ensures that they do not omit obvious parts of the assignment as easily. When they have time and opportunity to do so, self-assessment in this structured form encourages students to revise their work before they submit it. They perceive the most blatant and fixable errors in their own work, and thus my task as their teacher becomes guiding them through more subtle understanding of the assignment and concepts.

Students assess their own writing before they ask me to do the same. I end up with students who are more actively involved in their writing, who understand that mysterious grade they eventually receive, and who are directly involved in revising their own writing. Ahead of time, rubrics are time-consuming to create, but they pay back that time with an end result of easier grading and more effective writing. Formal rubrics also help different teachers in the department to be more consistent about our expectations. Though we can never make grading an entirely objective exercise, it helps to have a consistent basis for our grading decisions.

Revise the Exercise

As teachers, one of the most important things we can do with a large project like this one is learn from our experiences. What portion of the writing was weakest? If you found yourself writing reams of explanations in the margins again and again, look back to the process. What could have been more clearly explained? How did this student's misconceptions escape the earlier writing exercises? Did he grade himself accurately in his self-assessment? If she was inaccurate in her own assessment, did she misunderstand the criteria? How could the rubric be improved to communicate necessities and expectations more clearly? Just as students learn to write through attempts, revisions, and further attempts, our efforts to learn to assess and guide their writing are always evolving. We must be willing to reflect upon and revise our strategies as needed.

Keep Parents Out of It

The most gratifying changes I made in our science fairs in the last few years kept many more parents out of the fair. Their lessened involvement in our long-term project was a vote of confidence for our guidance as teachers, and helped to level the field between students with over-involved parents and those with absent, uninterested parents. Too often in previous years, I had overheard parents referring to their sixth grader's experiment as "our project" or quarreling with their son or daughter over the means and the method. On the other hand, we had some parents who ignored their children's struggles and left them to sink amid those buoyed up by inflated adult wording in their reports.

Determined to lessen parent involvement, I turned to the component that draws parents in the most rapidly: the dreaded Science Fair Paper. In recent years, as we have made this writing assignment simpler and clearer for the students, we have found the remarkable result that parents, less stressed over their children's writing competence, divested themselves from most of the project! This change has left us free to work with the students, and left the students free to pursue and complete the experiments and the writing with their own ideas. Keep it simple, keep it manageable, keep it relevant, and parents will trust their children to complete the project on their own.

Keep Your Goals in Mind

It is essential that science fair writing be clear and easy to understand. Science fair papers are often seen and perhaps even judged by many people beyond the classroom. However, science class is not grammar class. In assessing these papers, it is important to keep in mind the goals of the paper. If grammar obscures communication of ideas, or is sloppy enough to reflect poorly on the student, by all means ask for another revision. Nitpicking is not your job, however. Keep in mind the goal of your science fair writer: to communicate these ideas clearly and elegantly, but to retain ownership of the writing, and so to avoid undue help from parents or other adults (including their teacher). Look for and respond to substance in the paper. Does the writer communicate how the experiment was conducted? Does she relate her procedure in an understandable way? Does he reflect thoughtfully upon his results? Mark those passages that need another look with a more critical eye towards spelling and grammar, but don't feel compelled to turn a science fair paper into a narrowly focused mechanics exercise. Good transactional writing is about communicating clearly and elegantly. Mechanics are an important part of good communication, but be sure you can embrace the whole forest, instead of picking at the bark of the trees.

Why Assess?

Assessment is about more than putting grades on papers. As teachers, our assessment of student work has two goals. To assign a grade reflecting a student's progress in class is often one of the purposes, but it is not the only one. The other important goal of our assessment for us is to learn to teach the student more effectively. Writing gives us the opportunity to see what a student does or does not understand, and to improve our teaching in areas where we need to do so.

The other extremely important goal of assessment is to develop in students the ability to critically assess their own work, and then revise the work to improve upon it or bring it closer to the requirements for the assignment. The term "assessment" must include a student's own assessment of his/her work. In preparing students to assess their own work, we prepare them to use writing in the way they will most often use it outside of school: self-monitored and self-adjusted.

From introductory elementary school fairs to high levels of competition in regional and national high school fairs, students across our country practice creating experiments and communicating their results to teachers, judges, and their community. Through science fairs, students learn to dream up a problem, conduct their own experiments, clearly and attractively display their work, and communicate in writing. Through this once a year (or perhaps once in a lifetime) venture, we want them to develop and practice these skills into meaningful, long-term learning.

Chapter 13

Mathematical Essays: An Alternate View of Student Knowledge

Linda A. Bolte

What does it mean to understand mathematics; how does understanding develop; and how is understanding assessed? These are three significant questions that have emerged from the current efforts to reform mathematics education. To most mathematics educators understanding means that new knowledge is related to existing knowledge. One's understanding of an idea depends on how many *other* ideas it is related to, on the nature and strength of the relationships between the ideas in question, and on the overall coherence (or structure) of one's knowledge (Secada 1997, p. 8).

It is believed this type of understanding develops as the result of actively trying to acquire knowledge, constructing relationships among ideas, reflecting on one's own experiences, and communicating what one knows. For this reason, mathematics teachers at all levels must encourage students to investigate the connections between various mathematical topics, provide them with the opportunity to reflect on and clarify their own thinking about mathematical ideas and situations, and expose them to expressing mathematical ideas in writing (National Council of Teachers of Mathematics (NCTM 1989). Current recommendations not only call for changes in instruction to support this view of understanding mathematics, but also advocate the integration of instruction and assessment, the utilization of multiple methods of assessment, and assessing a wide range of aspects of mathematical knowledge (NCTM 1995).

One viable method of integrating instruction and assessment is the use of concept maps and writing. In a concept map, related concepts/topics are represented as nodes that are connected with linking lines. The words used as labels for these linking lines indicate the specific relationship between the terms. Concept maps have been used effectively in mathematics classes as a learning strategy, a means of identifying student misconceptions, and an assessment instrument (Bartels 1995; Kounba 1994; Wilcox 1998). The increased use of writing in mathematics classes is consistent with the current effort to utilize alternate means of assessment (Connolly and Vilardi 1989; Sterrett 1990).

The two types of writing most frequently used to develop and assess mathematical knowledge are journals and writing prompts (Borasi and Rose 1989; Miller 1991; Mower 1996; Pugalee 1997). Most mathematics educators characterize journals as open-ended dialogues between the student and the teacher; entries may discuss mathematical content or attitudes toward mathematics. Written prompts tend to be more focused; they are commonly used to stimulate student responses to specific questions, such as, "How is solving an inequality different from solving an equation?" or "Last night a friend of yours asked you to look over her algebra homework. She wrote that $\sqrt{x^2 + 4} = x + 2$. Is she correct? Explain your answer."

The use of mathematical essays, in conjunction with concept maps, provides an alternate view of students' mathematical knowledge. Although each can be used alone, the combined use of concept maps and interpretive essays has a number of advantages. Whereas the concept map provides a graphical representation of the mathematical connections perceived by the student, the interpretive essay expands upon these relationships and focuses on communicating mathematical ideas in writing. By relying on these two alternate avenues of expression, students can explicitly communicate aspects of their knowledge of mathematical topics. Both strengths and weaknesses can be communicated in greater detail and in a more personal manner. The dual approach enables teachers to monitor student progress and guide instruction, as well as encourage students to explore a variety of relationships between mathematical concepts and topics, develop missing connections, and clarify misconceptions. Although this method of instruction/assessment does not assess every aspect of students' understanding of a particular concept or range of related mathematical topics, it does address several frequently neglected learning objectives. These include the efficient and effective organization of knowledge, the ability to communicate ideas clearly, and creativity (Clarke, Clarke, and Lovitt 1990).

How to Use Concept Maps and Interpretive Essays in the Mathematics Classroom

Concept maps/interpretive essays can be used in a variety of mathematics classes, either at the beginning of a lesson to review past material, during instruction to develop understanding, or as a summative activity. For example, in an Algebra II or Precalculus course, students can base a map and essay on terms such as *mapping*, *graph*, *domain*, *range*, *inverse*, and *one-to-one*; a geometry class can utilize words related to polygons or quadrilaterals. Figure 1 below provides a list of terms that have been used in a variety of mathematics classrooms from junior high to the introductory college level.

Figure 1
Suggested Terms for Concept Maps

Functions				
table of values	one-to-one	equation	inverse	circle
independent variable	mapping	exponential	quadratic	rule
dependent variable	constant	function	linear	range
logarithmic	composition	ordered pair	domain	graph

Figure 1 (cont.)
Suggested Terms for Concept Maps

Linear Relationships

vertical	graph	equation	rate of change	zeros
horizontal	undefined	x-axis	y-axis	table
x-intercept	y-intercept	parallel	direct variation	slope
intersect	indirect variation	solution	perpendicular	dependent

Rational Numbers

fraction	numerator	least common multiple	ratio
proportion	decimal	greatest common divisor	part
percent	factorization	multiple	whole
equivalent	divisor	denominator	simplify

Triangle

angles	vertices	height	length of sides	base
equiangular	right	acute	line segments	isosceles
obtuse	equilateral	scalene	size of largest angle	regular

Polygon

angles	vertices	# of sides	n-gon	square
triangle	rectangle	rhombus	line segments	acute
obtuse	equilateral	hexagon	right	regular
isosceles	quadrilateral	trapezoid	parallelogram	pentagon

Quadrilateral

parallel	perpendicular	congruent	exterior angle	diagonal
rectangle	rhombus	bisect	polygon	obtuse
right	regular	isosceles	quadrilateral	trapezoid
convex	concave	parallelogram	interior angle	square

Students are introduced to concept maps by working through the multistep construction process as a class. First, students read a list of terms in order to become familiar with the general topic being explored (e.g., about ten terms related to a review topic). Next, the terms are sorted into clusters according to the extent to which they are related, and the clusters are arranged around the central concept or topic. Because the relationships between terms can be viewed as either hierarchical or web-like, students should be shown simple examples of both types of maps. Next, linking lines are drawn between terms, and labels indicating the relationships being illustrated are written on the corresponding linking lines. Although the use of linking words is critical to map interpretation, students have the tendency to omit these labels because it is difficult for them to specify some relationships they wish to express. Consequently, this aspect of construction is discussed at some length. The class generates possible linking words (e.g., *has the property, is an example of, is an alternate form of, involves*) and discusses the need to draw directional arrows on the linking lines to indicate the direction of the relationship being expressed. It is very important to stress the individualized nature of the task to students; there is no one correct map. You may suggest students write the individual words on pieces of paper to facilitate rearranging the terms, omitting any terms they are unable to use or adding additional terms and symbols. The goal is for students to construct a map that makes sense to them as a means of constructing their own knowledge and to provide the foundation for their written essay.

Once a draft of their concept map is completed, students are introduced to the writing component, an interpretive essay in which they clarify and expand on the relationships expressed on the map. These essays are not limited to merely explaining how the map is organized; they are meant to give students the opportunity to reflect on the relationships illustrated on their concept map and refine their thoughts. Students are allowed the freedom to set the essay in any context they choose. The resulting product is frequently more personal, informal, and creative than technical writing.

To assist students who are not comfortable writing about mathematics, the teacher can provide a few broad guidelines: (1) make your paper reader-friendly; try thinking of a classmate as the reader rather than the instructor; (2) be as thorough in your discussion as possible, including additional information you think is relevant and your personal insights; and (3) personalize your essay by making it into a story or setting it in a creative context. No page limit is imposed on the essay; the only requirement is that it effectively communicate the connections the writer perceives.

If more guidance is required, the teacher may provide students with short selections of previous students' efforts and creative approaches. Some students are uncomfortable with the open-ended aspect of the task; they are concerned as to whether they are doing it right and whether there is a prescribed length for the essay. These students can be counseled to begin with a few key terms and linking lines, and build their map based on these core concepts and relationships. Although some students will not be able to think of a creative setting that can be developed, their essays can nevertheless include personal reflections that move the essays beyond a mere listing of textbook definitions or a series of disjointed statements.

When students are familiar with the overall process of constructing a map and writing the accompanying essay, they are given a list of approximately 10 to 20 words related to the selected topic and asked to construct a concept map based on these terms. Students are advised to use their text, or other resources, to clarify the meaning of any terms they do not know; they are encouraged to explore several arrangements of the terms until satisfied with the organization of their map. Students may move back and forth between the map and the essay as they become aware of relationships they omitted or notice errors in their thinking. In this way, the concept map provides structure to the interpretive essay in the form of a graphical outline and the essay provides an opportunity for the student to communicate the depth of their understanding of the topic.

An alternate instructional approach is to have the concept map constructed as a group project. This can be approached in two ways: have the group use assigned terms, or let them generate their own terms. In either case, the group must reach a consensus as to the arrangement of the terms. Groups then share their maps with the whole class, which leads to a class discussion of the similarities and differences between group maps. A discussion of this nature can broaden students' perspectives as to the open-ended aspect of the activity and expose them to relationships they did not perceive. This also allows students who are less proficient with writing to communicate their knowledge orally. Another variation is to construct a class map, over time, as the topic is being developed. In this case, all students use the same concept map for organization of their thoughts, but individual understandings and reflections are communicated in the interpretive essays.

Each concept map and interpretive essay can be evaluated using focused holistic scoring criteria shown in Figures 2 and 3 below. The use of these specific trait-scoring rubrics allows the teacher to distinguish between different dimensions of a student's response (Taylor and Bidlingmaier 1998). The concept map criteria focus on organization and accuracy; the interpretive essay criteria focus on communication, development, and mechanics (grammar and punctuation). If used strictly as a learning tool, the descriptive portion of criteria can be combined with written and/or oral comments to provide qualitative feedback to the student.

Figure 2
Focused Holistic Scoring Criteria for Concept Maps

Organization: description of clusters and connections used

6— Excellent: shows complete, in-depth understanding of links among various terms; creates clear and insightful clusters of related terms; utilizes exemplary linking words; may add terms
5— Fluent: shows a thorough understanding of links among various terms; creates illustrative clusters of related terms; utilizes effective linking words; uses all terms
4— Good: shows a general understanding of links among various terms; creates adequate clusters of related terms; utilizes applicable linking words; may omit a few terms
3— Fair: shows a partial understanding of links among various terms; creates understandable clusters of related terms; utilizes adequate linking words; may omit some terms
2— Weak: shows a minimal understanding of links among various terms; creates deficient clusters of related terms; utilizes unsuitable linking words; omits several key terms
1— Inadequate: shows little understanding on links among various terms; creates ineffective clusters of related terms; utilizes inapplicable/no linking words; omits numerous key terms
0— Unacceptable: no attempt made or unintelligible

Accuracy: evidence of inaccuracies/misconceptions

4— Excellent: no errors
3— Fluent: few minor errors, no conceptual errors
2— Good: some errors
1— Weak: numerous errors
0— Inadequate: numerous major conceptual errors

Figure 3
Focused Holistic Scoring Criteria for Interpretive Essays

Communication: clarification of understandings and expression of mathematical ideas

- 6— Excellent: demonstrates interpretations and understandings in a clear, systematic, and organized manner; represents mathematical ideas accurately in an exemplary manner
- 5— Fluent: demonstrates interpretations and understandings in a clear and organized manner; represents mathematical ideas in an effective manner; may contain minor misconceptions
- 4— Good: demonstrates interpretations and understandings in an organized manner; represents mathematical ideas in a proficient manner; may contain some misconceptions
- 3— Fair: demonstrates interpretations and understandings in an understandable manner; represents mathematical ideas in an acceptable manner; may contain several misconceptions
- 2— Weak: demonstrates interpretations and understandings in a manner that is disorganized or difficult to understand; represents mathematical ideas in an inappropriate manner; may contain numerous misconceptions
- 1— Inadequate: demonstrates interpretations and understandings in a manner that is impossible to understand; represents mathematical ideas in an inaccurate manner; numerous misconceptions
- 0— Unacceptable: no attempt made or unintelligible

Development

- 3— Excellent: method of presentation clear and appropriate transitions
- 2— Adequate: relationships and transitions sometimes unclear
- 1— Poor: lacks coherence; disjointed statements
- 0— Unacceptable: no attempt made or unintelligible

Mechanics

- 1— Acceptable: few violations in grammar, punctuation, capitalization
- 0— Unacceptable: errors interfere with understanding; unintelligible

Depending on one's goal, the concept map can be used as an ungraded advanced organizer, (i.e., an outline), and only the interpretive essay is assessed as a finished product. However, in this case, a mathematical accuracy component should be added to the writing criteria listed in Figure 3. Relative weights given to each trait assessed (e.g. communication, development, mechanics) may vary depending on individual teacher's level of expertise and emphasis. Regardless of whether both map and essay or only the essay is scored, students should be given the scoring criteria prior to beginning the activity to allow them the opportunity to evaluate their work.

Using the Scoring Criteria

When grading a collection of student maps and essays, each map and essay are examined and given a preliminary score from 0 to 10. Maps and essays are then sorted according to their preliminary scores for each trait; anchor papers that illustrate the level of proficiency for each score are selected. To ensure consistency in scoring, the remaining maps and essays are then compared with the anchor papers, adjusting scores as necessary. This use of anchor papers is critical to the scoring process, particularly when distinguishing between excellent and fluent work. It is recommended that a score of 6 for organization (concept maps) or for communication (essay) be reserved for exemplary work. Additional comments and corrections can be written on each map and essay at the discretion of the teacher.

Unedited essay accompanying concept map

The land of Function is a complex region populated by two tribes: X's and Y's. The two tribes have distinct responsibilities, yet have rela-

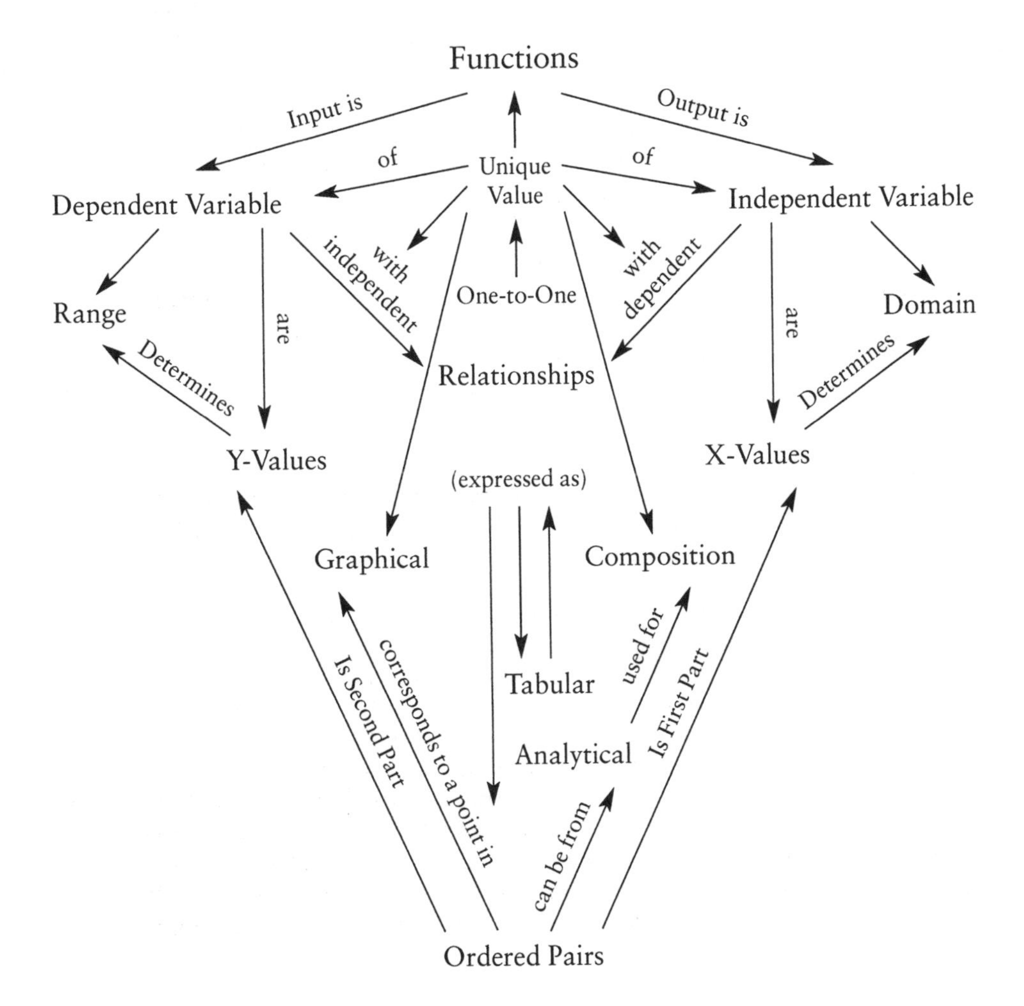

tionships that span between them. X's are extremely independent and only capable of providing input. They have formed relationships with the Y's, who, as everyone knows, are incapable of independent thought, and have become very dependent upon the X's. The Y's have realized their true role in life and become so dependent, in fact, that they are only capable of carrying out the wishes of X's in the form of output.

Being the dominant tribe, X's have set the boundaries for their domain of the land of Function. Recognizing the need to protect the superior X's, Y's have stepped into the role of determining the range within which they will need to defend the boundaries.

To maintain the dependence of the Y's, they have each been paired up with an X. These groupings are called ordered pairs (OP). OP's reside within dwellings in one (or more) of Function's housing units.

The first of these housing units, which is more of a hippie-type of communal gathering, is Graphical. Each OP is provided one specific point with Graphical. The OP's happily reside here, often drawing upon emotional connections with other OP's (*"Like, piecewise, dude."*)

Another housing unit found within Function is Tabular. Tabular is for OP's that prefer a more structured, rather listed living environment. OP's in Tabular are often caught in the trap of "trying to outdo the Jones's"; never happy with what they have, they are often comparing their relationship with those of other OP's.

The final Function housing unit is Analytical. Analytical is often a crowded crazy place where OP's are able to physically exert themselves. The pairing of OP's is often a temporary condition here. X's are able to participate in many different activities, such as division, addition, multiplication, and subtraction. Due to the limiting dependency of the Y, the X is encouraged to alternate partners depending on the current selected activity. The Composition Room is available for those OP's that feel up to the challenge of combining with other OP pairs. There is a waiting list for Composition, however, and the order is very important and strictly adhered to.

Although most Y's feel exceptionally honored by the attention of an obviously superior X, regardless of the lifestyle, some OP's feel a unique value for each other. In these cases, a one to one relationship is formed and the Y is granted the individual attention of an X who takes sole responsibility. In these relationships, no other X will violate the bond and request that particular to the company of that particular Y.

Life within the land of Function can be a complex situation, but as long as the relationships are clear and maintained, manipulation of the tribes is simply a matter of adhering to traditions.

The concept map shown previously received a total score of 6. The organization of the map (good) indicates a general understanding of multiple representations of functions and the meaning of domain and range. However, the map does not clearly illustrate that one-to-one is a special property of some functions and that composition is not limited to analytical functions. In addition, all terms relating to families of functions (i.e., linear, quadratics, absolute value), were omitted. The accuracy of the map was rated as good. Although the map indicated the output of a function is the independent variable and input is dependent, the essay expresses the correct relationship. The precise meaning of one-to-one and a conceptual understanding of composition are lacking.

The essay that accompanies this map received a total score of 9. Communication of the mathematical ideas is fluent; the analogy developed is well-based and the relationships between the terms is clearly expressed. The property of one-to-one is correctly interpreted, but there is some lack of clarity in the portion of the essay that discusses analytical functions and dependency of y on x. The method of presentation is clear with appropriate transitions (excellent) with few violations of grammar (acceptable).

Positive Effects on Learning and Assessment

There are numerous benefits to both students and teachers when incorporating these activities as part of mathematics instruction: students' learning of mathematics is enhanced, their view of mathematics is broadened, and teachers are provided with an alternate means of assessing understanding.

Enhanced Learning

Although constructing a map and writing an interpretive essay can be time-consuming, students generally report they enjoy and value both activities. Many students feel it encourages them to reflect on their knowledge and enhances their integration of this knowledge. When asked what, if any, do they see as the advantages of this activity, one student in an algebra course stated:

> It helps you realize that in order to work with mathematical operations you must understand the words in context. Mathematics is not just about numbers; there is really a whole language involved.

Another responded, the concept map, "made me organize the concepts and ideas. I am a visual person so this was very helpful."

Students frequently indicate they enjoy the opportunity to demonstrate their knowledge in a non-numerical way that allows them to be creative. One student stated "The creative writing project I did was more fun than any math project I've done since 6th grade." One geometry student developed a scenario based on a TV game show, Polygons 'R' Us Jeopardy. Another used the post office, the bank, and streets they are on to build an analogy for the three choices for a parallel postulate that result in Euclidean, hyperbolic, and elliptic geometry.

> In Euclidean town there is only one street which contains the post office and not the bank [i.e., for any point, P, not on line, l, there is a unique line through P that is parallel to l]. In Hyperbolic town there are many streets that contain the post office and not the bank [i.e., for any point, P, not on line, l, there are many lines through P that are parallel to l]. In Elliptic town every street contains both the post office and the bank

[i.e., for any point, *P*, not on line, *l*, there is no line through *P* that is parallel to *l*].

Concept maps and essays dealing with functions can result in stories in a variety of settings. Two students in an algebra class described a Functional Bakery in this way:

> Today's special is our Function Cake. With today's special you have a few choices. Let us tell you about them and why our options are the way they are. The box is the function, it relates to everything inside of it. The plate that the cake goes on is the relationship. The relationship describes how everything goes together. The analytical, graphical, and tabular are the frosting because it covers everything inside. The analytical describes the relationship in the form of an equation. The graphical used a graph to depict the function. The tabular describes the function in the form of a table ... Connecting the layers is the filling. The filling is the way the two layers are related. The filling may be linear which we consider strawberry. It is written as $f(x) = ax^2 + bx + c$. We consider the quadratic as blueberry filling. It is written as $f(x) = ax^2 + bx + c$. With strawberry filling there can be a one-to-one correspondence... The filling may be changed depending on the situation. For a different association between the x and y values, a different filling will be used. For the composition of functions you take the analytical view and apply two different functional processes. The output from the first one becomes the input for the second...

In addition to their concept map, these students also included a box from the bakery that contained cardboard cakes illustrating the relationships discussed in their essay. Two other algebra students wrote and illustrated a short story, "The Function Curse," which they submitted as a spiral-bound children's book.

Frequently students indicate they value the opportunity to personalize the content. One student wrote, "I will take this knowledge with me because it is mine. I didn't just regurgitate it through practicing equations." Two others who worked cooperatively felt the "project made us think about what we had learned and how we would explain it to someone else."

Students' View of Mathematics

The open-ended nature of this activity can counter students' conception of mathematics as a collection of isolated topics. Students frequently believe all mathematical activity is limited to recalling and applying learned procedures, and that mathematical knowledge is right or wrong, with no room for personal judgment. These beliefs are explicitly challenged by engaging students in reflection on past and current knowledge, by encouraging the creative and flexible expression of their ideas, and by not imposing a time restraint on the formulation and communication of their ideas.

This approach also reinforces students' basic understanding of the terms and encourages deep thinking and flexibility in the use of mathematical terms. Students must initially have a basic understanding of what each term means, but as they struggle to show the interrelationships between the terms, they must be prepared to look at the meaning of the terms from different perspectives. For example, on a triangle map, the terms *acute*, *obtuse*, and *right* can refer to a classification of triangles or the measure of individual angles. Omission of this type of linking lines and no reference to these relationships in the essay indicate a narrow or limited understanding of these terms. On a linear relationship map, students may be able to illustrate the relationships between the terms associated with *equations* and those associated with *graphs*, but be unable to define a connection between these clusters. Therefore, the *solutions* to linear equations and the *zeros* of graphs are viewed as separate, unrelated concepts.

Assessment Tool

This dual approach has benefits beyond using either method individually because the reliance on both visual and verbal communication of mathematical knowledge results in a more detailed representation of students' mathematical knowledge. Frequently students will omit certain relationships on their concept map because the map becomes too cluttered; however, they discuss these relationships in their essay. Other times students discuss a relationship in the essay, perhaps vaguely, but are unable to illustrate the relationship on their map because they do not have a clear understanding of the relationship. Each instance provides valuable information as to the depth of the student's understanding. The creation of the concept map gives an underlying structure to the essay without being overly rigid. By the same token, the essay justifies the organization of the concept map and clarifies possible technical inaccuracies in the construction of the map, such as inappropriate or missing linking lines. It allows the students to elaborate on the connections they see between the terms, to explain the connections they perceive in a specific context, and to refine their thinking.

A second benefit of the combined approach is that potential misconceptions can be readily identified by noting inappropriate or missing linking words, the omission of terms or linking lines, and overall organization of the concept map. For example, students may not link divisor and factor, nor indicate that fractions, decimals, and percents are multiple representations of the same ratio. Analysis of the interpretive essay can corroborate these misconceptions or indicate the error is an inaccuracy in the construction of the concept map rather than a conceptual misconception. A common error shown on the functions concept map is illustrating that all functions are one-to-one. However, many times in the context of the essay, it was obvious the student can distinguish between the defining characteristic of a function, single-valuedness, and the one-to one property. Subsequent instruction can focus on remediating these misconceptions individually or as a class. As patterns of misconceptions arise for given topics, teachers can alter their future instruction to incorporate additional examples and activities that focus on these issues.

Lastly, this task offers teachers sufficient flexibility to adapt either or both components to their individual needs. Concept maps can be constructed individually, in small groups, or as a class. For less proficient or younger students, fewer terms can be used, which results in shorter essays, drafts of essays can be submitted, and the mechanics of writing can be emphasized accordingly.

The use of concept maps and interpretive essays provides students with a rich learning experience and yields substantial insight into the degree of connectedness of selected aspects of their mathematical knowledge. Each method can be used effectively individually; however, when used in conjunction, students are given the opportunity to express their knowledge in different ways, allowing for individual differences in learning styles and verifying the relationships illustrated. In the process, they actively participate in the worthwhile task of developing connections between related concepts, reflect on their thinking, and become engaged in mathematical discourse. Although this approach does not encompass all types of mathematical knowledge, it does provide students with an opportunity to communicate some dimensions of their knowledge in a reflective manner, and enables teachers to assess student understanding at a more personal level.

Works Cited

Bartels, B. 1995. Promoting mathematics connections with concept mapping. *Mathematics Teaching in the Middle School* 1: 542–549.

Borasi, R., and B. J. Rose. 1989. Journal writing and mathematics instruction. *Educational Studies in Mathematics* 20: 347–65.

Clarke, D. J., D. M. Clarke, and C. Lovitt. 1990. Changes in mathematics teaching call for assessment alternatives. In *Teaching and learning mathematics in the 1990s, 1990 Yearbook*. Reston, VA: NCTM.

Connolly, P., and T. Vilardi, eds. 1989. *Writing to learn mathematics and science*. New York: Teachers College Press.

Kounba, V. 1994. Self-evaluation as an act of teaching. *Mathematics Teacher* 87: 354–58.

Miller, D. 1991. Writing to learn mathematics. *Mathematics Teacher* 84: 516–521.

Mower, P. 1996. Fat men in pink leotards or students writing to learn algebra. *PRIMUS: Problems, resources, and issues in mathematics undergraduate studies* 6: 308–24.

National Council of Teachers of Mathematics. 1989. *Curriculum and evaluation standards for school mathematics*. Reston, VA.

National Council of Teachers of Mathematics. 1995. *Assessment standards for school mathematics*. Reston, VA.

Pugalee, D. 1997. Connecting writing to the mathematics curriculum. *Mathematics Teacher* 90: 308–310.

Secada, W. 1997. Understanding in mathematics & science. *Principled practice in mathematics & science education* 1(1): 8–9. Madison, WI: Wisconsin Center for Education Research.

Sterrett, A., ed. 1990. *Using writing to teach mathematics*. Washington, DC: Mathematical Association of America.

Taylor, C., and B. Bidlingmaier. 1998. Using scoring criteria to communicate about the discipline of mathematics. *Mathematics Teacher* 91: 416–425.

Wilcox, S. 1998. Another perspective on concept maps: Empowering students. *Mathematics Teaching in the Middle Grades* 3: 464–469.

Suggestions for Further Reading

Ciochine, J., and G. Polivka. 1997. The Missing Link? Writing in mathematics class! *Mathematics Teaching in the Middle Grades* 2: 316–320.

Chapman, K. 1996. Journals: Pathways to thinking in second-year algebra. *Mathematics Teacher* 89: 588–590.

Crannell, A. 1994. How to grade 300 mathematical essays and survive to tell the tale. *PRIMUS: Problems, resources, and issues in mathematics undergraduate studies* 4: 193–204.

DiPillo, M., R. Sovchik, and B. Moss. 1997. Exploring middle graders' mathematical thinking through journals. *Mathematics Teaching in the Middle Grades* 2: 308–314.

Dougherty, B. 1996. The write way: A look at journal writing in first-year algebra. *Mathematics Teacher* 89: 556–560.

Elliot, W. 1996. Writing: A necessary tool for learning. *Mathematics Teacher* 89: 92–94.

Mayer, J., and S. Hillman. 1996. Assessing students' thinking through writing. *Mathematics Teacher* 89: 428–432.

Chapter 14

Mathematics the WRITE Way

Carol A. Thornton

Writing is both a catalyst for learning and
a forum for assessing mathematical learning

For years mathematics classes have been taught with a great deal of lecture, much dialogue between individual students and the teacher, a limited amount of small-group work, and very little writing beyond homework exercises. Times have changed. The call now is for more engaged learning that includes frequent and well-structured writing experiences to enhance learning and our assessment of student understanding in mathematics (National Council of Teachers of Mathematics 1998).

Writing in mathematics has received increased emphasis in the "writing across the curriculum" movement because of its demonstrated benefits to mathematics learning and its usefulness for assessing student thinking (e.g., Clarke, Waywood, and Stephens 1993; Shepard 1993; Waywood 1994; Yerushalmy 1997). Comparisons of classes with and without writing components confirm that students who write in mathematics learn and retain concepts better than students who do not write as part of their course work (Robertson and Miller 1988). The fact is that most individuals must verbalize ideas in order to internalize them, that writing provides this forum and encourages greater precision than speaking (Goeslin 1977).

Specifically, researchers have found that writing in mathematics classes provides opportunities for students to communicate, clarify, organize, and assess their mathematical thinking (Azzolino 1990; Drake and Amspaugh 1994), to reinforce mathematical language and vocabulary, and to construct a better understanding of mathematical relationships (Abel and Abel 1988; Shepard 1993). Student writing during and after a math activity can be used to bring unanswered questions to the surface and help a teacher decide how to follow through (Countryman 1992; Clarke et al. 1993) encapsulate the implications of well-structured writing experiences for learning and assessment when they say that (1) writing involves processes that are fundamental to mathematics learning and otherwise are not readily engaged; and (2) the process of writing both mirrors and supports the process of learning.

Classroom Episodes from the PUMP Algebra Project

This section shares ways that middle school and high school teachers in our PUMP (Peoria Urban Mathematics Plan) Algebra Project have incorporated writing activities into their classes to more actively involve their students and increase opportunities for critical thinking. This Project, funded by the National Science Foundation and led by staff from the Mathematics Department of Illinois State University, has focused on helping teachers make more students algebra ready by the end of 8th grade. PUMP is one of seven mathematics projects recently cited by the National Staff Development Council and the Edna McConnell Clark Foundation (Killion 1999) for effectively linking teacher enhancement with student learning.

The following types of writing activities implemented in their classrooms by PUMP teachers will be discussed briefly:

- Open-ended questions for pre/post assessment
- Math explanations
- Talk-write-talk
- Writing parallel or extension problems
- "Publication" (posting) of written solutions
- Quiz taking
- Test prep: Student's Choice and Walk About
- Problem analysis

Some of these writing activities involve whole-class interactions, others require collaborative teaming or individual work. Teachers report that all these writing activities provide rich sources for assessment and for student learning. In presenting the activity descriptions, only one PUMP teacher's version is provided. Pseudonyms are used rather than real teacher names.

Open-Ended Questions for Pre/Post Assessment

Writing can help teachers assess their students' learning both prior to introducing a topic and after completion. Open-ended questions or tasks are most appropriate for obtaining rich assessment information. Ms. Jacob's 8th grade students, for example, were to begin a review of similarity. For openers, Ms. Jacob sketched two similar right triangles on the board—one with side lengths labeled 3, 4, 5; the other with side lengths labeled, 6, 8, n—and directed students to "THINK a moment, then write all you know about these triangles."

Sometimes Ms. Jacob simply collects students' papers for overnight review. The day I was in her room, however, she gave her students time for individual work then asked them to compare notes with a partner. While the students worked, Ms. Jacob moved among the students to better observe them at work. She then recorded on the board what students reported as different students shared their ideas with the class. Finally, because ideas related to perimeter and area did not emerge in the discussion but were to be treated in the upcoming lessons, Ms. Jacob asked students to write how they thought the perimeters and areas of the two triangles compared.

This brief activity was enough to tell Ms. Jacob what most students understood well and where the trouble spots were. The initial directive was to *write.* Writing was the vehicle for inviting students to reflect on the mathematical ideas and formulate their thoughts. Writing was the medium for establishing accountability and challenging active participation by ALL students. Ideas important to the topic which did not emerge (in this case perimeter and area) were specifically addressed through teacher questions. As a result, the teacher was in a better position to decide what to emphasize during instruction.

At the end of a class Ms. Jacob often distributes 3 x 5 notecards or paper scraps and asks her students to take a few minutes to write (1) what they have learned that day; and (2) what they still have questions about. Asking students to write what they think they are learning requires them to organize their thoughts and confront their own learning. Asking them to verbalize their questions provides opportunity for self-assessment.

By reviewing the papers, Ms. Jacob can make a quick appraisal of students' confusion and points of clarity. This practice encourages *ownership* of the mathematics being learned; it puts students in charge of clarifying their own thinking and diagnosing their own misunderstandings. Ms. Jacob also learns a great deal by quickly reviewing what her students have written. Doing so helps her plan the quick recap that will open the next day's lesson, to select or create appropriate problem tasks, to determine appropriate homework assignments, to pose useful questions for informal or written assessments, and to identify students who may need special help.

Math Explanations

PUMP teachers try to keep paperwork manageable!—so writing assignments typically are short and focused; they are frequently done in class and take little time to read; they require thinking and are helpful in assessing what areas are still unclear or misinterpreted

Rephrasing. For example, PUMP teachers frequently ask their students to write a sentence or two to explain a mathematical concept (e.g., integer, surface area, ratio) *in their own words* or to tell how to carry out a procedure (e.g., solve for the unknown in a linear equation like $3t - 4 = 5$). Some special education teachers in PUMP have their students keep a notebook of "Math I Know and Can Do." Tabs are used to organize the notebook into sections (geometry, fractions, percent...); and students make their own dictionary of important math ideas or enter samples of computations and problems they can solve—with any notes they consider helpful.

Writing and rotating. The day I visited her classroom, Miss Canter gave each team of four students a Think Back Sheet containing four questions about a probability experiment they had just completed. Miss Canter frequently uses Think Back Sheets, so her students were familiar with the "write the rotate" procedure to be used in completing the sheet:

- Students number off 1-2-3-4 within each team.
- Students discuss question #1 and student #1 records the team response to the first question. Then, at the teacher's signal, all #1 students in the room rotate clockwise to the next group, taking the team's paper with them.

- Students discuss question #2 and student #2 records the team response to the second question. Then all #2 students in the room rotate clockwise to the next group, taking the team's paper with them. This procedure continues for questions #3 and #4.

The rotation in this process gives the students opportunity to engage in several verbal and written exchanges with different members of the class. Disagreements on one question do not interfere with discourse on subsequent questions; dominant personalities do not overshadow the expression of shyer students as they reflect back on the problem, task, or—in this case—the probability experiment.

Miss Canter concluded the lesson with whole-group discussion, during which each group was called on to share what was written on the paper their group had last. Because, for each question, there was only one response for every four students, the class exchange was manageable in the limited time. We also found that students who would not ordinarily volunteer to present to the whole class did so, perhaps feeling less awkward reading responses written by students other than themselves.

CONNECT Sheets. Mrs. Robinson typifies a group of PUMP teachers who emphasize the importance of making *connections* between (1) "real world" situations; (2) mathematics symbols; (3) diagrams, pictures, or graphs; and (4) students' own personal (written) explanations. To structure writing activities that emphasize these connections, Mrs. Robinson uses home-made CONNECT sheets. Students simply fold a paper into fourths—one for each of the four categories above. When doing a CONNECT sheet after a lesson on simplifying expressions, for example, one of Mrs. Robinson's 9th graders wrote the following:

- *Real world situation*: Sarah recorded the following as people brought cookies to the bake sale to be sold: 5 dozen chocolate chip (Mary); 2 dozen peanut butter (Yolanda); 2 dozen chocolate chip (Shelly); 1 dozen chocolate chip (Victor); 5 dozen peanut butter (Mia).
  Total: 8 dozen chocolate chip and 7 dozen peanut butter.
- *Mathematics symbols*: $5c + 2p + 2c + c + 5y = 8c + 7p$.
- *Diagram/picture/graph*:
  CCCCC PP CC C PPPPP → CCCCCCCCC PPPPPPP

My explanation: To simplify an expression, you just organize it better so it's easier to read and understand. You put everything that's "alike" together. Like you put all the c's together and all the p's together.

Whatever the context, student explanations reveal thinking and the quality of student understanding of the mathematics being addressed. Sometimes Mrs. Robinson merely collects the completed CONNECT sheets and reviews them privately to learn the current level of students' understandings and their misconceptions. She typically writes comments on the students' sheets to reinforce, congratulate, or redirect their thinking.

At other times Mrs. Robinson asks students to work together in groups (which she carefully forms to include capable students as well as those less comfortable with ideas) to compare what they have written. During the group discussions, the students are often able to expand their knowledge and understanding of an idea or procedure, and many of the misconceptions that surface are corrected by peers. In this part of the lesson, Mrs. Robinson moves among the groups, interacting as necessary. In whole-class wrap-up, Mrs. Robinson brings closure to the activity by having one or more groups summarize their examples.

Writing assignments which focus on student explanations furnish the teacher with insight into students' levels of understanding or misunderstanding. Information obtained helps the teacher decide how to frame the next lesson or help an individual student.

Talk-Write-Talk

I remember it well!—and so did the students—months later. They were 8th graders in Ms. Pearl's algebra class, using the graph function of their graphics calculators for the first time that day. Ms. Pearl moderated the activity and had students alternate between discussion and private writing in their math log. To start the activity the students teamed with two other students, copied, then graphed these equations on the same grid:

$$y = x, y = x + 3, y = x - 3$$

Within their groups students discussed the graphs and explained to one another how the graphs were alike and how they were different. Then Ms. Pearl told the students to think about what everyone in their group had said and, in their Math Logs, write several sentences to summarize how the graphs were alike and how they were different. To conclude this first part of the activity, Ms. Pearl called on several students to read their summary. Other families of equations were similarly analyzed.

This activity exemplifies one which a number of PUMP teachers have found useful. On this particular day Ms. Pearl kept a low profile during student discussion. She walked from group to group to observe, but refrained from interfering. Likewise, during independent "write" time, she moved between students to observe the thinking they displayed through their writing. The crux of the activity is the writing piece, for this is the time when students "pull the idea together" in their own minds. A final whole-group session provides important feedback for students as well as for the teacher on the accuracy and level of students' thinking.

Writing Parallel or Extension Problems

After students have solved a problem, a number of PUMP teachers have adopted the practice of having students create a related problem or one that extends the problem just solved. Participation in problem posing exercises like this offer several advantages for students as well as teachers. Students who are less comfortable with the ideas are provided opportunity to reinforce learning by creating and solving a problem quite similar to one just completed. More capable students are challenged to stretch their thinking—to "go beyond" the parameters of the present problem in a way that is somewhat related to it. In both cases, to assess students' abilities to compare and generalize in the context of the topic of study, many of the PUMP teachers ask their students to explain how their new problem is related to the original one and how it differs.

"Publication" (Posting) of Written Solutions

Consider these three scenarios:

- Mr. Mooney points to an algebraic equation on the board and challenges his 8th grade algebra students to work in teams to write word problems that can be solved using that equation. As students finish, Mr. Mooney asks each group to "publish" its problem on a large piece of newsprint and tape it to the wall.
- Mr. Wick gives his 6th grade students a circle graph showing how Leandra budgeted to spend the money she had saved for the December holidays. Categories shown are:

  —Videos/movies/snacks: 20%
  —Keep in savings: 27%
  —Comics: 27%
  —Clothes
  —Holiday basketball tournament: 15%
  —Presents to family: 108%
  —Miscellaneous: 5%

  Using the information shown, students work with a partner to determine (1) the dollar amount Leandra budgeted to spend in *each* category; and (2) the total amount Leandra planned to spend during the holiday season. On large newsprint students write and then post their report, which includes the graph itself, the dollar amounts they found, and a statement that clarifies to the reader *how* they determined each amount.
- Mrs. Gibson opens class by asking her 7th grade students to record in their Math Logs as many different equivalent ways they can think of to represent each measurement unit posted (foot, square yard, cup, meter, square meter, pound, cubic centimeter). Students can use fractions to describe a measurement. (For example: 1 cup is the same as 1/4 quart, 1/8 half gallon, and 1/16 of a gallon. 1 cup is also 16 fluid ounces.) Student teams are then each given a large sheet of poster paper labeled with *one* of the units. The challenge: to record and illustrate, if possible, the different equivalent measures for that unit. A large variety of measurement tools and devices are available.

In each of these instances, student teams are allowed to do a *Walk About* to examine the other posters as they finish. As they walk, students are given the option to leave "math edits" on post-it notes that start with a GOOD comment about a poster and then provide helpful math comments or corrections. Whole-class wrap-up provides further opportunity for student sharing, summarizing, and teacher feedback.

This technique of providing a public forum for displaying good student work has served many purposes. Teachers obtain a clearer understanding of student thinking as they observe students work and assess their finished product. Students are held to a certain accountability for collaborating in order to produce a written document that can be posted publicly aside those of their peers. In our experience this posting is accompanied by a sense of ownership and pride. When oral reports are made about a posted paper, most PUMP teachers allow student teams to elect a spokesperson and either stand by that person or not during presentation. Students learn from the feedback of their peers as well as from that provided by the teacher.

Quiz Taking

During the past semester Miss Robbins has tried a new kind of quiz with her Algebra I class: asking students to sort the different types of algebraic problems into categories and also to give a brief analysis of the approach needed to solve each, with no actual problem solving. She has included both review and new types of problems on the quizzes. Students know in advance that this type of quiz will be given and, during classes, tend to be much more concerned—in a positive way—about being able to verbalize their understanding.

Test Prep: Student's Choice

Mr. Underwood made the following announcement to his high school geometry class: "Now that we have completed this chapter on measurement, your last written assignment (worth 30 points) will be to select *one* interesting problem, solve, and comment on it. It's all right to work with a partner on this assignment, but you must each do your own write-up—which is due the day of the test." The assignment sheet provided further details and the grading scheme:

1. **5 points:** Identify chapter topic, page, problem number, important given information, and state the problem.
2. **Up to 10 points:** Calculations and explanation. (Use diagrams to illustrate your ideas if appropriate.)

Note: If the problem you select is too easy, you may lose points on these next sections:

3. **Up to 5 points:** "Big ideas" (up to three concepts or skills) from the chapter that you used to solve the problem. Elaborate enough to demonstrate your understanding of the concepts or skills.
4. **Up to 5 points:** problem you select is too easy; you may lose points on these next sections:
5. **Up to 5 points:** "Big ideas" (up to five concepts or skills) from outside the chapter (concepts or skills taught in previous math classes, other subjects, or other chapters of the text we are using) that you used to solve the problem.
6. **Up to 5 points:** Your thoughts on the chapter: write a paragraph reflecting your impressions of the chapter. What was hard? Easy? Why was it easy/hard for you?

Jordan's work for #3 and #6 will provide an ideas of what students have done with this type of writing assignment. Jordan chose a problem that involved designing an outdoor dog pen that would allow maximum play space for a pet dog using only 32 yards of fencing. The pen was to be a "stand alone" pen away from the house and other buildings. For #3 Jordan wrote:

> "Two 'big ideas" my partner and I used were areas of polygons and circles (inner space) and their perimeters (total distance around the outsides). A third "big idea" we used is that the more "squarish" rectangles have more area. At first we thought an 8 by 8 square pen was it: the perimeter is 32 and the area (64) is bigger than for any other rectangles. But then we experimented with regular polygons and got greater area as we increased the number of sides (for perimeter = 32). We saw a pattern and decided a circular pen would give the most play space."

In her chapter reflection (for #6) Jordan wrote:

> "The easy part of the chapter was the different formulas. I remembered them from middle school. But the problems were more complicated. They had fractions and decimals, and sometimes ratios and square roots. Using a calculator helped, but you had to do more than just work a formula. The hard parts were the applied measurement problems. They made you really think. Working in partners helped...and talking through the different ideas afterwards. I learn a lot from others and explaining my own strategies to them."

This type of writing assignment encourages student accountability for understanding major chapter concepts likely to be tested, provides insightful self-assessment opportunities for students, and encourages many students to work collaboratively to prepare for a test. In completing the assignment, students generally examine several problems before they select ONE that will satisfy all the conditions—and in so doing they review a substantial amount of the unit material!

Test Prep: Walk About

Mrs. Rivierra used a slightly different approach to help students review for a chapter test. She explained the math "Walk About" to her 7th graders this way:

"There are 8 problems on the sheet I gave you that samples the kinds of problems we've been doing in this chapter. You have about 20 minutes to walk about and find someone who can *use a pencil* to solve (and then autograph) each problem. It is all right to challenge and erase a solution, but you must explain your decision to the person who wrote it. In the end, you should have 8 *different* autographs."

After students completed their work, Mrs. Rivierra called on students to report on each part of the sheet in the following manner:

"Latoya, who did your #1?"

The student who autographed Latoya's #1 presented his or her solution at the overhead or board.

Mrs. Rivierra used writing to engage her students actively in chapter review. Students had the responsibility to seek out, question, and watch peers respond to questions based on important aspects of the chapter. As wrap-up, students in turn helped to summarize, repeat, or present key chapter ideas as they reported out. Mrs. Rivierra interacted as necessary in this final part of the lesson to modify, clarify, correct, or extend students' responses.

Problem Analysis

At the end of almost every test, Mr. Wang has his Algebra I students analyze the problem they think was "hardest" on the test. This analysis counts as a problem on the test. Students are required to identify the problem by type and describe the approach taken to address it. One student, for example, selected the problem $x2 - 3x < 15$ that was to be plotted on a number line. The student wrote:

> "This was a quadratic inequality. I needed to get standard form and factor to find the roots, then plot them on the number line. I also should check out a number in each part of the line to see what works."

Mr. Wang typically asks for the same type of analysis as part of each night's homework assignment. These analyses call for correct vocabulary and an ability to generalize on how to proceed. The teacher typically directs his comments on these analyses to the student's thought process and on helping the student verbalize how generally to proceed.

Looking Back

The call for increased writing to enhance critical thinking and learning on the one hand and opportunities for enriched assessments on the other has been examined. Classroom episodes illustrating effective ways middle and secondary teachers in the PUMP Algebra project have incorporated writing in their mathematics instruction have been shared. As we look for increased thinking and achievement in our mathematics classrooms, we need to consider and develop high quality writing experiences like those just shared—that offer rich opportunities for assisting and empowering teachers and students alike.

Works Cited

Abel, J., and F. Abel. 1988. Writing in the mathematics classroom. *Clearing House* 62: 155–158.

Azzolino, A. 1990. Writing as a tool for teaching mathematics: The silent revolution. In *Teaching and learning mathematics in the 1990's*, ed. T.J. Cooney and C.R. Hirsch, 92–100. Reston, VA: National Council of Teachers of Mathematics.

Clarke, D. J., A. Waywood, and M. Stephens. 1993. Probing the structure of mathematical writing. *Educational Studies in Mathematics* 25: 235–250.

Countryman, Joan. 1992. *Writing to learn mathematics*. Portsmouth, NH: Heinemann.

Drake, B., and L.B. Amspaugh. 1994. What writing reveals in mathematics. *Focus on Learning Problems in Mathematics* 16 (3): 43–50.

Goeslin, William E. 1977. Using writing about mathematics as a teaching technique. *Mathematics Teacher* 70 (February): 112–15.

National Council of Teachers of Mathematics. 1998. *Principles and standards for school mathematics: Discussion draft*. Reston, VA: The National Council of Teachers of Mathematics.

Robertson, Douglas, and Carol Miller. 1988. Integrating elementary algebra and writing for basic learning. Paper presented at the 66th Annual Meeting of the National Council of Teachers of Mathematics, Chicago (April).

Shepard, R. G. 1993. Phases of meaningful learning. *Journal of Mathematical Behavior* 12: 287–293.

Waywood, A. 1994. Informal writing-to-learn as a dimension of a student profile. *Educational Studies in Mathematics* 27: 321–340.

Yerushalmy, M. 1997. Mathematizing verbal descriptions of situations: A language to support modeling. *Cognition and Instruction* 15: 207–264.

Chapter 15

Story Writing in Mathematics

Carolyn Lott and Diane Burrell

Using writing as a tool in the mathematics classroom usually has two purposes: as a diagnostic tool for gauging students' understanding of mathematics concepts and for evaluating and changing pedagogy to meet students' needs for achieving that understanding (Millman 1999). In the past, students and teachers both have been reluctant to write in mathematics classes because it was not part of the traditional method of approaching understanding and teaching of mathematics. However, since the National Council of Teachers of Mathematics published *Curriculum and Evaluation Standards of School Mathematics* (1989), writing has become an accepted part of learning mathematics and connecting it to thinking/problem-solving processes. Teachers may further value writing assignments when they realize how writing clarifies student thinking, makes connections for students between mathematics symbols and real-world understandings, and helps them assess their own teaching and how they need to modify it to meet student needs. Still hard, though, is convincing mathematics teachers to use writing as a part of their methodology because of their lack of confidence in their own writing skills and their ability to assess the writing papers, as well as the perception of increased time necessary to evaluate the writing.

For these reasons, assessing student writing intimidates many mathematics teachers—just as the bank clerk who was opening an account for me this morning said I intimidated her because I teach English. Mathematics teachers need objectivity when grading writing; they need their criteria or rubrics to be clear, and they need point values attached to all graded parts. When Diane Burrell assigned her freshman/sophomore "integrated math" class at Hellgate High School a creative story to write, she made the assessment criteria as objective and clear as possible. Diane was not satisfied to grade only for mathematics content and "not grade for spelling or grammar," the usual interpretation of writing in English. As English teachers, we want students and teachers to understand that when they are grading for mathematics or all other curriculum areas' content, they are grading for "English," since development, organization, clarity, complete sentences, all are parts of communication we call English. Depending on the stage of the draft, students will need to be aware of their grammar, their spelling, their transitions, their completeness, their presentation, in any subject area and any writing assignment. If that communication is unclear for any reason or has distracters such as misspellings or grammatical errors, then the concepts may not be as obvious or as distinct.

The 1989 NCTM *Standards* correlate the writing process stages of pre- writing, writing and revising to problem-solving strategies in mathematics. Clarifying the thinking for both the writer and the reader, writing in mathematics assignments range from discussions, or explanations to outlines, posters of rules, justifications, arguments, descriptions, definitions, directions, or analyses. Note that creative writing—defined as creating story with dialogue, in apposition to the essay format—does not appear in the usual list of assignments that generate writing in the mathematics classroom. But, for Diane's students, "creative writing" was another mode for demonstrating their understanding of mathematics concepts.

Hellgate's Freshman and Sophomore Integrated Math 2

Diane's students at Hellgate High School write their mathematics biographies the first day of class. After sharing her own biography in relation to mathematics, Diane continues to model the constant interaction our lives have with mathematics. Through the course of study, Diane also assigns research papers on mathematicians and their contributions to mathematics and the world in general. She has students mix the mathematics with the life of a person, thereby giving "voices" to persons who discover mathematics concepts. Every test gives an added value to writing by asking students to "explain what you would need to solve. . ." or "analyze what was done incorrectly in this problem. . . ." At the beginning of their study of integrated math, students write simple explanations of their thinking about mathematics problems using complete sentences. They aim toward clear proofs, and clear understandings. Most writing assignments model short answers to mathematics questions about "why?" Usually, at the beginning, they write a paragraph, at most. As the year progresses, all proofs of geometric concepts are treated as essays, with the usual writing criteria and rubrics shared with the students as they write. Later, to give them some choices in their selection of data, Diane also assigns the following "story."

"Tell Me A Story Assignment"
Integrated Math 2

Write a story using geometric characters and/or a geometric setting. The story must meet the following criteria:

- At least 5 geometric properties must be used in the plot.
- All geometric properties and vocabulary must be used accurately and correctly.
- The story must be a minimum of 200 words.
- Your paper must be typed or neatly written in ink.
- You must use correct English usage, spelling, and grammar.

A rough draft of the story is due *Monday, March 1*. The rough draft will be worth 10 points and you must have a copy with you in class to receive credit. You will be given a final copy of the grading criteria at that time and we will peer edit the stories in class.

The final draft of the story is due *Monday, March 8*. The final draft is worth 30 points. 5 bonus points will be given if you attach a slip confirming that you have had the story edited at the Writing Center. No late papers will be accepted.

As with most writing assignments, Diane read these stories for their correct understanding of integrated mathematics. The grading criteria or rubric presented below was partially created by her and partially by the students: she wrote the first four areas of the rubric and the students created the last two in class.

Grading Criteria for "Tell Me A Story"
Integrated Math 2

__________ Geometric Properties (5 points total)
One point for each property used to a maximum of 5 points

__________ Accurate mathematical usage (5 points total)
All properties and vocabulary used accurately—5 points
Some errors in use of vocabulary or properties—3 points
Numerous errors in use of vocabulary or properties—1 point

__________ Length (5 points total)
Length _> 200 words—5 points
Length 100–200 words—3 points
Length < 100 words—1 point

__________ English usage (5 points total)
Correct spelling, punctuation and grammar used throughout—5 points
Some errors in spelling, punctuation or grammar—3 points
Many errors in spelling, punctuation, or grammar—1 point

__________ Organization (5 points total)
Story has a plot with a beginning, middle, and an end—5 points
Plot has organizational problems or is not coherent—3 points
Story has no organization or nothing happens—1 point

__________ Neatness (5 points total)
Story is neatly typed or written in ink and has a title—5 points
Story has no title or is hard to read in places—3 points
Story is extremely messy and hard to read—1 point

__________ TOTAL (30 POINTS POSSIBLE)

__________ 5 bonus points for visiting writing center

The first read by Diane was for the mathematics—did students use geometry properties? Were the relationships or the characteristics or the connections among the geometric properties used correctly? Just prior to the assignment used in this paper to show how writing affects learning, students studied quadrilaterals, nests, categories, not just as individual shapes, but how they fit together. So, one thing Diane was using the assessment for was to judge how well they demonstrated their understanding of these geometric concepts. One student clearly showed common characteristics of quadrilaterals when he wrote of the basketball team:

"Scott's [Square] diagonals are equal in measure, have the same midpoint, and his diagonals are perpendicular. Robb Rhombus was a great center. Robb's diagonals had the same midpoints and are also perpendicular. They have Paul Parallelogram and he is considered to be better than Scottie PiPen. Paul has only one good thing about him. His diagonals have the same midpoint. Last but not least was Dave's Rectangle. He was rad. Dave's diagonals have the same midpoint and are equal in measure. Since they all have one thing in common they are called the midpoints."

Another student's story related the quadrilaterals to the world of everyday objects in a scavenger hunt for specific shapes: a picture frame, a kite, a wall-to-wall carpet in a trapezoid room. Yet another student's characters calculated the size of their expected baby: "He used formulas like 1/2 b*h=A (in case the baby looked like him [a triangle]), A=pi*r^2 (in case the baby looked like Cindy [a circle]), and V=1/3pi*r^2*h (in case the baby looked like both of them, which would make it a cone)." Relating their geometric studies to the real world was a major objective of the writing assignment.

The next reading was for the other criteria in the rubric, holistically assessing the writing for usage and organization as well as length and neatness. Since the rubric clearly gave points to "degrees" of meeting the criteria, the papers could easily and quickly be scored. Beyond the scoring criteria, an interesting observation surfaced: many students addressed social themes in their stories. Different shaped figures were aware of belonging needs, recognized cliques, sympathized with outcasts, and discovered commonalties that gave them connections. Students seemed to be aware of the pain of uniqueness or loneliness.

Changing Teaching Focuses and Emphases

Many students did not demonstrate the connections among the quadrilaterals. Their stories met many of the other criteria, but either did not use relationships in their plot, or the relationships they did use were not correct. Diane decided not to "re-teach" the geometric concepts. Instead of immediately re-teaching, which was not appropriate for many of the students, Diane waited until two chapters later while studying logic. By using examples such as "If a figure is a rectangle, then it is a parallelogram," students could once again visit the relationships among geometric shapes and their connections to objects around them. As a result of discussion about the grading criteria, Diane learned that students did not "see" that connections were a part of the assignment. Most of them had the properties, but not the connections in their stories. Therefore, the assignment itself needs to be revised before it can be given again with the specific references to giving examples of connections in the stories.

Another factor in the decision not to re-teach was the pressure to keep a steady pace in their mathematics curriculum. Even the students themselves seem to resent covering the same material again immediately. But, they resent *not* "sneaking" the concepts in somewhere else later on. Diane had to figure a way to make the same concepts naturally come up later in their studies. She had to let the content settle, allowing students to begin making connections and understanding relationships with the same content but in a different emphasis.

Evolving from the assessment of this writing assignment also was the necessity to have students visualize how shapes looked and where there were incidences around them in their everyday worlds of geometric shapes. Shapes of doorways, driveways, houses, boxes, all became ways to illustrate the abstract visualization of geometric shapes. These figures added to what students understood about seeing the world differently—mathematically.

In this story assignment, Diane gave one week to write the rough draft. Then she divided the class into groups of three for peer editing and allowed one more week for revisions before the final draft was due. In the peer editing sessions, students used the scoring criteria and rubric on their peers' stories and on their own. The ones who took advantage of this class work had better papers. One student who learned in the peer editing session that his spelling disability was distracting readers from his story did not compensate for it by either asking for help via the Writing Center or by using the spell checker on his word processor successfully. Therefore, his low score reflected the total impression of the story: the mathematics content *and* the presentation.

Some of the students also took advantage of collaboration allowed in their English classes. When students suggested that they needed time for working together on their mathematics story assignment, one English teacher gave class time to work. Many teachers are becoming interested in interdisciplinary collaboration on assignments. This particular aspect of teaching writing across all the curriculum may be helped by the Senior Project that was just recently initiated by this mathematics teacher. All students will be expected to complete a formal research project.

Another change that may result from this assignment was requested by students: to write another story. They liked writing the story using their mathematics. Next year, students may write a story during their study of logic, maybe a mystery. Students enjoyed each other's stories and wanted Diane to read them aloud.

From the social themes evident in the stories, Diane learned that students are very aware of each other and their uniqueness. They seemed to notice the "silliness" in most of the disagreements among their characters and discovered that a way of addressing differences among groups was by talking: the answer to the violence in their stories. The stories usually ended in a peaceful resolution of the differences and misunderstandings that caused the violence. This specific writing assignment resulted in a discussion in the classroom about the school violence that had recently permeated news reports, an added bonus even beyond their growth in mathematics understandings and their writing skills.

All lessons in the mathematics textbooks used at Hellgate High School include questions which require some writing. Some teachers are reluctant to include the writing questions because they are uncertain about how to evaluate them. Most do assess for spelling errors and for incomplete sentences in their everyday assignments, but most do not assign longer writing samples nor do they use a valued rubric for scoring. Instead, they use a holistic Likkert scale to score the paragraphs explaining a proof. Teachers who do emphasize the writing questions have found that modeling responses for the class improves the quality of work the students produce.

Because technology has changed the face of mathematics teaching so much, more teachers may realize the value of writing as a way to make sure students understand mathematics concepts. When students can type into a calculator practically any mathematical formula and have the calculator compute answers for them, changes in pedagogy seem required. To address these changes in ways of "doing" mathematics and to compensate for the technological tools, verbal explanations of problem solving strategies may become routine. Writing as a tool in every curriculum specialist's teaching techniques makes for more successful communication by students and makes teaching a more exact science for all teachers.

Works Cited

Millman, Richard S. 1999. Using writing to assess mathematics pedagogy and students' understanding. In *Evaluating writing: The role of teachers' knowledge about text, learning, and culture*, ed. C.R. Cooper and L. Odell, 154–69. Urbana, Illinois: National Council of Teachers of English.

National Council of Teachers of Mathematics. 1989. *Curriculum and evaluation standards of school mathematics*. Reston, VA: National Council of Teachers of Mathematics.

Chapter 16

The Collage: An Alternative to the Book-Test or Book-Paper Assessment

Rebecca Sanchez

With the recent implementation of state standards in my state and many others, teacher are once again hearing a lot about authentic assessment and alternative assessment. We English teachers are being urged to move away from consistently using paper and pencil assessments that tend to measure in a one dimensional way what students retain on the given test day and toward other assessments that give students the opportunity to show what they think and feel about the material in a more long term way while interpreting the literature in valid, measurable ways. Since my students had already read books or plays and taken the tests and often written papers in addition, I was ripe for an alternative to the book-test and book-paper route.

Earlier in the school year, I began to ask students what they were interested in as far as the history of the twentieth century went. With the approach of the millennium in mind, I had them write to me in their journals by responding to the prompt: What historical events, eras, and personalities of the twentieth century are you interested in knowing more about?

Their number one response was the Vietnam War, closely followed by the Holocaust but in the sense of Adolf Hitler's rise to power and his magnetic personality as Germany's visionary. As far as twentieth century personalities went, Adolf Hitler, Joseph Stalin, J. Edgar Hoover, President Franklin Roosevelt, and Hollywood movie stars of the glamorous 30s and 40s rated high. Since we would later do a Vietnam War project, I immediately honed in on their interest in Hitler's rise to power. Little connective lights were going on in my brain as I read their journals and tallied their interests. The novel *Summer of My German Soldier* by Bette Greene came to mind. A quick rereading of the novel on my part reinforced my hunch that it would both support their areas of interest as well as provide a springboard for research. In addition, the novel would lend itself to a collage, combining writing and visuals, in lieu of a test or paper.

During this unit, the students were working on several fronts to generate products which would be fused later into the collage. First of all, students read the novel both in-class orally and out of class as homework. Students often had pop quizzes and journal writes in order to keep them accountable and to ensure effective classroom discussions. As every teacher knows, when the students don't do the reading, classroom discussion is rather pointless.

From time to time, the students were asked to write poetry based on the novel. Essentially any kind of poem, free verse or formula, can be applied to the novel and its characters. One of the most successful poetry assignments I gave for the novel was my own Two Tone Poem. I asked students to think of a character who had two sides to his/her personality or who lived in one reality but had dreams or fantasies of something greater or better. Students could also consider the way a character was and the way the character could be or should be. The first stanza of their free verse poem corresponded to the second item or tone." In this way, each poem showed two tones of a character. Out of four poetry assignments, students had to have taken two to final draft stage, complete with titles, interesting language, images, and effective organization. Here are two samples:

Monster or Man?

A Nazi, what do you expect?
They're all the same; Anton's no different,
A monster out to kill innocent victims
Like his leader, the mass murderer Hitler.
He escaped from the prison camp
To unite the German saboteurs
Who landed on American soil.
The FBI captured the saboteurs,
They will capture him, too.

He's no monster, just a fellow human being,
He's German but speaks flawless English.
He liberated himself from the prison camp
To be free like the wind,
He has befriended Patty Bergen,
A Jewish girl as lonely as the Ugly Duckling,
He risked his chance at freedom
When he left safety to rescue Patty.

Patty's Flight of Fancy

I realize that I'm homely
And that is what you see.
I know I will never be brilliant,
Or beautiful or sweet.
My hair is unkempt
And my body is frail.
I want you to love me
But why can't you see?

He's holding me tightly,
I feel safe and warm.
He tells me I am lovely
And I know that's what he sees.
He listens to my dreams
And calmly soothes my fears.
I am appreciated and valued,
That's the way it should be.

About midway through the reading of the novel, I generated a list of every actual event, person, group, law, and movement mentioned in the text. I asked the students to self-select a topic that interested them. They were quick, I observed, to select the same topics they had earlier listed in their journals as their interests in the twentieth century.

Students then did research on the Internet and in hardback libraries, one of which I had in my classroom on a cart, to basically answer the who, what, where, when, and why of their topics. Along the way, I asked that they record their information under those categories and that they also print out or xerox photographs, maps, charts, drawings, and symbols that connected to their topics.

Once the research was complete, the students sat in a circle in my classroom and presented their research by talking about their topics. They were allowed to use their note-taking sheets, any additional notes, and Internet printouts. Each research talk lasted about five minutes. While presenting, the students passed their visuals around the room. Since every topic was lifted from the novel, every report enhanced our reading of it by adding to our knowledge base. Each student had the topic of his/her choice, and each report was individual and fresh.

After students made their presentation, I asked the students to type a list of ten facts in sentence form about their research topic. When those lists came in, I filed them with the poetry drafts. The students, at my request, saved their visuals from the oral reports, recorded helpful web sites and book titles rich in visuals, and held onto any World War II artifacts from home. At the conclusion of the novel, we then moved to the collage as the culminating activity. Students were told from the onset that the collage was in place of a test or paper and that the collage as a product would be assessed for as many points as a paper or test. Their oral presentation of the collage would also be evaluated.

Since the collage was a fusion of the reading of the novel with writing, researching, visuals and their own art work, and presenting orally, the students followed a checklist of instructions to ensure a strong product:

1. The students divided a piece of cardboard, 18 inches high by 30 inches wide in half, with each half measuring 18 inches by 15 inches.
2. The right side of the collage pertained to the novel. On this side, the students mounted their best two poems about the novel's events or its characters. They also featured visuals of the characters (likenesses cut from magazines, xeroxed from historical sources, or hand drawn) beside the poems.
3. Students then added to the right side of the collage any two of the following writing options: a letter Patty writes to Ruth from the reform school, a page from Patty's diary in the reform school, a letter to Patty from Anton's parents after they find out what she did for their son, a letter from Ruth any time after she is dismissed from the Bergen household to Patty, a letter to Patty from her parents or grandparents while she is in the reform school, or a news article about Patty's arrest and punishment.
4. The right side was then fleshed out with any other tie-ins to the novel such as Patty's dictionary list, Patty's seventh grade report card, a train ticket from Jenkinsville to Memphis, or a restaurant receipt for the Peabody Hotel's Skyline. Students also added artifacts from

home from the World War II era such as ration stamps, war bonds information, and metal buttons recalling Pearl Harbor.

5. The left side of the collage, pertaining to the research done by the students, featured the list of ten facts lifted from the research report and the visuals generated for the report plus any student art work.
6. In addition, the students had to have a written piece explaining their research topic's connection to the novel. Some connections were very direct such as Patty's mention of Joan Crawford, Shirley Temple, and Betty Grable as standards of beauty much more within her sister's grasp than hers. Other connections, less direct but no less powerful, such as the Gestapo or the book burnings of 1933 tied into Anton's discussion of Hitler's rise to power.
7. I urged students to consider the collage's background before they began to mount their writing and visuals. I suggested they think about such things as colors, a tiny repeating background motif, or flags; that they consider newspaper pages, charred newspapers, pages from books, maps, and even fabric.
8. Students were allowed to use three dimensional objects in their collages as long as the objects could be attached. FDR campaign buttons, World War II military medals, the star flags placed in windows by parents of servicemen, and pieces of vintage army blankets gave collages a three dimensional touch.

The students presented orally by essentially reading their original poetry to the class, sharing other modes of writing generated for the novel, and explaining the extra details on the "novel side" such as Patty's history grade or the last dictionary words she was calling her own. They then moved to the "research side" of the collage by revisiting their research topics with the list of ten facts. They connected their visuals to the topic by discussing each one. Finally, they connected the research to the novel by reading their connection piece. Students took all questions about their collages, dancing around with more knowledge, I might add, than any test or paper would demonstrate.

I displayed all the collages in my classroom for a number of days, giving each English class time to read the writing pieces and appreciate the visuals and artifacts. One teacher asked if telling the students there would be no test or paper made them less accountable for the reading of the novel. My experience was absolutely not. The students were into the reading, on task, and busy every day of this unit, constantly generating a piece of work that would ultimately become part of the collage. Because the students had the instructions for the collage since the beginning of the novel, even the locating, collecting, and creating of visuals suddenly became viable, important work. By fusing their interpretation of the novel through poetry and other modes with research products, my students found a refreshing alternative to the test or paper routine.

As Mike, a first period student, put it, "The whole time I worked on this novel, I felt like I was Patty. I will never forget what we learned. There are different ways to look at everything. I thought all Germans were Nazis, and I thought the test always came after the book."

And how does one evaluate work such as collages? With my students we identified the traits we were looking for in effective collages:

- all parts of the assignment as stated in the instructions
- ample details and description and especially word crafting in the writing
- appropriate and accurate content and language
- no mechanical errors
- innovative and unique perspectives
- a sense of time and effort invested in the task

I then used the following categories and points, the latter based on maximum of 50 points; students received a score sheet along with some comments:

STRONG

50 49 48 47

GOOD

46 45 44 43

MIDDLE

42 41 40 39

WEAK

38 37 36 35

WEAKER

34 33 32 31>

Something I really liked about your collage:

Something for you to work on in your future products:

Chapter 17

The Titanic Project: A Voyage in Time

Rebecca Sanchez

Over eighty years after her sinking, the legend of the *Titanic* is as strong as ever, certainly stronger than the 45,000 tons of hammered and riveted steel that shaped her doomed but magnificent form in the Belfast shipyard of Harland & Wolff over the three years of her birth. "The *Titanic* was no ordinary ship—she was a floating hotel, even a small town at sea. At the time of her launch in Belfast in 1911, she was not only the biggest existing ship, but also was the largest movable object ever built... the ultimate symbol of luxury and power" (Tibballs 1997, p. 7).

Who did not want to sail on the *Titanic*? Who did not want to be part of her maiden voyage and part of history, steaming into New York harbor in record time? Imagining a kind of floating town with three ticket classes representing a cross section of society from top to bottom, contemporary students studying the *Titanic* can easily calculate their own ticket classes and what that would have meant in terms of the tragedy. And therein lies the public's steadfast attraction to *Titanic*, and, more importantly, the reason why students are attracted to all things the *Titanic*. In short, they can be on board and ultimately perish or survive on the *Titanic* of their imaginations. In a classroom project that involves the *Titanic* and her 2,201 passengers, students can recreate her maiden voyage.

In the *Titanic* project, which I created for my tenth grade classroom, students select a person connected to the tragedy and write in the voice of that person in the mode(s) of their choice. By interweaving historical details and information about the ship, passengers and crew with the mannerisms and language of the Edwardian era, students generate writing that smacks of authenticity, as if it had been found in the attic of a *Titanic* survivor. Often I feel as though I am reading people's private papers as I read and assess my students' products.

The catalyst for the *Titanic* project, or any other historical project modeled on it, then, is to focus on a historical event that affected people across social classes. I have had the same success with projects focusing on historical events such as World War I and II, the Vietnam War, the Depression, the Holocaust, and the wave of immigration to the US around the turn of the century. The approach requires the teacher and students to study the historical event in great detail by using sources beyond the content area textbook. What naturally occurs is a rich merging of print, photographs, film, and primary sources such as maps, letters, diaries, and on the spot accounts as the teacher and students bring resources to school. The classroom becomes an in-class resource center where all the students share their findings with each other.

However, students need a starting point for a basic informative reading on the historical event. I recommend that the teacher choose the reading, assign it for everyone, discuss the reading, and add details from additional sources where appropriate. In respect to the *Titanic* project, a manageable and high interest narrative essay by Hanson Baldwin (1934), "R.M.S. *Titanic*" works well to provide information regarding the ship, its route, the events of its maiden voyage, and, most importantly, many names and descriptions of the passengers and crew. Students connect with historical events when they become knowledgeable about the people involved. A kind of internal gallery of personas must take root inside the students, making them savvy as to the history and also sensitive to the fact that history affects people, be it the sinking of the *Titanic* or the stock market crash of 1929. When students can imagine in a rather accurate way their historical counterparts in past society and how they may have been affected by the event, they are ripe for writing historical fiction shaped by that event.

After my students read the Baldwin essay, they work in small groups to generate lists of specific personas mentioned in the essay such as First Officer Murdoch, Benjamin Guggenheim, and the Countess of Rothes and nonspecific personas, or those without specific names, such as stewards, shoeshine boys, nannies, immigrant mothers, and teenagers. When we pull together to make a persona bank, I often find that some plot situations have evolved on the nonspecific persona list. For example, students have offered the persona of a young boy traveling with his grandfather to meet his parents, who had immigrated to New York two years earlier.

As a short follow-up activity to the persona bank, I ask the students to go through the essay and lift nautical vocabulary, list the terms, and define them. We normally display this list in the classroom, since students need to refer to specific parts of the ship very often in their writing, especially those students writing as crew members.

After the persona bank has been built by all the classes, I then present the concept of RAMPS to the students. Developed by Duke (1983), RAMPS enables students to lay the groundwork for their projects by deciding on the following elements before writing:

***R**ole*	The persona or person in whose voice the student decides to write; for example, the student chooses to write as *Capt. E.J. Smith.*
***A**udience*	The persona's intended listener or receiver; for example, Capt. Smith will be writing to *his wife.*
***M**ode*	The form the writing will take; in this case, Capt. Smith will write *letters* to his wife.
***P**urpose*	The reason or motive for the writing; here Capt. Smith is writing *to capture the details of* Titanic's *maiden voyage for his wife* and sadly enough, *to say his final good-bye to her.*
Situation	Any special circumstances that influence Capt. Smith and his writing; for example, *he is to retire after this voyage* and *he knows that Titanic does not carry enough lifeboats for her passengers*; ultimately, *as captain, he will go down with the ship, and he does.*

Students exchange RAMPS charts with each other for feedback before they hand them in to me. I read over their ideas to approve them or to point out snags before they occur. The most common snag is not realizing the logical audience for the mode selected. The next day students adjust the RAMPS set-up as the last step before moving into the writing.

At this point, I notice that students proceed in different ways. Before going to paper, some students must see photographs of the specific persona selected, so they will locate photographs of Frederick Fleet, for example, or Molly Brown as a kind of prewriting activity. Those who have chosen a nonspecific persona such as the young boy traveling with his grandfather will look through books and my box of antique photographs to find "*the* boy" and "*the* grandfather" before drafting. Other students, more linear, will read everything in the room about their persona before inspiration hits. Meanwhile, tactile students will touch antique clothes I have hanging in the room, run their fingers over a woman's sterling change purse or imagine how small were the child's hands that fit into a pair of old gloves pinned to a turn of the century shirtwaist.

Those students choosing nonspecific personas consult the *Titanic* passenger list, at my request, for an authentic name. They already have decided on the ticket class for their persona, the gender, nationality, and age. Scanning the passenger list of 2,201 yields up endless possibilities for names. Since the list is arranged by ticket class, students have no problems finding an entire family traveling together, a mother with children or a single person. I insist that they use only names on the passenger list or the White Star crew list so that their writing recognizes real people who met their fate in *Titanic*, people who may have very well thought in their final moments that their names were to disappear with the ship forever.

After establishing a due date for the first draft, I give students workshop time in class to write, conference with me, and look for information. When the first drafts come in with the RAMPS chart attached, response groups give feedback to each other. I travel the room, listening, commenting, and conferencing as needed. Essentially, students hone in on the focus and content of the first draft. Does the writing accomplish what the student indicated as the purpose for it? Is the persona clear? Is the audience for the writing clear? Are there gaps in information or does it provide all the needed details? Is the information appropriate for the selected persona? Is the information accurate historically and factually for *Titanic*?

Once these focus and content areas are strengthened, the students move to draft two of the project. Typically, the second draft features more writing than the first draft, both on length generated in any one piece and in the number of pieces in the draft. Students often begin to mix modes with draft two. For example, draft one may have featured a set of diary entries for the persona of a teenage girl. With draft two, we find poetry written by the girl tucked into her diary and even a newspaper clipping about *Titanic*'s maiden voyage. Of course, the student who chose the persona of a teenage girl has written all of the pieces and in various modes, but the voice of the teenage girl lost to the depths of the Atlantic Ocean on April 15, 1912, gains strength and lives on.

Around this time in the project, we begin to look at the organization of the entire draft of the project as well as its individual components. I want to make sure that whoever would pick up the project to read it would have a strong sense of who is writing and for what reason and also a strong sense of the time and place for the writing. In short, the project should not sound contemporary. Students, as well, have a concern for authenticity, and most of my conferences at this point focus on an individual but believable voice telling the events of *Titanic* in their proper order (Sanchez 1994).

As a kind of preface for the project, students construct a *Titanic* biopoem, the formula a customized version of Barbara Page's biopoem format featured in *Plain Talk* (Virginia Department of Education 1987). I ask students to combine facts with appropriate creative information when using the following customized formula:

Line 1 Persona's first name
Line 2 Native of ________
Line 3 Age and occupation
Line 4 Who travels in (ticket class)
Line 5 To (state the reason to be on *Titanic*)
Line 6 Who loves (three items)
Line 7 Who fears (three items)
Line 8 Who survives/perishes (choose one)
Line 9 Who wrote/thought the following ___________(name the mode/modes)
Line 10 Last name

If choosing personas who perish, students must add a "Please Note" tag to their biopoems to explain how the writing survived when the personas did not. A sample explanation might tell us that steerage class passenger Stella Sage gave a letter written to her husband in New York to a crew member after asking him to please give the letter to someone in a lifeboat who will mail the letter in New York to her husband. Reading the following biopoem as a preface gives any reader, including the teacher who will eventually assess the projects, a clear context for the writing.

Stella
Native of Limmerick, Ireland
32 years old, wife of John, and mother of 5 children with her
Who travels in steerage
To immigrate to America where her husband waits
Who loves her husband, her children, and her dreams of America
Who fears water and darkness
Who perishes with her 5 children on *Titanic*
Who wrote the following letter and diary entries
Sage

Clearly, Stella Sage did not survive the tragedy, but her writing did, so the "Please Note" tag explains how that occurred and, in the spirit of the project, how the writing exists for the teacher to assess.

While still working with the trait of organization, students check to see that the organization in their modes is appropriate for the modes selected. Does a letter have the place and date in a heading? A closing? Is it correctly paragraphed? Does each diary entry feature the place and date in the heading? Does an interview article feature an introduction as to who is being interviewed and why? Do dialogue tags throughout indicate who is speaking in the interview?

Students next address style through vocabulary items, language constructions, and sentence structure to give that 1912 ambience to the writing. We first look at language items in resources such as *The Social Studies Teacher's Book of Lists* (Partin 1992), which provides words and expressions in vogue around 1912. We discuss the effectiveness of a light touch with 1912 slang vocabulary and expressions, and students judiciously insert items such as "long green," the verb "ankle," and "geezer" into their writing. I also point out that the higher the persona's social class, the less likely he or she would be to use slang.

We also read examples of letters and journal entries written during the era to examine how the language differs from ours, particularly in sentence construction and word choice. *This Fabulous Century 1910-1920*, the second volume in Time-Life's century by the decade series, offers many letters and journal entries of the era. For models written by actual *Titanic* survivors from all ticket classes and also the crew, *Titanic Voices* (1999) and *Titanic: An Illustrated History* (1992) work well. When examining these real life examples, students notice a lack of contractions in writing, many compound complex sentences, and many words pertaining to etiquette and social formalities. Students also notice how much time people in 1912 devoted to describing people and things on paper. So with attention to language and style in mind, students enter a wonderful stage in the project: they really don't need me to write draft three. The classroom hums with industry; it is as if the *Titanic* is about to leave the port of Southampton once more. My students are on their way, tickets in hand.

After draft three comes in, I read with one purpose in mind and that is to observe what editing items I need to present in mini-lessons, on newsprint about the room, and in handouts to the students. Each year presents a different crop of weaknesses and strengths. However, the entire project is ultimately to contain no errors in mechanics and usage, and students edit in that spirit. Response groups help one another. I also hold editing conferences where I edit a paragraph with a student and then have that student edit the next paragraph alone while I observe. Students consult grammar books and spelling tools, such as *Webster's Instant Word Guide*, and check *Titanic* resources to see examples of mechanical items such as underlining the name of a ship or the spelling of "Cherbourg," France, *Titanic*'s first port of call.

Students often become quite involved in the "packaging" of the final product. Those writing on the computer choose elegant script fonts while those writing by hand often use a calligraphy pen. Students cut down Xeroxed pictures of passengers to glue into lockets or place in frames. Sometimes students find an old wooden box, perfect for stashing their *Titanic* artifacts. Although additional touches to the final draft to enhance the 1912 feel of the project—aged paper, pressed and dried flowers, antique stamps, *Titanic* souvenirs, and White Star luggage tags—show extra effort and a seriousness of purpose on the part of the student, in no way do they take the place of effective writing. The writing is the project; the visuals are embellishments for the writing. Teachers need to discuss the difference since students may overfocus on the latter. Teachers, when assessing the final product, must focus on the writing, which can, at times, be weaker than the nicely done visuals that package it.

Over the years, I have recreated and refined my assessment tool for *Titanic* in an effort to make it define as closely as possible what the project is. I develop the rubric on a base of 100 points, which I can double in the grade book to make the project worth 200 points, a fair point value considering that multiple drafts and in-class writing workshop time are integral to the project.

I share the rubric (Figure 1) with the students directly after discussing the project and showing exemplary models of past projects to them. In this way, the students are clear as to the criteria for the project, and they know that there are different levels of performance or degrees of quality for the project. When responding to their project drafts in person or on paper, I use the language of the rubric and often refer to the levels on the rubric to indicate where the draft falls at that particular time.

Figure 1
Analytical Assessment Tool For The *Titanic* Project

Focus

6
- establishes and maintains a clear purpose as per the biopoem
- writes from a single point of view appropriate for the mode(s)
- shows clarity and originality of ideas within the realm of possiblities for *Titanic*

5
- a thinner version of 6

4
- establishes and maintains a clear purpose most of the time; may stray from the biopoem facts
- varies occasionally in keeping a single point of view in the mode piece(s)
- presents ideas which are clear but not especially original to the *Titanic* assignment

3
- a thinner version of 4

2
- shows uncertainty about the audience for the mode(s) and about the assignment in general
- typically shifts the point of view in the writing
- shows little if any clarity or originality of ideas

1
- a thinner version of 2

Content

6
- delivers unique, original ideas
- provides excellent development of those ideas with abundant details, explanations, examples, and historical information concerning the 1912 era and *Titanic*
- offers information appropriate for the audience, mode(s) and historical era

5
- a thinner version of 6

4
- delivers ideas that are more predictable than original
- provides adequate development of those ideas with some details, explanations, examples, and historical information concerning the 1912 era and *Titanic*; although typically some sections of the project could use more

Figure 1 (cont.)
Analytical Assessment Tool For The *Titanic* Project

3
- a thinner version of 4

2
- delivers under-developed ideas which are predictable and boring
- tends to provide skimpy development with details, explanations, examples, and historical information concerning the 1912 era and *Titanic* typically appearing as random lists of information

1
- a thinner version of 2

Organization

6
- offers a clear and complete biopoem with a "Please note" section if needed
- maintains a logical order for the mode(s) utilized and for the unfolding plot
- uses correct paragraphing
- uses transitions from sentence to sentence and between paragraphs for flow

5
- a thinner version of 6

4
- offers a reasonably clear yet complete biopoem with a "Please note" section if needed
- most of the time maintains a logical order for the mode(s) utilized and for the unfolding plot
- uses correct paragraphing most of the time
- uses transitions from sentence to sentence and between paragraphs inconsistently, which interrupts the flow

3
- a thinner version of 4

2
- tends to offer an incomplete biopoem, which creates confusion for the reader from the onset
- tends to disregard logical order for the mode(s) selected; tends to ignore any order of events in the plot development
- tends to use little to no paragraphing
- overlooks transitions which creates a choppy and abrupt effect for the reader

1
- a thinner version of 2

Style

6
- shows great care in word choice
- selects words to match the personality and biographical facts of the persona selected
- creates an effective voice and tone in each section of the project
- offers a wide variety of sentence types

Figure 1 (cont.)
Analytical Assessment Tool For The *Titanic* Project

5 • a thinner version of 6

4 • shows some care in word choice
- sometimes selects words to match the personality and biographical facts of the persona selected
- typically creates an effective voice and tone in some sections of the project
- tends toward less variety in sentence types with a frequency in structural errors
- such as run-ons and fragments

3 • a thinner version of 4

2 • shows little, if any, care in word choice
- rarely selects words to match the personality and biographical facts of the persona selected
- fails to create any effectiveness in voice and tone throughout the project
- tends to offer sentence types confined to simple and compound structures with repetitive run-ons and fragments

1 • a thinner version of 2

Conventions

6 • exhibits no errors in spelling, punctuation, and capitalization
- demonstrates excellent control of grammar and usage items
- makes no errors in sentence structure

5 • a thinner version of 6

4 • exhibits some errors in spelling, punctuation, and grammar
- demonstrates adequate control of grammar and usage items
- may have errors in sentence structure such as run-ons and fragments

3 • a thinner version of 4

2 • exhibits repetitive errors in spelling, punctuation, and capitalization
- demonstrates far less control of grammar and usage items
- makes repetitive errors in sentence structure, especially in runs-ons and fragments

1 • a thinner version of 2

After honing this project for more than ten years, I suggest that teachers address the analytical traits of focus and content first, moving to organization next. Once those three traits are in good shape, teachers should work on the trait of style, which takes on word choice, 1912 era vocabulary, sentence structure, and individuality in expression. This trait, more than any other, makes the persona come to life on paper, and my students rise to that challenge. As always in the stages of the writing process, editing comes last after the students have worked on all of the preceding traits. I want the focus, content, organization, and language locked in before we edit.

Teachers often ask me how long I spend on the project. The length varies from year to year and is dependent upon the amount of supplemental work I do after we read the Baldwin essay and upon the number of days I schedule for an ongoing in-class writing workshop. The simple truth is that with the plethora of materials in local bookstores as well as in educational catalogues, one could spend months on *Titanic.* My project tends to last four weeks from the introduction to the due date for the final draft. I try to give the students supplementals, including film clips, that are not in the mainstream. For example, a teacher can normally assume that nearly everyone has seen James Cameron's film *Titanic* and that far fewer students have watched documentary films by *National Geographic* and *The Discovery Channel.* When the teacher's intent is to *add* to the students' knowledge concerning *Titanic*, the choices for film become much clearer and ultimately more effective.

No matter how long the project runs or how many resources we have used, my students and I are always a bit sad to close it down. They tell me, "But, Mrs. Sanchez, this is so real," and it is to us. So real, in fact, that we take a moment every year on April 15 to remember our personas. In the 1912 press the first class passengers received all the attention, and second and third class passengers were often not even mentioned in news articles. Passenger lists for those classes were omitted not only from the newspapers but also from the various *Titanic* memorial books published in 1912. Yet each year in my classroom, steerage passenger Stella Sage, comes to life on paper, tending to her children and looking toward New York, as did they all.

Works Cited

Baldwin, H. 1934. R.M.S. *Titanic. Harper's magazine.* Reprint. in *Appreciating Literature.* New York: Macmillan, 1984.

Duke, C. 1983. *Writing through sequence: a process approach.* Boston: Little and Brown Company.

Forsyth, A., D. Hyslop and S. Jemima. 1999. *Titanic voices.* New York: St. Martin's Griffin.

Lynch, D. 1992. *Titanic: An illustrated history.* Toronto: Madison.

Partin, R. 1992. *The social studies teacher's book of lists.* Englewood Cliffs, NJ: Prentice Hall.

Sanchez, R. 1994. The voyage between truth and fiction. *English Journal* 83 (2): 40–42.

This fabulous century. Volume 2, *1920–1920.* Morristown: Time-Life Books, 1970.

Tibballs, G. 1997. *The Titanic.* Pleasantville: Reader's Digest, Inc.

Self, Judy, ed. 1987. *Plain talk about learning and writing across the curriculum.* Richmond: Virginia Department of Education Press.

Chapter 18

Assessing K-12 Schools' Use of Writing to Learn as a Tool for Comprehensive School Reform

Joseph Milner

Back in the early eighties, I thought that I understood what writing across the curriculum was, but almost every time I encountered someone talking about writing across the curriculum it seemed to greatly diminish the concept I had. When I was asked in 1989 to serve as a leader at a North Carolina Institute of Government's Principals' Institute on the campus of the University of North Carolina, I found myself time and again taking issue with the main speaker William Zinsser. His consistent emphasis was learning to write, almost never writing to learn. A few years later when my own university began to focus attention on writing, the sessions were most often led by the English faculty members who repeatedly hammered colleagues in other disciplines about their need to use tougher writing standards with students in science, art, and anthropology. Some of the more altruistic colleagues in other disciplines were cheered as they spoke about their devotion to the conventions of standard English. No one talked about the benefits writing could offer to learning in those other disciplines. No one said anything about writing's effect on concept validation. Altruism rather than self-interest was always the spur that was meant to prick non-English colleagues' intent. I wondered if I was missing something; I began to almost distrust my understanding of this bold learning tool.

Then, a year later, Neil Griffiths, Headmaster of Westlea School in Wiltshire, England, visited Wake Forest University to work with elementary teachers on math. My belief in writing to learn was fully resurrected. Neil was a bright, jolly, over-the-top teacher whose work as Headmaster included contact with Jimmy Britton, Douglas Barnes, Pat D'Arcy, and others who championed that fundamental exploratory way to learn. He showed teachers in North Carolina and elsewhere how deeply his students conceptualized and controlled new ideas when they discovered them through their language. He let elementary and secondary teachers work through difficult problems and articulate familiar concepts, like what is an "angle," that seemed at first transparent to them but were not, in fact, fully grasped. Neil would also let teachers work toward a solution to a mathematical progression problem involving tiles and then read his students' written statements that edged toward a full understanding of the progression at work here.

Figure 1
Tile Problem

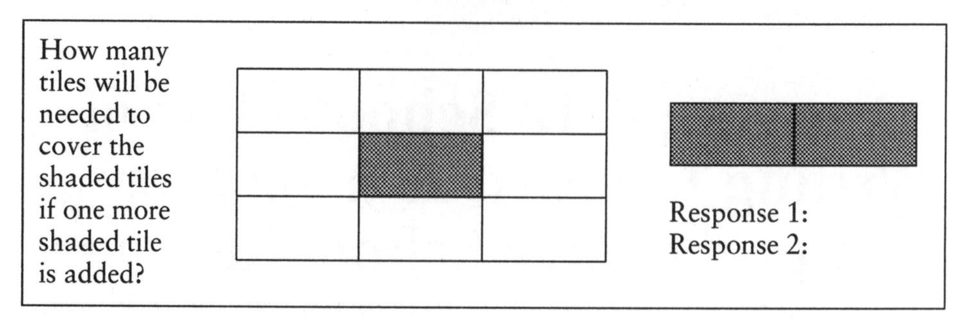

Neil's buoyant teaching style and the obvious impact on his students' conceptualization provided by such writing solidified my belief in writing as a powerful tool for learning.

Bob Tierney, another terrific teacher, helped me see the power of writing in science. His stories that feature the indomitable Fred and the whiz kid Charles are full of humorous vignettes, but more than that, they always illustrate the way he uses writing to help both the best and the brightest learn science in his classroom. Talking with Bob over the years encouraged Becky Brown and me to dedicate our Writing Project's 1997 Summer Institute to writing in science. Bob and a number of able consultants visited our site and I became not only more dedicated to writing to learn but more able to use it well in my own writing and teaching. So when a former fellow from our project called to ask for help at her school, I listened to her success story at her former school and told her I would come to her new school to help in any way I could. Her leadership in writing to learn as an assistant principal at her former school had caused the school's writing test scores to rise remarkably, and she wanted to do the same with the teachers at her new school. I told her that the only way I could offer a convincing and useful after school session for her faculty was to work with them on a number of problems scattered across the disciplines as a way to demonstrate the power of writing to learn for their students. This was to be the first of four schools that I would help in building writing to learn into their comprehensive school reform.

Writing to Learn Problem Solving

I decided to create a set of seven problems that ranged in difficulty from fairly simple to very complex so that the teachers could experience the challenge that they would want their own students to feel. The problems were also scattered across the curriculum so that all of the teachers could identify directly with at least one of the problems they encountered and, thus, know the usefulness of such writing in their own subject area. The problems looked like this:

1. The captain of a Dutch cargo vessel was concerned that the water level in the canal lock was too low for his heavily loaded vessel. He was not sure what to do when the lock commandant, who spoke a language he did not understand, tried to offer a solution. A young

deckhand finally came up to suggest a solution: Toss the two extremely heavy but worthless lead cylinders overboard. Should the captain follow the suggestion? If he does, will the water in the lock rise, remain the same, or fall? Explain your answer in a clear written statement below. Use two baking tins, two batteries, water, and a pencil to test your previous thoughtful response. Be sure to fill the larger tin almost 3/4 full when you start your experiment. Write your new explanation of what happened in your test if it is different from what you wrote above.

2. Write a brief definition of what you believe to be cruelty to animals. Each of the following cases involves the issue of cruelty to animals. For each situation, decide whether or not the action is an act of cruelty to animals and explain in a few written words why you made that decision.
   a. Exceeding the speed limit by 20 mph, a man is driving down a country road. He sees a sign that says "Deer Crossing." He then proceeds into the "Deer Crossing" area at which point a deer runs across the road in front of the car. Unable to stop in time, the driver hits the deer. Although the driver does not stop his car, he notices from his rearview mirror that the deer staggers into the ditch beside the road.
   b. The animal shelter has a policy of putting to sleep all animals who are not adopted after 30 days.
   c. A local farmer's cornfields are being destroyed by jack rabbits. He pays a bounty to anyone who brings him a rabbit carcass.
   d. Every winter hunters kill baby Harp seals for their fur. They are killed by a blow to the head with a blunt stick. The hunters argue that the seal's deaths are painless, that the Harp seal is not an endangered species, and that selling the pelts is their primary means of livelihood during the winter.
   e. In order to verify the workability of a new procedure for voiding the bladders of paraplegics, researchers in a medical school replicate the conditions of a paraplegic by breaking the spines of dogs. The spines are broken while the dogs are anesthetized, and the dogs feel no pain as a result of the operation.
   f. The ears of boxer puppies are clipped (cutting and shaping their naturally long, floppy ears into short, pointed ones) and their tails are bobbed. After their ears are clipped, the boxers' heads must be bandaged and taped for several weeks until they are healed.
   g. To determine the effects of isolation on humans, baby monkeys are separated from their mothers at birth and raised in total isolation. The monkeys develop mental disorders which render them unable to relate to other monkeys even when they are placed in a normal environment later on.
   h. A woman goes shopping in the grocery store. Intending to be gone only a few minutes, she leaves her dog in the car. She meets a friend in the store and doesn't get back to the car for nearly an hour. The temperature outside is close to 95 degrees F, and when she returns to the car, she finds her dog has collapsed.

i. A man returns home from work to find that his dog chewed a hole in a chair. In anger, the man kicks the dog several times until the dog runs to the basement to hide.

Write a new definition of cruelty to animals stating the criteria that allow you to decide whether an act is or is not cruelty to animals.

3. Build a barometer to measure atmospheric pressure using a balloon stretched over the opening of a jar, and a straw to measure the rising pressure on a gauge you have created. After your team has built the barometer, use the space below to write an exact explanation of how you did this.
4. On a jetliner to Europe there are 9 boys, 5 American children, 9 men, 7 foreign boys, 14 Americans, 8 American males, and 5 foreign females. How many passengers are there on board? Explain in writing the thinking that allowed you to find that answer.
5. Find the next number in this series: 7, 12, 27, 72, 207, _____. Explain in writing how anyone can find that answer.
6. A camper has 3 fish to cook on her campfire and needs to cook each of them for two minutes on each side but can only cook two fish at a time on her small grill. Explain in writing the most efficient sequence for cooking the 3 fish.
7. Three baskets sit on a high ledge with a sign over each that correctly marks the contents: Apples, Pears, Mixed. A clever child mixes up the signs so that none of the signs correctly indicates what is actually in the basket below. The orchard owner decides to make a game of it by allowing you to reach into one of the baskets above you and without being able to see what is in the basket pick one piece of fruit out. The challenge is that if then you can put all the signs over the correct baskets, you can have all three baskets without charge. Explain in writing how you might beat the orchard owner at this game.

You can see that some of the problems were quite complex and would take a great deal of time to work through while others require a relatively brief amount of time to solve.

Middle School Response

I wanted to mix problem-based learning where possible with writing to learn, so I started with the ship in the lock problem. To illustrate the power of minds-on and then hands-on learning, I asked the teachers to listen to the problem, think about it carefully, and then write an answer that included an explanation of how they arrived at their answer. Einstein was famous for these *gedunken* experiments, those performed only in his head. John Keynes tells us that Newton was even more neurologically muscular than Einstein; he had the discipline to work a problem over in his mind until he had the answer. For most of us, however, we need more concrete ways to deal conclusively with such difficult problems. So, after the middle school teachers thought about the boat in the lock problem and had written up their responses, I asked them to work in large groups with a 1 inch baking pan (the lock) bread loaf pans (the boat), and two batteries (the lead cylinders). With these everyday items they were able to simulate the problem and test their old thinking and writing with the stern facts of reality. Even with a too large group, the teachers talked, challenged one another, and scratched their heads to try to come up with a written explanation that satisfied their assumptions about displacement and their careful measurements when the cylinders are on the boat or in the water. They generally came to discover that the weight of the two cylinders displaces more water when they are on board than when they are in the water. Teachers felt a bit shaky in the field of physics, but the crucial experiment using a floating boat and real lead cylinders engaged them fully in their learning.

With the *Cruelty to Animals* problem they were put at ease. They were sure that they knew what cruelty was. When they had worked a while to write out a definition, we stopped to discuss their definitions and then they individually reviewed the list of varied instances that involved pain for animals to determine if each was cruel or not and why they judged it was or was not cruel. When they worked through the decisions with two or three colleagues, their disagreements made them focus on the detriments of cruelty. They had to develop criteria or they could not defend their choices. As the groups talked to work through their decisions about each of the instances, they began to agree upon the essential criteria that determined if an act was cruel. In many groups, the contest of ideas was vigorous. In one group, we had a teacher, who felt it was cruel to prune trees, talking with a colleague who only ate what he had killed. When they completed their work after such vigorous debate, they then discussed the criteria from which each small group was working. Only then could they write up their individual criteria; at this juncture, they each began to form a much more solid definition of cruelty. They began to write about cruelty to animals in a way that was far clearer and far more precise than their first rambling uncertain attempts had been. Some were embarrassed by the contrast, but they were all quite pleased with their final piece of writing.

We also worked with math problems like the airplane, fruit basket, and fish fry problems. These were challenging in a different way. The teachers needed more than everyday language (labels, arrows, directions, schematics) to think through the problems, but when they solved them, they turned back to language again to explain in step-by-step fashion how they arrived at their answers, and how someone else could discover that answer. Writing to learn how to solve and explain these problems was crucial and the clarity and elegant simplicity of the written answer told observers how well they had learned and how great was the promise for long-term conceptualization. Some of them seemed to come to the correct answer without being able to convey their thinking process clearly to the rest of us; others had the answer and could communicate clearly the process they used to arrive at their answers.

A Secondary School's Response to Writing to Learn

The most important result of my work with writing to learn was my understanding of how the faculty and administration of these very different schools responded to the concept. I was involved in very different ways with each of these schools from start to finish. After my work at the nearby assistant principal's school, the first school I helped was a very exciting secondary school in the western part of my state. An assistant principal had attended a retreat where I asked school leaders to focus on writing in their schools. He liked what we were doing and encouraged his principal to ask me to work with the school's entire faculty on writing. I accepted their invitation, but said that I believed that writing to learn was the only approach that would make sense for the people who taught in disciplines other than English. He initially responded that writing across the curriculum might be good for his teachers; he felt that they needed to emphasize things like punctuation and grammar in all of their classes. I responded that I believed students would learn to write better because of my session, but that my emphasis would be placed on using writing as a tool to help all students learn in all of their classes. He liked that idea and thought that his teachers would buy into it, too. I think they did.

Our session was very lively. The boat in the lock created a hubbub of thinking out loud, challenging one another, building on each others' good ideas, and huddling in small groups to settle on some agreed upon conclusions. The enthusiasm, energy, and hard thinking continued throughout the afternoon; they liked the idea that the writing prompted their conceptualization and solidified it in their memory. We talked a good bit about their interest in the process and their belief that they could use it in all of their classes. Because we had actually dealt with problems from science, math, and social studies that were a challenge for them, they could see very clearly how the writing worked to solidify their own conceptualization. They came to understand the concept of displacement and the role of weight and volume in a way they never had before. The same could be said about cruelty to animals, which they had often considered but never before pondered with such care.

Two Elementary Schools' Responses

When the Porter/Obey bill on Comprehensive School Reform emerged in North Carolina, I was asked to represent the National Writing Project at a Southeastern regional meeting for "providers" and individual schools. The National Writing Project was a provider designated in the legislation, so I asked a director, the successful middle school assistant principal, and a teacher to join me in explaining how writing to learn could provide a successful platform for comprehensive school reform. Schools across the state attended our four sessions and were attracted to the energy and intelligence of our team, but, most of all, to the teacher driven quality of the institutes and the impact of writing to learn on learning across the curriculum. I have had calls from schools across the state and some of these have resulted in partnerships between Writing Projects and schools seeking comprehensive school reform. I also have worked with schools in our region of the state, and the results of our collaboration were quite different and most informative.

The first school was up front about its interest in the Writing Project as the means for comprehensive school reform. The principal of this "low wealth" school had been a participant in a Writing Project seven years earlier and still remembered the vitality and strength of those summer days. She asked me to come to their school to demonstrate some of that power to her faculty, none of whom had been Writing Project participants. We arranged an early morning session where she hoped I could show them the power of writing to learn and the generativity of working together in a Writing Project way to bring about continuous reform at their school.

The sessions at the elementary school were full of energy and challenging thinking. We worked through many of the same problems that I used with the teachers at the secondary school in the mountains. The way the teachers worked individually and together told me quickly about the good feelings they had for their school and their role in the total learning program that was underway there. A number of the teachers, curriculum leaders, and assistant principals at the school took leadership roles in my visit there; I could feel their support of what we were undertaking together. The morning went very well.

The next elementary school encounter was very different. The principal had not attended the providers conference, but had heard from the school system's Federal Grants Coordinator that schools like hers were good candidates for Comprehensive School Reform funding, if they used the Writing Project as a big part of their proposal. The initial phone contact was strange because the principal was not clear about what the Writing Project was, how it would serve as a provider, what we did to create school reform, and how our Summer Institutes operated. I tried to explain what we were, that we operated in a teacher-centered fashion, and that our basic impact would result from teacher ownership of the project and writing used as a tool for learning. I did not feel that we were communicating very well, but agreed to come to her school for a session with her faculty. I had a relationship with her school that preceded her being principal there, so I had fond memories that made me want the new relationship to succeed.

I planned for a morning much like the one at the other elementary school, but found they were not very much alike. I had little or no contact with the principal; she spent some time in the room with us, but seemed to spend all of that time working on a schedule or a list of some kind. She was not involved with our problem solving activities. I felt good about our session; it worked well. But I entered and departed as if I had come to fix the sink. I did not feel her presence enlivening our efforts nor much interest in what might happen next.

Assessing the Responses

The four experiences were all very different and evaluating them can only be done by intuition along with a kind of ethnological study of each of the four different cultures. The first of my four encounters was delightful. The nearby assistant principal, who was a part of our earliest Writing Project Summer Institute, had by sheer force of will and without any funding incentives taken her first school to new heights on the end of course testing. She had pleaded, promised, placated, and persuaded her faculty to do what she called writing across the curriculum until their writing test scores were the most improved in her school system. In a state environment where gain scores mean everything, she drove her faculty to accomplish amazing things. The common writing activities they employed were not spectacular, but there was a common purpose that made them work. The teachers who may not have been impressed with their leaders' strategies were attracted to her passion for writing. The principal at her middle school was totally aloof or even indifferent to the task at hand, but he knew that something good was happening with the school's test scores and that made him content to accede to all of her requests. She has kept up with me since that visit and has continued to do well at her new school.

The mountain school administrators were very aware of the power of professional development. They knew writing was important, but they had more of a pragmatic sense of the impact of the entire host of dog and pony shows that came to their school than a belief in one approach they wanted to emphasize. They introduced me with great fanfare and were enthusiastic about my session with the teachers. They called to follow-up the visit and wrote to request that I return to work with the faculty on another aspect of writing. I was flattered, but did not see any way to make writing important to their entire faculty other than the writing to learn approach we used on my initial visit.

The first of the two elementary schools was an exciting place to work not only because the teachers were so receptive, but because the initial session was just a first step toward all of us working together on comprehensive school reform proposal. I met with school leaders on two or three other occasions where we built a loose plan for writing to learn as a foundation for changing the face of learning at their school. We worked back and forth as colleagues seeking a common end. The principal kept us focused, but other curriculum leaders played a strong role in directing and shaping our plans. They wanted to develop their own writing project on the second year of the grant after a few leaders had attended the summer institute of our local site. They all took part in this free flowing kind of planning session and, then, as individuals, wrote pieces of the proposal. Sadly, they did not receive funding, but seemed not to be deterred by that bit of political bad luck. They wanted to continue the plan as much as possible with or without the funds to help them.

The other elementary school was the obverse of this existing school. The principal was lame in her support of the writing to learn session, but even more confounding was the fact that I had a call from the school secretary (not the disinterested principal) the next week to ask that I write a statement of support from the Writing Project. I wrote back to say I wanted to do good things to help their school in its reform, but that the Writing Project could not write a letter of endorsement unless its ideas were an integral part of the school's plan for comprehensive reform. I heard nothing for a month or more. Out of the blue, a month later, I had a note in my office that the same very nice secretary at that elementary school had called to ask for a letter of support. I returned the call and said I had a warm place in my heart for her school because of my long-term relationship with it, but had to reiterate the terms of my letter that said I could only offer my endorsement if writing to learn and the Writing Project were seriously involved in their plans for reform. That was the last chapter in that story—or so I thought. When the state released the writing test scores for our local schools, the uninspired school was at the bottom of the list. The inspired school was in the middle of the pack, moving toward the top.

The four encounters are representative of how schools adopt new teaching strategies like writing to learn to reform themselves. Their concern and understanding run the gamut from deep collaboration with full implementation to superficial encounters looking only for funding support that will have little impact on the school and the learning within.

Chapter 19

Assessing Writing Across the Curriculum as Dialogue: Considerations for Staff Development

Collett B. Dilworth

At a recent state level conference for K-12 curriculum leaders, I surveyed the educators attending a concurrent session, asking them what teachers wanted most from a writing across the curriculum program. The first requirement, the educators agreed, was that such a program not place onerous burdens on teachers in the content areas. The next most important objective was to improve "basic writing skills." Said one participant, "I just want them to be able to write a correct sentence and a real paragraph, topic sentence and so forth." Another said, "It's unbelievable what they turn in," to which a third responded, "But whatever it is, it's not spelled like English!" As a member of my university's Writing Across the Curriculum Committee for over a dozen years, I have found similar objectives and objections cited by my colleagues in higher education. Such responses show that content area teachers are certainly concerned about their students' writing abilities and that they tend to seek as direct an approach to writing instruction as possible.

The nature of this direct approach is evident in the responses to another question posed at the conference session: "What's the most important means teachers need to be able to teach WAC?" A representative reply was, "If I'm going to teach writing, I'm really not sure what specifics to focus on. I mean, how much should I count off for mistakes and which kinds of things should I count off for in the first place?" Here we can see the common assumption that to teach writing is essentially to highlight error. Under this assumption teachers deduce that because students of writing must learn from their mistakes, writing pedagogy should proceed through a tough love formative assessment. Surely, the reasoning continues, the "skill" of writing comprises a set of patterns and principles (as in the physical and social sciences), and so teaching should be a matter of applying these patterns like templates laid upon student papers. To turn formative assessments into grades, therefore, instructors may simply discern departures from the template, subtract the relative values of departures from some criterion total, and award the number left. Because this model focuses on the piece of writing as product, it is familiarly known as "the product approach."

The problem with the product approach is that research can find no evidence that it helps students learn to write. Since the 1960s the English/language arts education community has concluded that students actually tend to write more poorly when they write mainly to avoid error. In the seventies and eighties, English/language arts teachers focused the writing curriculum on the processes used by real writers in the real world. The "process approach" guides students in thinking up content and putting it down in tentative drafts, then revising, then rethinking and redrafting and, along the way, editing for correctness and convention. Problems of coherence and error are treated during the revising and editing. Teachers have found, however, that focusing only on the "process" can have almost as desiccating an effect as focusing only on the product. Drilling on tactics for getting ideas (brainstorming, etc.), inculcating patterns of organizing, and urging revision may direct students to useful skills, but students still find it difficult to see the point of it all. Long-term effects of instruction remain difficult to discern.

Today the model many English/language arts teachers are turning to is one that brings the processes of the writer and the characteristics of products to the context of audience. By highlighting the reader, a writing curriculum encourages students to understand the actual function of processes and products. The idea is to move from a monologic perspective in which the student is writing merely to get the writing done, to a dialogic perspective in which the student is writing to communicate. In a monologic curriculum, the teacher assumes the role of supervisor, encouraging and policing student behavior. In a dialogic curriculum, the teacher assumes the role of accompanying guide; both the teacher and the student shift perspectives between writer and reader, focusing on lessons made necessary by writer purposes, reader needs, and subject matter realities.

Relevance of English/Language Arts for Writing Across the Curriculum

The insights of English/language arts teachers surely have implications for all teachers participating in writing across the curriculum programs. Unfortunately "writing across the curriculum" is often understood as a disjointed hybrid. Being independent, tied to no particular context, composition comes to a content area as if it were a second bird to be set next to the bird of content, so both might be rocked in one throw. Seeing composition as an interloper from the English/language arts, content area teachers are daunted by what they construe as its baffling set of principles, exceptions, and codicils. The principles have to do with sentence level grammar, paragraph coherence, and mysteriously circular constructs such as "introduction" and "conclusion." They loom like dangerous weapons for which an educator must somehow become qualified before such powerful devices can be wielded with the authority of those Spartan adepts, the English teachers.

No wonder, therefore, that many content area teachers in WAC programs are too concerned with teaching writing to rethink the role of their content curriculum. They naturally want their inservice workshops to give them portable tactics useable tomorrow to elicit and improve student writing without interrupting content learning. My experience, however, suggests that a WAC program will enjoy little success when content area teachers simply apply tactics from language arts education. I believe WAC programs succeed most when teachers shift their concern from writing to the curriculum as a whole. Doing so makes it easy for them to discard those apprehensions about "which kinds of things to count off for."

To accomplish this shift, WAC program teachers should adopt a dialogic perspective not only on writing, but also on the science, art, technology, or social science that they teach. Students and teachers view course content not as matter to fill the vessel—students—but as information that comes alive when used in actual communication. One means of encouraging this perspective is to develop "rhetorical environments" for students to enter when they write. To establish these communications spaces, the teacher specifies circumstances in which the writer has a particular role and a particular audience in mind, an audience that needs to be addressed for purposes related to course content. Teacher and students also specify the most important criteria for a successful writing product in terms of those qualities likely to best serve the intended audience.

Instruction then proceeds with the teacher acting as accompanying guide toward the goal of effective communication with that audience. The class is structured to foster the writing processes of researching and planning, drafting, revising and editing in the context of serving the assignment's rhetorical objectives. Students indeed learn from their errors, but only when they discern how errors frustrate readers. Formative assessment, therefore, acts to focus on what is effective and what is ineffective from the viewpoint of readers with whom students learn to empathize. In such a curriculum, all the writers in the classroom, especially the authors of the course's textbook, produce text relevant for lessons in how writing can achieves its purposes.

A Pattern for the Writing Assignment

A crucial tool for WAC teachers is the writing assignment. The dialogic assignment's purpose is to create a context for writing, to thoroughly set the scene, and to provide the grounds for guidance and assessments that follow. The following pattern has worked well in WAC courses at East Carolina University:

1. *Preparatory experience*—Give students grounds for writing by providing relevant experiences: reading of all kinds, films and videotapes, audio tapes, exploratory discussions in class, lectures, debates, reports, and other public affairs.
2. *Rhetorical orientation*—Define the rhetorical environment students are expected to enter:
   a. *Topic and circumstances*—Give the general subject matter they are to address. If you want a narrow assignment you might even provide the title of their essays, but you should usually have students learn to focus their work by narrowing the subject matter and determining an appropriate title themselves. The general circumstances for the writing might be realistic settings such as committee reports, interoffice memorandums making recom-

mendations, letters to the editor, formal presentations with high stakes riding on successful impact.

   b. *Audience*—Specify for whom they are writing. Of course, their work is ultimately for the teacher, but the teacher should assess the writing for how well it addresses the specified audience. For example, if a college first-year English paper aims to persuade high school students to eschew drugs, the instructor should assess the paper by how well it serves that audience. This part of the assignment is often the longest, as the audience's characteristics and expectations should be rather vivid.
   c. *Writer's role*—Common roles for writers (and types of writing) are salesperson (persuasion), advocate (argument), teacher (exposition), critic (interpretation and evaluation), confidant (expressive writing), and artist (poetry, fiction, etc.) For example, in assigning an exposition (reporting a series of events or explaining a reality, or comparing two different things or tracing a process, etc.), you might recommend that students plan and develop their essays as a good teacher would develop a clear lesson for a group of people who need to learn about the subject.
3. *Mechanics*—These are important details, but we don't want this tail wagging the dog.
   a. *Scope*—For many students, the most pressing question in the composition classroom is "How long does it have to be?" One of your goals in the writing curriculum is to develop students' attitudes so that they ask instead "How broadly and deeply should the topic be developed?" Number of pages is a way to answer both questions, but the latter needs more analysis in terms of the objective and the audience. (For example: "Write a narrative of this episode in your life descriptive enough for your reader to be able to enjoy an imaginative experience but not so detailed that the reader can't enjoy the story in a quick reading: 400 - 500 words.")
   b. *Format*—How should the paper look? How specific you get depends on the writer's role and objective. For expressive writing, manuscript format can be left up to students; for certain kinds of expository writing such as reports, format may be highly specified.
   c. *Schedule of process*—When will students invent, plan, draft, revise, and edit? Specify deadlines or dates and times for these activities, reminding students that they share a "looping" relationship (e.g. part of revising can be reinventing and replanning; some writers edit throughout the process; etc.).
   d. *Criteria*—What in principle is "excellent" versus "poor"? By specifying these two criteria, the assignment brackets the range of quality concisely but efficiently without binding the assessor with too many preset qualities. Criteria should be worded in terms of the writer, the reader, the thinking, the organization, and the style required by the aim of the piece of writing. For example, "excellent" on a particular expository assignment might be specified as follows: "An excellent paper will make clear for your audience how several articles explore the concept of

[________]. It will support its general points with specific examples from the articles we have read. The paper's organization will make it easy for the reader to follow the sequence of main points and to recall them after finishing the essay. A poor paper will read as if the writer has no interest in teaching his or her reader. Either its main ideas will not help the reader understand the concept or they will be so poorly worded and organized that the reader will have difficulty understanding them. A failing paper will not demonstrate how themes function in our stories." If you wish a more detailed set of criteria, an evaluation guide is better appended separately rather than thickening the assignment's main text.

Here are some examples of assignments for dialogic writing and assessment:

Environmental science

We have been studying the water cycle and water management. We have learned how water cycles from standing liquid, to evaporation to precipitation and how it interacts with the ground. We have examined how various environmental influences affect the quality of water, and we have looked into the very important problem of how humans draw on available water for various uses.

Your writing assignment is to assume the role of an informed citizen preparing a position paper to be presented before the city council. Your circumstances are these:

A developer is proposing to build a housing development near the city's main water reservoir. You see that a housing development in that locale might affect the drinking water. You need to prepare a statement that will explain to members of the council the potential dangers of such construction and the reasons for these dangers. You respect the developer, however, and know that people need houses and streets and parking lots. So you also want to suggest what the developer might do to insure the water will not be affected.

The council members despise having to listen to disorganized, inaccurate and hard to understand statements. They never have enough time to take care of all the city's business at their meetings, so they do not want to waste time with statements that beat around the bush. Yet they are very serious about insuring that all the citizens of the town live in a healthy, supportive community. They are constantly trying to get all the information they need to make important decisions, so they appreciate full information given clearly. Since these are educated adults, you need not explain all the details of the water cycle as if the members were hearing about evaporation for the first time. Yet you will want to remind them of the processes affecting water supply, and how these processes affect us.

Your statement, which will be delivered both orally and in writing, will probably not serve the council in less than 500 words or in more than 750 words. To insure your most useful organization, you might consider adapting the pattern for research reports and the patterns for formal recommendations we have used before.

We will spend the first part of class tomorrow in small groups brainstorming and drafting. The last half of class we will discuss some of the points we've thought of. On Monday next week, you should bring your completed first drafts to class to share in small groups and then to discuss major points and problems with the whole class. On Wednesday, final drafts are due.

An excellent paper will make the members of the city council very grateful the writer-speaker showed up. The members will be impressed at how clear the points are, with what good sense the points were selected and organized, how well standard English was used. They will feel the time they have given to the statement has benefited the city. A poor paper will not give the members of the city council the information they need. Some points may be worth making, but they will be worded ungrammatically or inaccurately or in sentences hard to figure out. When the members will have finished with a poor statement, they will wish it could have been clearer, more to the point, more thorough, or easier to see how the points make sense together.

Psychology

We are completing the unit on "Motivation and Emotion." We have examined biological, social, and cognitive explanations of human emotional responses. We have paid special attention to our textbook's summaries of studies that have led to these explanations. Our text has demonstrated how a person's behavior can be partially explained by several different theories and that these theories need not contradict each other. We have also read the Grimm brothers' folk tale about the sparrow and the dog. [The sparrow nurtures an abused, runaway dog and wreaks total vengeance on the man who thoughtlessly runs his heavy wine wagon over the dog sleeping in the road.]

Your role is to be a psychologist-in-training who is preparing an analysis of the sparrow's motivations for his actions. Your audience is people interested in folklore (the way the Grimm brothers were). These people like to study stories that have been told and retold until the stories are a part of the culture. The characters in such stories usually demonstrate traits that the culture believes are very significant, traits such as jealousy, love, selfishness, pride, generosity, and greed. It has not occurred to many of these people, however, that the field of psychology can provide very interesting perspectives on the characters in the literature. Because this audience is already familiar with this tale, you need not summarize it for them. Your readers will want you to explain one theory of motivation and show how the sparrow's actions can be at least partially explained according to the theory. Your readers are people who really like for someone to interest them in something new. They appreciate clear explanations organized so that the points make sense and so that the ideas can be remembered. You will probably not serve your readers well in fewer than 300 words.

Tomorrow you should come to class with a theory tentatively selected. You will want to re-examine our textbook to see which of the studies and theories are relevant to the sparrow. For example, you might analyze the sparrow's behavior in terms of drive reduction theory, expectancy-value theory, intrinsic-extrinsic motivation, self-actualization needs, or opponent-process theory. We will spend some time in pairs exploring our ideas and preparing statements applying the theories to the story. Then we will share statements and ideas. In five days we will bring rough drafts to class to share and to revise. Final drafts are due in seven days.

An excellent paper will interest readers so much and give them such a clear idea of how psychological theories can inform our daily lives, that they will want to read more of the writer's ideas. They will easily finish the essay without having to stop to figure out what it means, and after they finish reading, they will find it easy to remember the main points and examples. There will be too few grammatical errors to distract readers. A poor paper will make the reader wonder what the writer means. The readers of a poor paper might be discouraged from turning to psychology for interesting ways of understanding behavior.

Formative Response and Assessment

Teachers assessing student writing for the assignments above will put themselves in the role of the intended audience and will assess merit according to how well writers fulfill the roles they have assumed (teacher, confidant, critic, advocate). Such assessment demands that content area teachers offer honest responses to features of the writing without having to depend on complex grammatical or rhetorical concepts. So in assuming the role of intended audience, a teacher responds to writing not as an instructional authority but as a real reader by portraying pleasure in encountering the writing's virtues and by asking questions to guide students in revising and editing.

Questions addressing problem areas in student writing can suggest alternative strategies to resolve reader difficulties, but teachers should not do all the writer's thinking. If the teacher enters full corrections and revisions on students' papers, students will learn how to wait for an authority to do their work but will learn little about how to revise with a rhetorical purpose in their own minds. Solving rhetorical problems under guidance helps; giving directions does not help. To effect this approach, therefore, teachers should maintain the spirit of dialogue, of give and take between reader and writer, especially when responding to student writing.

Two tactics are especially useful in responding to student drafts turned in to the teacher or shared during small group revision.

Trace Anticipations and Fulfillments:

"Your title makes me anticipate that most of the paper will be on the sparrow's personality. So when I first began this paragraph, I got ready for a brief explanation of what Maslow meant by self-actualization, a brief review that would lead to how this theory applies to the sparrow. But for three paragraphs the paper concentrates not only on Maslow but also on several other theories. Do you think your reader will lose track of the paper's main purpose? How much of these three paragraphs can you cut and still give your readers the background they need to understand your analysis?" [The problems of getting the big picture are the crucial problems and need to be solved first. The most important teacher response, therefore, shows the writer how a reader processes the paper and where the writing succeeds and fails to help the reader make meaning. Often when students' focus clarifies, so does their grammar. Ask students to revise major content problems before worrying about the little problems that remain.]

"Wait a minute, I'm going to reread the second page, because I thought you said this sort of thing doesn't matter when people don't figure they will get any reward. Yes, you did say that, and it makes sense. Do you think these two sentences here will confuse your reader?" [The teacher in a conversational tone gives a running commentary of how the reader's understanding develops and just where and when understanding gets derailed.]

Portray the Psychological Effects of Sentence Constructions and Suggest Effects of Possible Revisions:

"I got confused right at this point in the sentence where I've put the slash. Do you think your reader might understand more completely if you made two sentences out of this really complicated one?" [The teacher marks places where confusion kicks in, but doesn't bother with analysis in grammatical terms. The question leaves the specific solution up to the student.]

"I had trouble figuring out who the circled word refers to, the dog or the bird." [Rather than a cryptic "ref" put above a pronoun whose reference is not clear, the teacher states the effects on the reader.]

"These three sentences really work for me. I think your reader will appreciate how the long one sets up a generality, and the two simple, direct, short ones show a positive and a negative example." [Comments are not confined to weaknesses. The reward for good prose is an impressed reader.]

"Would something like the wording you use here work in the paragraph below where I've put the three slashes (///)? Those slashes are at a place where I lost track of the topic. I don't know, maybe those same words you use here would be too repetitive used again only a short distance away. Would synonyms be appropriate?" [The teacher models the kind of thinking mature writers do when they revise.]

Giving Grades

One way to understand a final letter grade is to realize that a grade is given when teaching is finished. Once a paper gets a grade, students consign the paper and all its potential to the trash heap of history. Out of sight, out of mind. Since each course has a relatively tiny number of hours during a school year, we don't want to quit teaching during any of them. Papers, therefore, should be works in progress for as long as possible so students will have a chance to deepen their aptitudes, especially for revision, by continually applying them. To satisfy students' need to know how well they're doing, teachers might give papers tentative characterizations that may change after subsequent revision. These characterizations are not letter grades but they can suggest the paper's present merit, and for very good drafts, they can suggest ways to test strengths. For example: "I think this draft will achieve your purposes with the audience quite well. Can you think of any other analogies that might be more clear, perhaps even more exciting for your young readers than the one you use to explain transverse fission?" If students maintain their work in portfolios that will be submitted for assessment at the end of the grading period, they have at least some opportunity and incentive to revise.

Still, the adamant constraint remains. Most of us teach in schools where the final grade is the bottom line. We must, therefore, give an ultimate grade when it is no longer possible for us to directly educate our students. When that time finally arrives, when the last item of the portfolio has been reviewed, it is time to sum up the performance to date. But we "sum" only figuratively. The most valid grade relates to the teacher's holistic understanding of the student as writer. The question is this: Given the expectations we can have for students at their age and stage, has a given individual's service to intended audiences been "excellent, good, fair or poor?" In a monologic WAC program, formal assessments offer students grounds for smugness or rancor. In a dialogic WAC program, formal assessments offer them grounds for growth.

A most effective strategy in fostering this kind of growth are rubrics which provide information to the student writer, not merely a grade. A rubric of general qualities might look like the following:

Excellent (A): A great pleasure to read and share, this writing excites the reader by how well it achieves the purposes required by the assignment.

Good (B): Well worth reading, this writing makes it easy for the reader to gain new experiences and knowledge and to respect the writer's point of view.

Fair (C): Not so good, but not poor, this writing gives us something for our efforts but not as much or as well as readers have a right to expect.

Poor (D): Lacking significant thought and hard to understand. Typically such writing has inaccurate word choice, weird syntax, grammatical errors and mispunctuation.

Failing (F): Not enough of the assignment was accomplished to warrant evaluation. The purpose is not clear, and the intended audience is not served.

Examples of more specific rubrics can be found in those designed for the earth science and psychology assignments described earlier in this chapter.

A Rubric for the Sample Earth Science Assignment

Excellent: Makes the members of the city council very grateful the writer-speaker showed up. The members will be impressed at how clear the points are, with what good sense the points were selected and organized, and how well standard English was used. An excellent paper will make city council members proud to represent citizens such as the writer.

Good: Presents all essential information clearly. The audience will have few if any questions about the paper's content and will find it easy to remember main points. They may come upon some problems with language, but these will not distract them. They will feel the time they have given to the statement has benefited the city.

Fair: Gives most of the information the council members need, but does not make it easy to understand or remember. The audience may have to ask questions to understand what the writer means in certain places. Some language usage and sentence structure may puzzle the audience.

Poor: Does not give members of the city council the most important information they need. Some points may be significant, but they may be worded ungrammatically or inaccurately or in sentences hard to figure out. When the members will have finished with a poor statement, they will wish it could have been clearer, more to the point, more thorough, or easier to see how the points make sense together.

Failing: Does not help at all. The audience may feel the presentation should not have been on the agenda.

A Rubric for the Sample Psychology Assignment

Excellent: Interests readers so much and gives them such a clear idea of how psychological theories can inform our daily lives, that they will want to read more of the writer's ideas. After they finish reading, they will find it easy to remember the main points and examples. There will be too few grammatical errors to distract readers.

Good: Helps readers understand a theory of human motivation and makes them comfortable with the idea that psychology applies to our daily lives in interesting, helpful ways. Although there may be some problems with individual words and sentences, these will not get in the way of the main content: Readers finish the essay without having to stop to figure out what certain parts mean.

Fair: Applies a theory of motivation to the story, but leaves the reader with incomplete understanding. The sentences may make the reader pause to figure out what they mean. Readers get something from the text, but not as much as they need to feel interested and well informed.

Poor: In important places, makes the reader wonder what the writer means. Information needed to understand the subject is either missing or incomplete. When the members will have finished with a poor statement, they will wish it could have been clearer, more to the point, more thorough, or easier to see how the points make sense together. Readers of a poor paper might be discouraged from turning to psychology for interesting ways of understanding behavior.

Failing: Readers have real trouble figuring out what the text is about. They may be inclined not to finish the piece.

Chapter 20

Weaving and Stitching to Assess Writing Across the Curriculum

Shirley J. McCann

We were all weaving our way through the process wanting to make a difference, believing that students' information writing is important and that together we could make a difference. During our off-campus curriculum and staff development time for assessing and developing writing, we bantered, debated, questioned, told stories and laughed sometimes hysterically, especially on the two days that our rookie teachers were frisked as they entered the government building with their laptop computers! We were all there trying to thread together the writing until it resembled the finest tapestry. But what was going on? Who was involved? How was it done? How did it go? During the 1998-99 school year, Robinson Secondary School began a three-year informational writing initiative in which cross-disciplinary teachers collaborated to find out about the writing competencies of their high school students. The initiative included writing assessments, curriculum and staff development in writing, and a teacher researcher project.

The project included ninth grade teaching teams from five core subjects, Algebra, Biology, English, Foreign Language, Geometry, and World History plus a multidisciplinary writing team with representatives from each of the core subject teams. The premise was that if all disciplines require information writing and teachers analyze and critically review that writing collaboratively, students will realize that good writing is essential in every subject. Throughout the year, the teachers met together to assess writing samples collected from assigned subject writing, current instructional strategies used in each core subject, and the implementation of the writing process in the classroom.

Time for curriculum and staff development was provided off-campus for all participants. The five core subject teams analyzed student writing samples, developed appropriate instructional strategies, writing tools, and rubrics based upon the results of the teams' assessment of the writing samples .In addition to the core teams, the multidisciplinary writing team participated in in-house staff and curriculum development to identify and develop writing strategies across subjects, to develop universal writing rubrics, and to conduct a schoolwide assessment of writing samples.

The interrelationship among the different teams and the support of the foreign language department, who were already involved in the development of rubrics, the liaison from the school system's Office of Testing, Planning and Evaluation, and the writing coordinator are depicted in Figure 1. The weaving together of ideas from all of the disciplines was the primary factor that contributed to the success of the project. All of the findings and recommendations of the core subject teams and the multidisciplinary team were woven across teams through team leaders, written summaries of findings, conversations with teachers, and on-going collaborations with the liaison from the Office of Planning, Testing, and Evaluation.

As the coordinator of the writing project, I incorporated an action research model which was guided by three research questions, "What's going on?" "What needs to be done?" and "How do we get there?" My goal was to have a collegial, teacher-driven approach to the assessment procedure. I believe strongly that if teachers are given time to reflect, analyze, and plan, that the instructional outcomes are more meaningful, valuable, and appreciated. My approach was relatively simple: weaving and threading ideas, strategies, and methodologies across subjects and teachers, carrying information from team to team, watching and waiting for things to occur, acting and planning on the basis of this data, and lastly, rejoicing when so many good things happened.

The chapter describes the process of implementing the initiative, and the findings and implications of this in-house approach to assessment, curriculum and staff development, and teacher research. Specifically, I address the implementation plan, data, collection and analysis, in-house curriculum and staff development, multidisciplinary and core team discoveries, summary of overall project findings, and the role and discoveries of the writing coordinator (see Figure 1).

The Implementation Plan

The writing initiative began during the 1998-99 school year and will continue for the next three years. The initial steps included:

- Coordination with school planning team, department chairs, and administrators
- Formal presentation of the three year plan to the five core content teams
- Development of an in-house approach to evaluating schoolwide informational writing
- Development of in-house curriculum and staff development for planning informational writing strategies, tools, and rubrics
- Establishment of a summer curriculum development workshop to design an on-line Robinson conference site with teacher-developed writing lessons, writing process strategies, and writing rubrics.
- Coordination with the Office of Planning, Testing and Evaluation liaison, school planning team, and teacher researcher model.
- Establishment of a Teacher Researcher group at Robinson to model the school planning process with an action research approach.

Data collection analysis

The first year of the three-year plan focused on the core subjects at the ninth grade level and in subsequent years will include the tenth and eleventh grades. The overall year's plan consists of three stages:

Figure 1
Interrelationship: Core, Multidisciplinary, and Instructional Support Teams

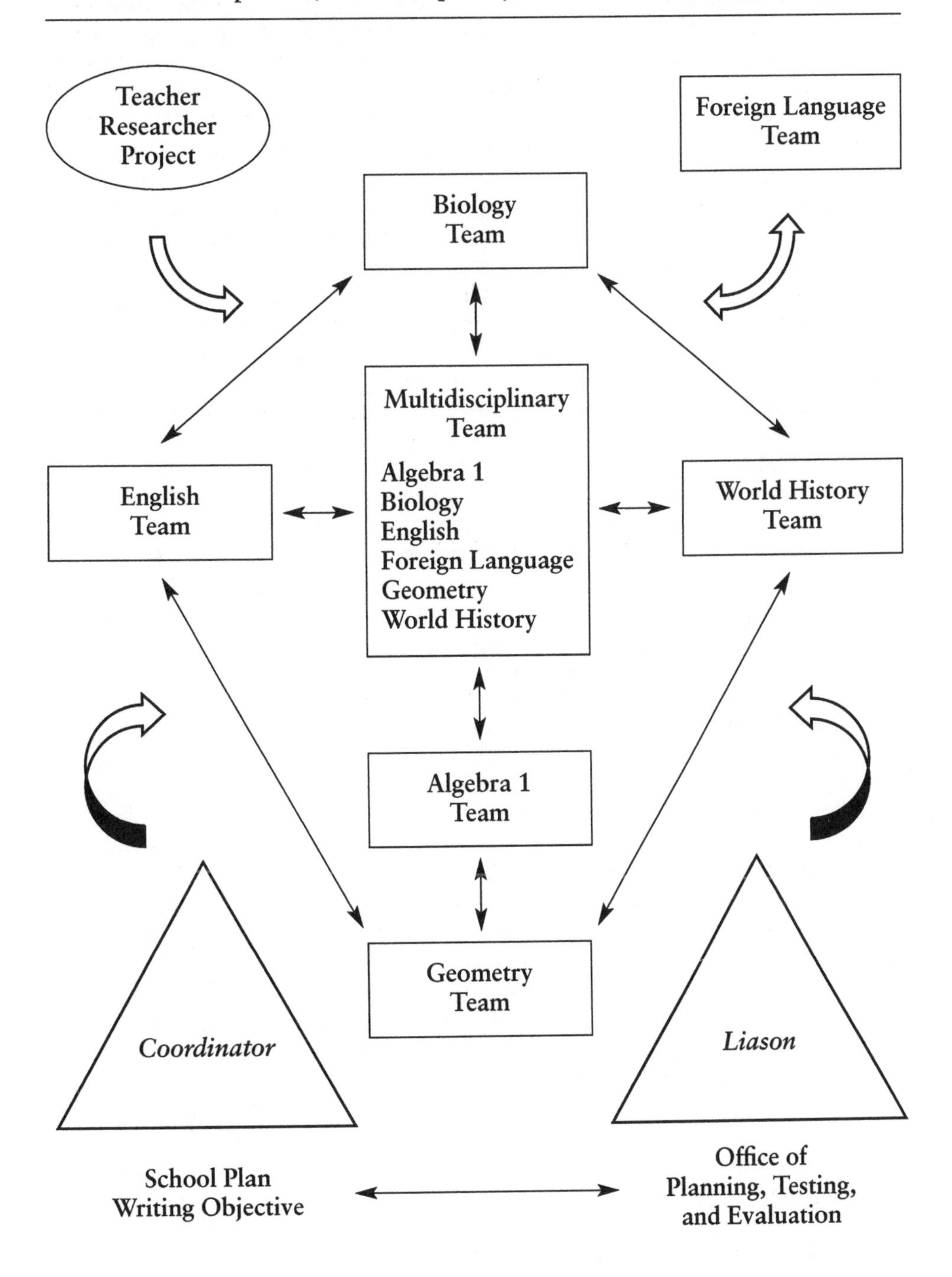

Baseline data	Collection of three writing samples (top, middle, bottom) from each core teacher to identify current content writing assignments, tools used to assist student writers, and criteria used for assessment.
1st semester data	Based on the baseline analysis, core-teaching teams selected a particular type of writing to assign to students and designed rubrics to assess the writing. Three writing samples (top, middle, bottom) were collected from each core teacher. Teachers reviewed the samples based upon the criteria identified in the rubric.
2nd semester data	Based on the 1st semester analysis, core teaching teams selected new writing assignments, modified first semester writing assignments, and enhanced current writing assignments with pre-write or editing tools.

Data was collected from the multidisciplinary meetings, core team meetings, individual conversations with teachers, and discussions with Office of Planning and Evaluation liaison. The analysis entailed primarily a constant-comparison approach; that is, looking at previous data to determine differences and similarities and planning new data collection based on the results. This analysis and planning was repeated throughout the assessment process. For example, each of the core teams examined its baseline writing samples to discover the types and forms of writing that were assigned to students in different subjects. Through the comparison of the baseline writings, teachers recognized patterns of writing behaviors that existed across all of the student writings. From this analysis, teachers identified specific writing assignments that each core subject would develop for its students for the first semester.

Upon the completion of the first semester writing assignment, the teachers again through a constant-comparison approach examined the first semester writing samples by contrasting their assumptions about student writing with the students' actual writing results. Teachers reviewed differences and similarities among the highly effective, effective, and least effective writers. Based on the results of this analysis, the teachers identified the writing behaviors that they would focus on for the second semester.

Using the same approach, they collected, ranked and examined the second semester writing samples. The process became more extensive because the second semester writing samples were not only examined, but also reviewed for the differences and similarities between the first and second writing assignments. The results of this assessment provided direction for next year's writing emphasis within each core subject.

Teachers seldom engage in this type of formal assessment of students' work with their colleagues because of their regimented schedules. Even when they are given staff development days, often the objectives are determined by county or state mandated agendas. The opportunity for in-house staff and curriculum development at Robinson, however, gave teachers the opportunity to focus on writing skills directly related to their students and their classroom. They were able to share with other teachers at the school their concerns about student writing, and to discover common issues across and within disciplines.

In-House Curriculum and Staff Development

An important aspect of the writing initiative at Robinson was the in-house staff and curriculum development component. Three features of the approach affected the successful completion of the first year of the project. First, a teacher-driven approach promoted an exchange of concerns and observations related to student writing, verification of teacher beliefs through a systematic assessment of student writing, and teacher-designed strategies to improve student writing. Second, teachers were given released time during the school day to critically examine student writings. Funding for substitutes was acquired through a county teacher collaboration project, which encourages teachers to mentor with other teachers to share successful teaching techniques and methodology. Third, an action research model was followed for the staff and curriculum sessions. All of the decisions about student writing included a systematic approach of data collection, analysis, and development of instructional programs based upon the results of data findings.

The teacher evaluations indicated that the sessions were productive and meaningful because they had uninterrupted time to delve into the essentials of teaching and learning that often become secondary because of the minimal opportunities for reflection and introspection. If given the opportunity to critically examine student performance and progress, then teachers are able to identify patterns of learning and behaviors occurring in their classroom and to adjust their instructional programs accordingly.

Multidisciplinary team discoveries

As part of the writing initiative, a multidisciplinary team of teachers was established to develop consistent writing guidelines across subjects. The team's primary focus was to identify the elements of the writing process unique to their curriculum and to distinguish differences among core subject writings. The eventual outcome was to develop universal criteria for assessing information writing in all core subjects.

Off-campus curriculum and staff development was provided for the team. The purpose of the off-campus staff development day given to each core subject was to identify the components and implications of the writing process across disciplines, to examine previously developed tools and rubrics, and to develop individual content specific rubrics and a universal rubric for assessing student writing.

The team identified the basic elements of the writing process related to their subject. The results of the team analysis of the writing process as they were written on newsprint and hung on the wall of our meeting room are listed in Figure 2.

All five core subjects felt that pre-writing was essential to getting students to maintain a central focus for their writing. For instance, in math the teachers said that when students are writing an explanation for a procedure for completing a problem, the pre-write activities concentrate on the identification of the appropriate terms and the information given. If students correctly perform this preliminary step, they are prepared to solve the problem.

In social studies, the teachers indicated that the pre-write steps of completing a library report require previous research and/or discussion related to the topic,

Figure 2
Notes from Multidisciplinary Team's Discussion of the Writing Process

Prewriting

- Identify assignment objectives via rubrics
- Identify reader (audience)
- Do research
- Take notes
- Outline and prioritize
- Use graphic organizers
- Discuss ideas and related concepts
- Choose appropriate voice
- Decide on the purpose
- Identify the problem
- Use appropriate language of the discipline
- Choose focus and/or controlling idea
- Identify given information
- Free write

Drafting

- Structure, organize, write prewriting materials into sentences and paragraphs
- Explain and elaborate ideas through illustrations, examples, and facts
- Make connections between major ideas and supporting details
- Include all requirements of the assignment
- Add new approaches, evidence or solutions
- Include documentation or citations

Revising/Editing

- Check logic.... Does it make sense?
- Rearrange paragraphs for organization and clarity
- Make connections and transitions
- Read and re-read out loud... Does it sound right?
- Use peer, teacher, and other adult editing
- Use grammar and usage handbook and dictionary
- Check punctuation and word choice
- Revise and/or reselect ideas
- Check style and voice
- Use grammar and spellcheck

Final copy

- Prepare paper to go public
- Make legible
- Check draft against rubric and assignment

Note: All figures as they appear in the paper are drafts and are revised and edited through use in the classroom.

narrowing the topic, and arranging ideas through the use of graphic organizers. They also noted that this step must be incorporated into the writing process through direct instruction and with writing aids that assist the writer in limiting, arranging, and ultimately focusing on a central idea.

The science teachers indicated that their pre-write steps in writing a lab report were the purpose and hypothesis steps of the lab. They reported that this step is essential to guide the student through the interpretation and analysis of the lab. They, too, agreed that direct instruction and a guided activity are essential.

All of the core teachers agreed that organization is the key to a comprehensive and cohesive piece of informational writing. They believed that the orderly presentation of ideas with supportive details is the essence of coherent and substantiated writing. Additionally, they emphasized the importance of making connections between ideas through the use of transitional devices. The English and social studies teachers mentioned the importance of documentation of sources within the paper to verify references. They felt that students should follow a consistent format for documenting their sources.

All teachers said the revising and editing stage is crucial. They listed different strategies, such as reading out loud, checking with another adult or peer, and using a grammar and spell check. They suggested that students ask questions to see if their writing makes sense, "Is my procedure clearly defined?" "Is the reasoning logically derived?" "Do the main points support the thesis?" and "Is there adequate evidence to support the thesis?" In the last step of the writing process, the submission of the final copy of the paper, the teachers stressed the importance of following the specific guidelines for the writing assignment. They also emphasized the bottom-line of ink (except in math), legibility, neatness, and if typed, a twelve point font. They referred to this stage as "going public."

The team examined writing "tools," teaching strategies that assist students with the entire writing process. In particular, they discussed pre-writing and editing techniques. They expressed concerns that student writing often appeared incoherent and disconnected. They mentioned that when they attempt to suggest a preliminary organizational step before writing that many students indicate that it is unnecessary. Several teachers said that most students would complete prewriting only if required.

As a result, the team decided that more deliberate planning tools needed to be introduced to students when given writing assignments. The team concluded that differences in pre-write activities depend upon the topic and the type of writing assignment. For example, in world history, before writing an essay related to the cultural aspects of India, students might participate in a scenario related to the culture of a country as a pre-write activity. As they discover elements related to India, they acquire knowledge to formulate a thesis for writing an essay. The team reviewed graphic organizers, concept guides, advanced organizers and planners that assist students in developing a topic, identifying relationships between and among ideas, and logically developing a thesis. For example, in Figure 3, three-comparison/contrast organizers developed by the world history team demonstrates to students a format for organizing their thoughts before they begin to write. The three-prewriting activities assist students in organizing their ideas through a categorizing, questioning, and sequencing approach. This type of organizer also models metacognitive thought processes, which helps students systematically organize their ideas prior to writing.

Figure 3
(a) Pre-Writing

Feudalism Comparison Chart	
Europe	**Japan**
Who rules the government?	Who rules the government?
How is the ruler chosen?	How is the ruler chosen?
Who works for the ruler?	Who works for the ruler?
What do you call the land they own?	What do you call the land they own?
What type of building do they have on their land?	What type of building do they have on their land?
What is the name of the warriors?	What is the name of the warriors?
What is the code of duty for the warriors?	What is the code of duty for the warriors?
What must warriors do who follow this code?	What must warriors do who follow this code?
What type of weapons do the warriors use?	What type of weapons do the warriors use?
What is the reward for being a loyal warrior?	What is the reward for being a loyal warrior?
Whom do the warriors fight? Is the threat from foreign invaders or civil war?	Whom do the warriors fight? Is the threat from foreign invaders or civil war?
How was this society ordered?	How was this society ordered?
What was the role of women in this society?	What was the role of women in this society?
What was the religion?	What was the religion?
What type of economy did this society have?	What type of economy did this society have?

Figure 3 (cont.)
(b) Prewriting

CHART ANALYSIS QUESTIONS

Answer the following questions in complete sentences. Use the information on your Feudalism Comparison Chart to determine the answer. Some questions may have more comprehensive answers than other questions.

1. What were the *similarities* between the government in Europe and the government in Japan?

 ____

 ____

2. What were the differences between the government in Europe and the government in Japan?

 ____

 ____

3. What were the similarities between the European and Japanese warriors, their codes, their weapons, their rewards for service, and their enemies?

 ____

 ____

4. What were the differences between the European and Japanese warriors, their codes, their weapons, their rewards for service, and their enemies?

 ____

 ____

5. What were the similarities between European and Japanese societies and the role of women in those societies?

 ____

 ____

6. What were the differences between European and Japanese societies and the role of women in those societies?

 ____

 ____

7. How were the religions in Europe and Japan similar or different?

 ____

 ____

Figure 3 (cont.)
(b) Prewriting

---

8. How were the economies in Europe and Japan similar or different?

____

____

(c) Prewriting

Annotated Outline

THE QUESTION: Examine your Chart Analysis Question sheet. The answers on your chart demonstrate that there were many similarities and differences between European and Japanese Feudalism. Now, the question is this: how do you compare European and Japanese feudalism? In your judgment, what are more significant—the similarities or the differences?

YOUR ANSWER: There is no right or wrong answer. You must examine your chart analysis answers and make a decision. If you judge that the similarities between European and Japanese feudalism are more significant, then this is the position which you must prove in your paper. On the other hand, if you decide that the differences were more important, then you must prove that position in your paper.

YOUR THESIS: Your answer is the thesis. It is the main point which you want to prove. Therefore, your thesis is either that European and Japanese feudalism were primarily similar or European and Japanese feudalism were primarily different. Your paper will prove one position or the other.

INTRODUCTION: Before you state your thesis, you must give the reader some background. You should tell the reader that feudalism existed in both Europe and Japan. You should provide a short and general description of feudalism in these regions. Also, you should make the reader aware that there were similarities and differences between European and Japanese feudalism. In your introduction, you are moving from the general back towards the specific.

____

____

____

____

____

____

Figure 3 (cont.)
(c) Prewriting

THESIS: The last sentence in your introductory paragraph is your thesis. It tells the reader the specific position which you will prove in this paper.

____

____

____

SUPPORTING PARAGRAPHS: Now your job is to persuade someone who reads your paper that you made a good judgment. You want the reader to agree with your thesis. Therefore, you must give the reader evidence which will persuade him or her. The purpose of the next three paragraphs is to provide evidence or support for your thesis. Each supporting paragraph should begin with a topic sentence.

TOPIC SENTENCES: Topic sentences tell the reader how a paragraph is going to support or prove the thesis. Therefore, your topic sentences should tell the reader how that paragraph is going to demonstrate the similarities or differences of European and Japanese feudalism.

First Supporting Paragraph

First Topic Sentence: State here how European and Japanese feudalism were similar (or different) using information from your chart analysis sheet.

____

____

Supporting Sentences: Now you must support your topic sentence. You need to provide several specific examples which prove the above topic sentence.

- ____________________________________
- ____________________________________
- ____________________________________

Second Supporting Paragraph:

____

____

- ____________________________________
- ____________________________________
- ____________________________________

Figure 3 (cont.)
(c) Prewriting

Third Supporting Paragraph:

____

____

❖ ______________________________________

❖ ______________________________________

❖ ______________________________________

Concluding Paragraph: This paragraph should restate your theses and review your evidence. It should move from the specific to the general.

____

____

____

____

____

____

The team felt that students were not routinely editing and proofreading their papers. They appeared to use spell check on the computer, but often did not check their writing for organization, mechanics, form, or content accuracy. As teachers conversed with students regarding this aspect of the writing process, the students readily admitted that they are inclined to accept their first draft as their final draft. Furthermore, some of the team members reported that when students do peer editing, their recommendations are generally non-constructive and lack substance.

After this discussion, the team decided to consider strategies to promote the use of editing and proofreading. They previewed different examples of checklists that English teachers use with their students. The English teachers reported, however, that students often do not take the checklist seriously and simply check criteria with minimal attention to the task. One member of the team, a biology teacher, distributed a peer-editing strategy that he developed which included more interactions on the student's part. The guidelines were developed for a letter that the student had to write to a famous scientist. As shown in Figure 4 students were required to justify their responses and cite explicit references in the paper to justify their critique of the paper.

Figure 4
Peer Editing Guidesheet

Biology Conclusion Writing

Name of writer ______________________________

Name of reader ______________________________

Directions: Read the conclusion carefully and use the checklist to decide if the conclusion is complete. Check YES or NO and give reasons under the comments column to support your answer.

1. Is the purpose of the lab stated? ___ Yes ___ No	Comments:
2. Is the hypothesis stated? ___ Yes ___ No	Comments:
3. Is there a description of the data and lab results? ___ Yes ___ No	Comments:
4. Is there a comparison of the hypothesis and actual results? ___ Yes ___ No	Comments:
5. Is there a comparison of the student's lab results with the expected results of the experiment? ___ Yes ___ No	Comments:
6. Is there a statement about the accuracy of the student or class results? ___ Yes ___ No	Comments:
7. Is there an explanation of the causes of experimental error? ___ Yes ___ No	Comments:
8. Does the final statement summarize the answer to the problem question? ___ Yes ___ No	Comments:

The English teacher on the team developed an interactive peer-editing sheet that placed the student/author in a constructive role as editor. As seen in Figure 5, the student editor is asked to defend, verify and identify within the writing specific elements that need revision.

Figure 5
Peer Editing

English

Author's Name ________________ Editor's Name ________________

Literary Essay: Editing

1. Is the essay written in present tense (with the possible exception of quotations)? If there are exceptions, please note them.

2. Is the essay written in third person point of view? (*No* I, me, we, you, your, etc.) If there are exceptions, please note them below.

3. Is there a title? Write it.

4. Write the paper's thesis statement.

5. Introduction: How did the writer get the reader's attention and introduce the topic? Did the writer effectively lead to the thesis statement? Was the thesis the last sentence of the introduction?

6. Body Paragraphs: Write the topic sentence of each body paragraph. Does the entire paragraph develop this topic? If not, note the problem. Did the writer use paraphrases or quotations to support ideas? Did the writer effectively summarize, explain, analyze, and give commentary about ideas? Was the paragraph concluded with an appropriate concluding sentence? For each body paragraph, please answer the questions asked above.

Figure 5 (cont.)
Peer Editing

7. Concluding Paragraph: Did the concluding paragraph begin with a restatement of the thesis? Was the topic summarized and main points reiterated? Did the writer leave the reader with a strong impression of the validity of points made?

8. Write the restated thesis statement.

9. Indicate the technique used to summarize and reiterate main points. How did the reader leave you with a favorable impression?

10. Sentence Structure:

    Did the writer have any run-on sentences? If so, write them below.

    Did the writer have any fragments? If so, write them below.

    Did the writer have any misspelled words? If so, write them below.

    Did the writer use a variety of sentence structures and sentence beginnings? Write three varied structures below.

    Did the writer use descriptive adjectives and effective adverbs? Write three examples of each below.

Consistent writing guidelines

Through the discovery of similarities across disciplines the team of teachers realized that competent student writing could be reinforced if teachers emphasized consistent writing guidelines in all core subjects. For instance, if all teachers follow similar approaches for writing a thesis statement, then students will not only have practice in formulating thesis statements with different topics, but also with different subjects. The team also recognized that in addition to the development of similar instructional approaches that the establishment of universal criteria for evaluating student writing would provide a framework of expectations for students. As a result, the team developed drafts of both subject specific rubrics and a universal rubric which are available on the Rams Writing Conference site for feedback from the Robinson faculty. (Access to the Ram's Writing Conference is currently restricted to Robinson faculty and resides on the school district's employee e-mail system.)

The generic rubric is displayed in Figure 6. Although the rubric is not appropriate for all writing assignments, it offers a basic organizational structure for informational writing.

Figure 6
Rams Ⓡiting Rubric

Holistic View	
4	**Exceeds expectations, fully accomplishes the task, highly effective** Highly effective and accurate content, exact vocabulary Unity achieved through highly effective organization and focused central idea Highly effective, detailed supporting evidence appropriate to the assignment Consistent correct use of sentence structure, spelling, and mechanics
3	**Meets expectations, accomplishes the task, effective** Effective and accurate content and correct vocabulary Effective organization and focused central idea Substantial development with supporting evidence appropriate to the assignment Usual correct use of sentence structure, spelling, and mechanics
2	**Almost meets expectations, limited accomplishment, moderately effective** Partially accurate content and vocabulary Partially effective organization, stated central idea Partial development and/or some inappropriate supporting information Occasional correct use of sentence structure, spelling, and mechanics
1	**Meets very few expectations, engaged the task, ineffective** Inaccurate content and vocabulary Ineffective organization, unfocused central idea Minimal development and little or no supporting information Rare or sporadic correct use of sentence structure, spelling, and mechanics
0	**Meets no expectations, fails to accomplish the task**

Figure 6 (cont.)
Rams Ⓡiting Rubric

Analytic View

Content (includes concepts and vocabulary)

4 Highly effective and accurate content, exact vocabulary
3 Effective and accurate content and correct vocabulary
2 Partially accurate content and vocabulary
1 Inaccurate content and vocabulary
0 No understanding of content, vocabulary used incorrectly

Unity (includes organization, central idea, transitions, and purpose)

4 Highly effective organization, focused central idea
3 Effective organization, focused central idea
2 Partially effective organization, stated central idea
1 Ineffective organization, unfocused central idea
0 No central idea or organization pattern discernible

Supporting Evidence (includes examples, illustrations, reasons, events, and documentation)

4 Highly effective, detailed supporting evidence appropriate to the assignment
3 Substantial development with supporting evidence appropriate to the assignment
2 Partial development and/or some inappropriate supporting information
1 Minimal development and little or no supporting information
0 No development

Control of Language (includes sentence structure, spelling, mechanics

4 Consistent correct use of sentence structure, spelling, and mechanics
3 Usual correct use of sentence structure, spelling, and mechanics
2 Occasional correct use of sentence structure, spelling, and mechanics
1 Rare or sporadic correct use of sentence structure, spelling, and mechanics
0 Excessive errors in sentence structure, spelling, and mechanics

Subject differences and similarities

Through the multidisciplinary team meetings, both similarities and differences were identified across the core subjects. For example, in writing a proof in geometry, a student writer is expected to explain a theorem, which entails a detailed explanation of the process, logical supports to verify premise, and a final conclusion to solidify the premise statement. In writing a persuasive essay in world history, however, students are expected to persuade or convince based on a thesis statement, but the approach follows the same syllogistic reasoning. In both instances, the writers build a case with support to verify their premise or thesis.

In contrast, in foreign language, students are expected to compose descriptive paragraphs that do not require expanded thesis statements and detailed support. The writing assignment, however, does focus on the logical development of ideas, but the emphasis is placed on coherence, unity and grammar. For example, in writing about themselves, students are asked to use descriptive words and phrases that include their friends, family and personal interests. They are expected to write in complete sentences, use appropriate punctuation, and previously acquired vocabulary.

In English, the focus also is on coherent writing, including a logical development of ideas supported with evidence and, of course, correct grammar, but the writing is more in depth than foreign language, since the student is proficient in the language. For example, when students write character sketches, they establish a controlling idea and develop a sequence of major points, which elaborate upon details that support the thesis.

The team's primary discovery was that many of the concerns and requirements across disciplines were alike. All teachers felt that writing was an essential part of their subject. They all stressed the importance of students writing cohesively and organizing their thoughts in a logical way. During the process of identifying criteria for assessing writing, although the delineation of the specifics for a comprehensive writing appeared to take different directions for each subject, the emphasis was similar.

Overview of Core Teams' Discoveries and Findings

The core teams consisted of groups of teachers from the ninth grade core subjects—Biology, Algebra, Geometry, World History, English, and Level 1 Foreign Language. The responsibility of the team members was to assess student writing within their discipline and to develop writing strategies, lessons, and rubrics to enhance student writing. They examined baseline, first semester, and second semester writing samples from each of their students.

Through an analysis of the baseline sample papers, the core teams identified the aspects of the writing process that they needed to focus upon in order to assist students with their assignments. Subsequently, after reviewing the first semester writing assignments, the core teams selected the second writing assignments based upon their analysis of the first semester sample writings. The team members did all of the decision- making and the selection of writing, types, strategies, and tools was the result of the critical assessment of the student writing.

Biology team

The biology team recognized that students needed to become better writers and that teachers need to provide writing samples to assist students in recognizing the expectations for writing effectively. As a result, after the analysis of the first semester writing assignment, which was the writing of a comprehensive lab conclusion, the biology team decided that the rubric which they developed for the first semester writing assignment was not enough and that the students needed to see models of writing in relationship to the rubrics. Consequently, for the second semester writing assignment, they provided sample conclusion writing to demonstrate effective and ineffective conclusion writing. They reviewed a lab that students had previously completed and analyzed three different conclusions as illustrated in Figure 7. The students reviewed each of the writing samples with the rubric shown in Figure 8. Through this activity, students were able to recognize differences among the sample writings and to learn to incorporate the approriate performance criteria for writing a lab conclusion.

Figure 7
Sample Lab Conclusion: Time and Absorption

Complete conclusions:

The purpose of the lab was to test the amount of absorption of one type of paper towel strip using different time intervals. The data clearly shows that more absorption occurs the longer the towel strip is left in the liquid. A possible explanation of these results is the amount of fibers in the paper towel strips that allow for absorption. Possible sources of error include paper towel strips being unevenly cut and inaccurate timing. To solve these problems the paper towels need to be cut into evenly measured strips. Massing the towel strips might give information regarding the amount of the fibers in a single paper towel strip that allows for absorption. Using a stop watch at interval lab stations would allow for more accurate timing.

Partially Complete:

Allowing more time for the fibers to absorb the liquid allows for a higher absorption concentration. Possible sources of error include paper towel strips being unevenly cut and inaccurate timing. The paper towels need to be cut into evenly measured strips. Massing the towel strips might give added information about the absorbency of the fibers. Using a stop watch might allow for most accurate timing.

Incomplete conclusion:

First we collected our materials. We cut the paper towels into strips, and dunked them into the cups of water. Our time keeper told us when to remove the strips. We replaced each time variable three times. We filled in our data chart and answered the questions at the end of the lab. We all had a job to do in this lab. Everyone in the lab worked very hard.

Figure 8
Scoring Rubric

Name: ______________________
Lab: ______________________
Date: ______________________
Quarter: ______________________

Biology Conclusion Rubric				Score
Answer the Hypothesis or Purpose	Completely 3	Partially 2	Not At All 1	
Explanation of Results	Completely 3	Partially 2	Not At All 1	
Sources of Error/ Improvements	Completely 3	Partially 2	Not At All 1	
Presentation (Clarity of thoughts and ideas, legible)	Acceptable 1	Not Acceptable 0		
Mechanics (Complete sentences, spelling, punctuation, capitalization)	Acceptable 1	Not Acceptable 0		
Total Score				

Best part of writing:

Suggestions for improvement:

World history team

The world history team also discovered writing inadequacies through their examination of their baseline writing samples. The most common error across all of the papers was the students' difficulty in organizing their ideas in a logical order. After assigning students thesis-based essays for the first semester with writing prompts and or questions given to the students, the same phenomenon occurred; students still were writing essays that lacked organization. As a result, the team designed an explicit process lesson that not only assisted the students with organization before they wrote, but also guided them through the prewriting, drafting, and editing processes. The lessons that the teachers developed are included in the Ram Writing Conference site under the district's employee e-mail system. Again, all of these decisions were derived through the team's data analysis and discussion.

Math teams

Most of the math baseline writing assignments were given to students to satisfy the school-wide informational writing objective. The writings were usually not integrated into the math course requirements. They included, for example, an essay about a famous mathematician, a summary statement of a student's progress in math, or a journal entry discussing how students could improve their study habits in math. After a further examination of the writing objective and a realization that writing could possibly improve math problem solving, both the geometry and algebra teams refocused their writing assignments.

During the first semester, the algebra team gave students a writing assignment in which students critically reviewed completed problem solutions and recommended alternative approaches for solving the problem as shown in Figure 9. Teachers introduced the assignment with several model problems that were previously solved. Teachers and students critically reviewed the attempted mathematical solution together; then students were asked to write an analysis of the approach and to suggest alternative solutions. The geometry team's second semester assignment was also aligned with the content requirements. Students were given an assignment to write a cohesive paragraph explaining the logic behind a problem that required knowledge of the measurement of an arc. The assignment sheet and the rubric are shown in Figure 10 A & B.

Figure 9
Algebra 1 Writing Assignment

Linear Systems of Equations

Ashley received this question on an assignment.

Solve this system of equations using the linear combination, substitution, or the graphing method. Show all work. Show an algebraic check. Write your solution as an ordered pair.	$3x + 6y = -15$ $-6x + 4y = -18$

Figure 9 (cont.)
Algebra 1 Writing Assignment

Below is Ashley's work. What method did Ashley use? Explain each step of her work. Did Ashley make any mistakes? If she did make mistakes, explain what was done incorrectly, complete the problem correctly, and explain the correct steps.

$$3x + 6y = -15$$
$$-6x + 4y = -18$$
$$6x + 12y = 30$$
$$\frac{42}{4} + \frac{18}{4} = -15$$
$$\underline{-6x + 4y = -18}$$
$$\frac{16y}{16} = \frac{12}{16}$$

$$-6x + 4\left(\frac{3}{4}\right) = -18$$
$$-6x + 3 = -18$$
$$\frac{-6x}{-6} = \frac{-21}{-6}$$
$$x = \frac{7}{2}$$

Check:

$$3\left(\frac{7}{2}\right) + 6\left(\frac{3}{4}\right) = -15$$
$$\frac{21}{2} + \frac{18}{4} = -15$$
$$\frac{60}{4} = -15$$
$$15 = -15 \ (?)$$

Sample Answers: *Please note: These are unedited versions, typed as written by students.*

Low (Score 1/5):

Ashley used the linear combination method. The first mistake I found on her paper was that I have no clue how she got 12y when +6y + 4y = 10y. So that's where her whole problem started for the answer to y. She should've gotten 6/7. Then solve for x by plugging it in to get -6x + 4(6/7) = -18. Then you get -6x + 24/7 = -18. Then subtract 24/7 by both sides and her answer should've been -6x = -6. Then x = 1. You check for your answer and it should come out right. If it didn't then I know I did something wrong.
But I don't think I got the answer. I needed my calculator to check it.

Middle(Score 3/5):

Ashley used linear combination to solve $\begin{matrix} 3x + 6y = -15 \\ -6x + 4y = -18 \end{matrix}$.

Explanation:

Ashley began by multiplying the first equation by 2. She got 6x+12y=30. But, the thirty should have been a negative thirty. Next, she subtracted the final numbers in each equation and got a fraction, the wrong number. She should have added the two numbers. Ashley used the fraction, by putting it in a completely wrong equation. She then simplified the outcome and made a mistake in that, too.

Figure 9 (cont.)
Algebra 1 Writing Assignment

Ashley's algaebraic check should have told her that the equation was wrong. She came out with a wrong answer and didn't do anything to fix it.

Did well on the first part.

The correct steps are shown below: Should be written in explanation form

(2) $3x + 6y = -15$ $3x + 6(-3) = -15$ $-6(1) + 4(-3) = -18$

$-6x + 4y = -18$ $3x + (-18) = -15$ $-6 + (-12) = -18$

$+18$ $-18 = -18$

$6x + 12y = -30$ $\frac{3x}{3} = \frac{3}{3}$

$-6x + 4y = -18$ $3(1) + 6(-3) = -15$

$\frac{16y}{16y} = \frac{-48}{16}$ $x = 1$ $3 + (-18) = -15$

$-15 = -15$

High Score(5/5):

Ashley started off using linear combinations. When she multiplied everything in the top equation 3x + 6y = -15 she left off the sign on the -30 she got. That messed up the whole problem. What you do is multiply 3x + 6y = -15 and you get 6x + 12y = -30. After that you add the 2 equations together and the 6x + -6x cancel to leave you with 16y = -48. From here you have to get the variable by itself. Divide each side by 16. You get a solution of y = -3.

With y equaling -3 you can now solve for x. Take the bottom equation -6x + 4y = -18 and sub in -3 for y. When this is done the equation becomes -6x + -12 = -18. You have to get the variable x by itself so you have to add 12 to -18. You end up with -6x = -6. Divide both by -6 and get x = 1.

Now you need to check. Sub in the values into the top equation like so: 3(1) + 6(-3) = -15. You get 3 + -18 = -15. 3 + -18 does equal -15 so your answer checks. Now sub in the 2nd equation: -6(1) + 4(-3) = -18. You have a solution of -6x + -12 = -18 and -6 + -12 does equal -18. Both answers check so your solution to the problem is (1,3).

Scoring Rubric
Algebra I Writing Assignment
1st Semester

The rating of a student's response to an item is based on a six point scale from zero to five, with five (5) being the maximum rating given and a rating of zero (0) indicating no response. Specific criteria for awarding a 5, 3, or 1 rating are described below to assist both the student and teacher to assign a rating to the writing sample.

5 **Fully accomplished the task**
- Is complete in responding to all aspects of the question
- Is clear and unambiguous
- Communicates effectively
- Shows mathematical understanding of the problems, ideas, and requirements
- Shows strong reasoning
- Uses grammar and vocabulary correctly
- Focuses on the important elements of the problem

4 **Assign at your discretion to those responses falling between 5-3**

3 **Substantially accomplished the task, an adequate response**
- Is not totally complete in responding to all aspects of the problem
- Shows some deficiencies in understanding the problem
- May present information that is only partially correct
- Uses grammar, language, and mechanics appropriately
- Indicates some understanding of required mathematical ideas, but misconceptions are evident
- Contains computation errors, either major or minor

2 **Assign at your discretion to those responses falling between 3-1**

1 **Engaged the task but with no focus, an inadequate response**
- Attempts but fails to answer or complete the question
- Contains little supporting information
- Includes explanations or reasoning that is not understandable
- Contains major computational errors
- Demonstrates limited to no understanding of the concept, procedure, or application
- Shows copied parts of the problem with no attempt at a solution

0 **No Response**
- The question was left blank
- No attempt was made to solve the problem
- No information was given to allow for any judgment

Figure 10a
Geometry Writing Assignment

Directions: Your answer to the following question should be in the form of a carefully planned paragraph. It will be evaluated according to the rubric on the back of this sheet. While content is important, remember that how you present your ideas is important, too. Pay attention to organization, supporting information (illustrations are always helpful), and correct use of the English language.

Figure 10a (cont.)
Geometry Writing Assignment

It was 1:00 PM on a sultry, Robinson afternoon. Beetle and Bughead happened to glance up at the clock as two ladybugs landed on the minute hand of the classroom clock. (No one has ever been able to satisfactorily explain why the glass was missing from this particular clock.) One of the bugs landed at the very point of the minute hand while the other lighted near the middle. At 1:15 PM, noticing that both bugs were still on the minute hand, Bughead remarked, "I know that both bugs have traveled the same distance because they have both moved 90°."

Beetle disagreed and said, "Something is wrong with your logic. Can't you see that the bug on the end traveled further?"

Question: If you were Beetle, how would you explain this apparent paradox to Bughead?

Sample Answers: ***Please note: These are unedited versions, typed as written by students.***

Low (Score 1 out of 4):

I think one of the bugs stopped and didn't move the other one just kept on going

Low (Score 1 out of 4):

I would tell Bughead that his logic cannot work. While one angle of the Δs is the same, they are similar, they are not congruent. The bug that is further away is on the angle with the larger triangle. Therefore, his distance is farther, although the angles of their 2 Δs are the same.

Low (Score 2 out of 4):

The two ladybugs have traveled the same distance because they are both traveling in arcs with the same midpoint. Although, the lady bug on the end has traveled twice the distance of the one on the middle. It is similar to a track & field has varying starts.

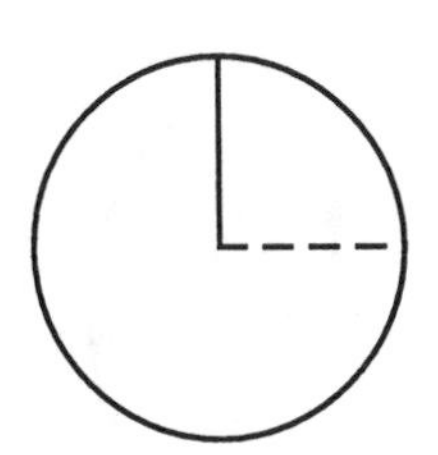

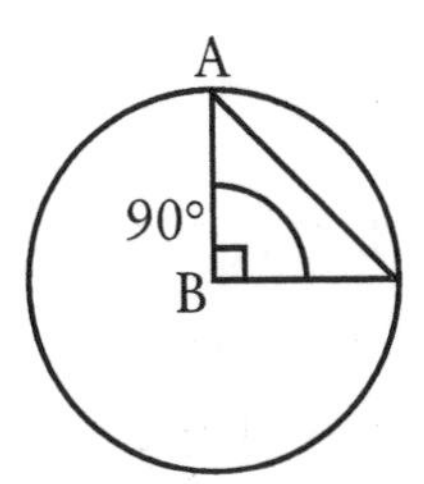

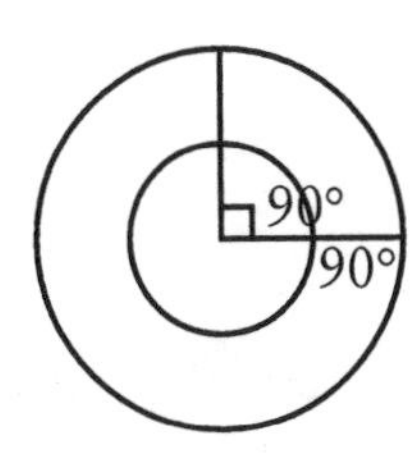

Middle (Score 3 out of 4):

Beetle is correct. The bug on the end of the minute hand is on a bigger circle, therefore the circumference is bigger and the arc is also bigger. We know that the circumference of the circle for the bug on the end is larger than the circumference for the bug in the middle because the radius is larger. The area for circumference

Figure 10a (cont.)
Geometry Writing Assignment

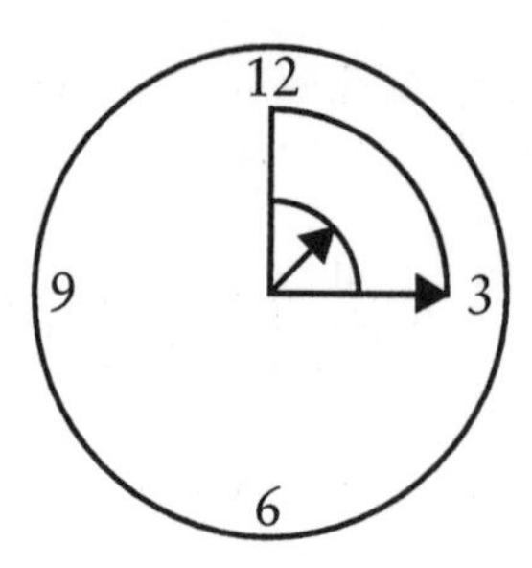

High (Score 4 out of 4):

If I were Beetle I would explain to Bughead that his logic was wrong, the bugs did not travel the same distance at all. The bug on the end traveled much further than the bug in the center of the hands. This is because an ARC LENGTH is different from an ARC MEASURE. An arc measure is measured in degrees, and an arc length or distance is measured in units (inches, centimeters, feet, meters, ect.). My friend Bughead made the mistake of confusing arc length and measure. The bugs did turn the same arc measure, but did not go the same distance. For example, lets make the clock hand 10 inches long. On bug is 10 inches up on the hand and the other is only 5 inches up the hand. To figure out how far each bug traveled, you first must figure out how far they would travel if they went a full rotation around the clock. To find this, you just find the circumference of circles with 5 and 10 inch radii. The circumference of a 10 inch circle is 62.8 inches. The circumference of a 5 inch circle is 31.4 inches. To find the length of an arc, you multiply the circumference by the ratio of the arc measure to the entire circle, which is 360°.

$$62.8 \text{ x } \frac{90}{360} = 62.8 \text{ x } .25 = 15.7 \text{ inches}$$

$$31.4 \text{ x } \frac{90}{360} = 31.4 \text{ z } .25 = 7.85 \text{ inches}$$

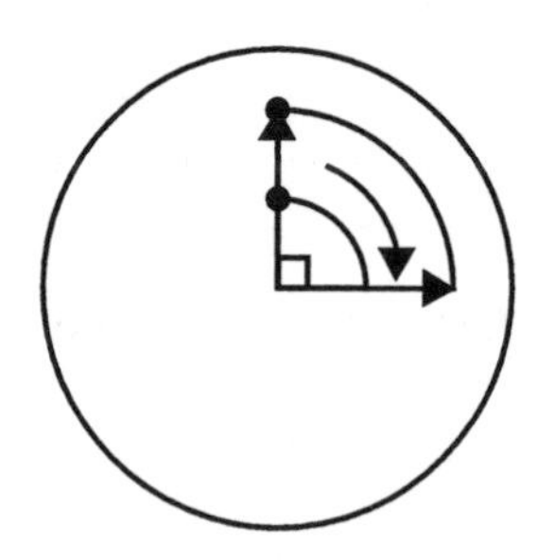

The bug on the end of the minute hand traveled 15.7 inches. The bug in the middle of the minute hand only traveled 7.85 inches, which is half as much as the one on the end traveled.

Figure 10b
Geometry Scoring Rubric

Score 4
Content:
Demonstrates full understanding of the concept, procedure, or application.
Uses content-related vocabulary correctly.

Writing:
Demonstrates clear organization and logical development of ideas.
Supports each central idea with examples, illustrations, reasons, or events appropriate to the task.
Uses grammar, language, spelling, and mechanics correctly.

Score 3
Content:
Demonstrates substantial understanding of the concept, procedure, or application.
Uses content-related vocabulary effectively most of the time.

Writing:
Demonstrates organization and logical development of ideas most of the time.
Does not consistently contain supporting information appropriate to the task.
Uses grammar, language, spelling, and mechanics correctly most of the time.

Score 2
Content:
Demonstrates limited understanding of the concept, procedure, or application.
Uses content-related vocabulary inappropriately.

Writing:
Demonstrates limited ability to organize ideas logically.
Contains little or no supporting information.
Uses grammar, language, spelling, and mechanics ineffectively.

Score 1
Content:
Demonstrates minimal understanding of the concept, procedure, or application.

Writing:
Engaged the task but had no focus.

Score 0
Made no attempt to accomplish the task or gave an irrelevant solution.

As a result of these assignments, the teachers discovered that writing allowed students to concentrate on the logic of each step of the process and to think about the reasoning required solving the problem. If they were unable to explain the problem, they probably were unclear about the way to arrive at the correct solution. Several teachers commented that they observed significant changes in math calculations as a result of the writing requirement.

English team

From the English team's data analysis emerged the discovery that student in-class writing assignments were different from the out-of-class assignments. Although the students do have additional time and resources when they do assignments outside of class, and more editing time is provided, the contrast was significant enough for the teachers to investigate more thoroughly the differences. They eventually decided to design an in-class timed writing, which modeled procedures for preparing, organizing, editing and proofreading. The two "tools" shown in Figure 11a were provided to students for organizing their ideas before they start to write. A model organizer was presented to the students as a guide in developing their own prewrite tool—see Figure 11b. These were metacognitive tools, which assisted the students in seeing the relationships between causes and outcomes as they developed their essays. The prewriting was completed outside of class, but the remaining steps were completed in class.

Figure 11a Cause and Effect
Annotated Outline

Question:

____

____

Thesis Statement (created from your question)

____

____

Major evidence (supporting ideas)

	Causes	Effects
1.	____________________	____________________
	____________________	____________________
2.	____________________	____________________
	____________________	____________________
3.	____________________	____________________
	____________________	____________________

Figure 11a Cause and Effect (cont.)
Annotated Outline

Conclusions: (Restatement of thesis, echoes from main points, closure)

____

____

As a result of.. or ..therefore..

____

____

Figure 11b
Cause and Effect Essay Model Organizer

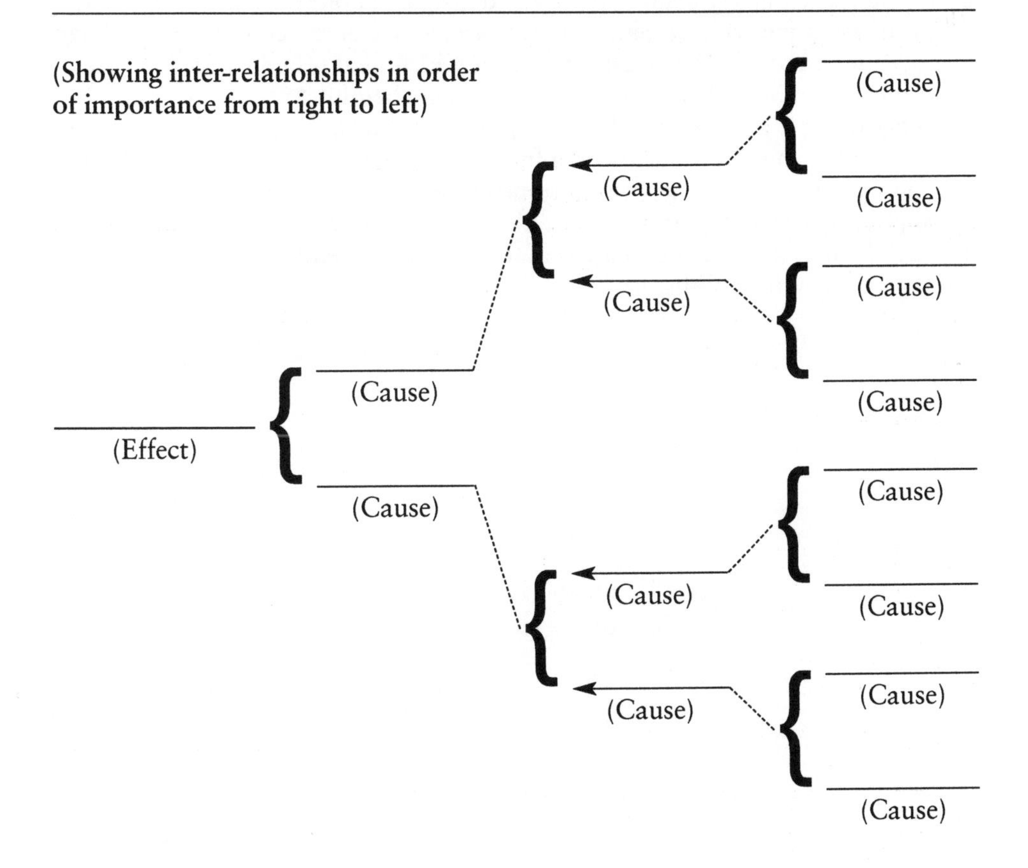

The English team's meetings away from campus allowed teachers to assemble together in a relaxed way and to focus on "What's going on" with their student writing. It was the opportunity for team discussion and data analysis that provided the forum for teachers to discover that student writings were somewhat different in-class vs out-of-class. Perhaps the finding of in-class vs out-of-class may have been mentioned previously in the faculty room over lunch, but ended with the discussion, simply because of teachers' limited time for common sharing and exchanging of ideas.

Foreign language

The foreign language department was already engaged in a four-year project with writing and the assessment of writing. They had developed writing rubrics and were already using writing prompts and field testing county-wide rubrics. Since they were ahead of the other core subjects, they were extremely helpful in a variety of different ways in supporting the school's plan. They provided examples of county-wide rubrics, which were organized as both analytical and primary trait rubrics, for the other core teams to examine as a model.

A representative from the foreign language department also was a member of the multidisciplinary team and provided insights about the use of rubrics as a means of assessing writing. Since she was a member of the county-wide foreign language instructional development project which field tested rubrics for use in the classroom rubrics, her support was extremely helpful.

Since the foreign language department had used a field-tested rubric, they decided to collect more formalized data from the student writing. The record keeping chart used to report the scoring results is shown in Figure 12. The results of the analysis gave the department a profile of the writing skills of the students and assisted them in deciding upon areas that they need to reinforce with students to improve their writing skills.

Figure 12
Task Scoring Rubric

(Teacher's Name Here)															
	Exceeds Expectations					Meets Expectations					Does Not Meet Expectations				
Period #															
Task Score															
RUBRIC CATEGORIES:															
Task Completion															
Comprehensibility															
Vocabulary															
Grammar															
Mechanics															
Level of Discourse															

Chart by Michael Campana

Discoveries about informational writing

Overall, the baseline data analysis from the Robinson project has revealed that the use of writing in the classroom is related to an individual teacher's prior involvement with writing, knowledge of the writing process, and recognition that writing can enhance subject matter knowledge. English and world history teachers, for example, assign writing every quarter; therefore informational writing is threaded into their content, although their approaches to writing are different. In English, the writings are literary-based essays with documentation based on evidence from the literary piece. In world history, the writings are usually research -based essays with documentation from resources beyond the textbook. In both English and world history, teachers emphasize the importance of organization, supportive and verified details, and conclusive endings, but the implementation is different. The English teachers deliberately design exercises and activities that include procedures for effective writing while typically, the world history teachers remind students about the importance of coherent writing and sometimes include prewrite and editing tools, but not as a distinct and separate lesson.

One of the most significant differences between the English and world history writing assignments is the way the thesis is derived. In English, most of the thesis statements are generated from a perspective question. For example, an essay related to the *Odyssey* requires the writer to critically review the elements of a hero and provide evidence to support heroic traits based upon the writer's or hero's view and perspective. On the other hand, in world history, students are given a prompt which helps students with the direction of the thesis. In one assignment, the students were asked to write a five paragraph essay on the roots of democracy with the following given thesis: "The origins of democracy can be found in ancient Athens during the successive leadership of Salon, Peisis, Tratus, and Cleisthenes."

Most of the information writing completed in biology requires the recording of information related to lab experiments. The process of writing a conclusion, the component of the lab which the biology team decided to critically examine, includes a purpose statement, verification of the hypotheses, analysis of data, and implications of results. The emphasis is primarily on the accuracy in reporting results, understanding of scientific processes, and drawing the specific conclusions.

The biology teachers are more focused on the experimental process and the correct interpretation of the lab. Although an actual write-up of a lab is required for most labs, the emphasis is on the understanding of the variables tested. During the review of the writing samples, which included the writing of a lab conclusion, the teachers expressed concerns regarding students' disorganization of thoughts, insufficient documentation to verify their results, and incoherent reporting of findings. Although these findings are indicative of inadequate writing skills as well as misinterpretation of the lab, the teachers tend to focus on the content rather than the written expression.

Familiarity or previous experience with assigning writing to students appears to be a contributing factor affecting the extent and frequency of writing in the classroom. As the project progressed this first year, however, a difference emerged from the integration of writing in the classroom. The major influence that encouraged more deliberate instruction was the opportunity for teachers to critically examine their own students' writing, to make their own instructional decisions for designing strategies to improve their students' writing, and to designate criteria for evaluating student writing through the rubrics which the teams developed. This entire process immersed teachers in the writing process and gave them more confidence in planning, developing and assessing student writing in their subject.

Overall Findings

Two major findings were discovered through the writing initiative. The first finding focused on the craft of writing. The teams found many similarities as they examined student information writing. Teachers agreed that organization and editing were essential for effective writing. As a result, it was unanimously concluded by all of the core teams that more deliberate prewriting and editing needed to be incorporated into the writing assignments. The teams also agreed that students need to be shown sample writings and to practice evaluating their writing through criteria established by a writing rubric. Another extremely important finding related to the writing process was the fact that the teachers reported that writing was helping students improve their basic understanding of subject content and that writing enhances student's critical thinking abilities.

A more detailed listing of these findings is shown below:

Information writing

Writing process across disciplines appears to have these similarities:

- Central focus unifies the direction of the writing;
- Logical organization helps to make the writing meaningful and connected;
- Prewriting is essential to the development of a coherent composition;
- First draft is often considered to be the final draft.

Integration of writing into teaching:

- Writing helps content mastery;
- Writing assists students in distinguishing between known and unknown facts;
- Writing improves critical thinking and syllogistic reasoning.

The second finding emerged from the actual work plans and how they were implemented. Four aspects of the work plans which contributed to their successful implementation were (1) a teacher driven approach, (2) an investigative strategy, (3) in-house staff and curriculum development, and (4) the weaving, threading, and carrying of ideas across subjects. The teachers were the primary decision-makers throughout the project. They examined the student papers, identified the strengths and areas that needed improvement, and then they developed the tools and strategies to improve their students writing. The action research model of trying to figure out what's going on through constant comparisons of data made the findings realistic and meaningful to teachers. The in-house-off-campus staff and curriculum development provided time for teachers to relax with their colleagues and to conduct business at the same time. Lastly, the continuous coordination across subjects allowed teachers to keep in touch, make sure their approaches were consistent, and to let the students know that we were all working together to make a difference in their writing. Characteristics of the successful work plans appear below:

Implementation of work plans

- Collegial teacher-driven plan
- Time to talk
  - Useful accomplishments........rubrics, prewriting organizers, writing lessons, editing tools
  - Uninterrupted time away from campus
- Action research approach guided by the following questions:
  - What's going on?
  - What needs to be done?
  - How do we do it?
- Staff and curriculum development
  - Resources used as jumping-off point for creative development
  - Teacher as investigator and inventor
  - Expertise shared and synthesized within and across disciplines
  - Teacher as resource to each other
  - Respect for each other's knowledge
- Coordination/leadership approach
  - Weaving and threading it together
  - Watching and waiting for things to happen
  - Carrying information among teams
  - Relating information through memos

Writing coordinator's role

As the new role of writing coordinator and teacher researcher evolved, my position shifted into that of curriculum, assessment, and staff development. I was primarily responsible, along with the leadership team, for establishing procedures for implementing the schoolwide information writing objective. I planned the curriculum and staff development retreats, coordinated with team leaders and department chairs, "carried" the assessment and instructional development across the disciplines, and worked with the school planning team and the liaison from the Office of Testing, Planning, and Evaluation. One of my primary roles as coordinator was to assist with communication across core and interdisciplinary teams. I kept running records of all of the curriculum and staff development sessions, and compiled drafts of documents as teachers developed writing tools and rubrics.

I also was responsible for planning team meetings and curriculum and staff development sessions with the team leaders. The purpose and agenda were established with the team leaders. Most importantly, however, I chatted with teachers regularly to get their reaction, suggestions, and recommendations about the approaches, strategies, lessons, and assessment tools they were developing for the writing project. Lastly, as a direct result of my involvement with the teacher researcher project, I was able to analyze the relationship of school planning, inhouse assessment, and teacher research. The office liaison not only met regularly with me, but also attended most of the curriculum and staff development sessions. During the year, she also conducted research related to the correlation of the school plan and the teacher researcher process.

What's next?

The writing coordinator and the multidisciplinary team will continue with the informational writing project in the summer through an administrative funded curriculum and staff development workshop. The outcome will be a conference site set up through our district's First Class e-mail system that will include all of the instructional and assessment tools, which were developed throughout the year by the core teams.

The project will continue next year with the emphasis on tenth grade and the continuation of the ninth grade assignments that were developed this year. Quantitative data as well as qualitative data will be collected next year. The generic rubric, which was developed by the teachers, will be the measurement tool used to assess the difference in both the ninth and tenth grade students writing skills. And I will continue to "weave and thread "my way through the process and will invite the ninth grade team to assist with the carrying-on role, since it was through their investigation of writing that so many new discoveries and ideas evolved.

Chapter 21

The Open Conspiracy: One High School's Effort To Assess and Improve Informational Writing Across the Curriculum

Marian M. Mohr

If schools are to be judged by what their students are able to do, what exactly will they judge and whose standards and measures will be used for making the judgment? All over the country, state legislatures and school boards are choosing test scores as measures and threatening to punish schools that do not meet the standards.

Suppose the subject to be judged is secondary school writing, a particularly slippery skill to assess. Even if the school's English Department has reached some agreement on process and product, grammar and usage, expression and exposition, that is no guarantee that teachers in other disciplines will see the very same students as writing competently in math, science, social studies, and foreign language classes. Suppose everyone thinks that the students do not write well enough in any subject. What should be done about it? How?

School administrators and teachers need to know how and why learning takes place at their schools to decide how best to improve. School improvement plans and teacher research are two ways that a school can gather this information and learn to use it wisely. I will describe a year of such an effort at Robinson High School and the discoveries we made during the process, in the hope that other schools will find useful information here for their own efforts at assessing and improving student writing across the curriculum.

School improvement plans are required by the Fairfax County Public Schools, of which Robinson is a part, and are monitored by the school system. Schools draft their objectives for improvement, create work plans to fulfill their objectives, and assess their progress over a period of three years. This procedure happens with more or less faculty input according to the leadership of each school's administration. The School Improvement Plan of Robinson High School for the years 1998-2001 has an objective to improve students' informational writing across five disciplines—Science (Biology), Social Studies (World History), Foreign Language, Mathematics (Algebra and Geometry), and English.

The reading specialist (Shirley McCann) at Robinson was given the responsibility for planning and leading the implementation of the writing objective and an associated staff development effort (see Chapter 21 for her account). I was a liaison between Robinson and the school district's Office of Planning, Testing, and Evaluation with the responsibility for leading a teacher research group and, working with the reading specialist, to support the school plan implementation. The reading specialist's research topic was the assessment itself, along with its staff and curriculum development components. I planned to study the connections between teacher research and the assessment and improvement effort.

Since 1980 I have been involved in teacher research in my own classroom as a high school English teacher and as a leader of teacher research groups. I see teacher research as a way to discover and disseminate teachers' knowledge and understanding of teaching and learning. My experience with teacher research has led me to believe that the understandings derived from it are vital to the improvement of schools, especially to improved student learning. Because of this background, I was interested in how teacher research could become more a part of the general knowledge of schools, particularly through the school planning process.

The Plans

Since improvement plans are for three years, a focus on the ninth grade was chosen for the first year. The ninth graders will eventually be tested as 11th graders by the new state tests of the Standards of Learning which include a writing sample evaluation. The ninth grade teachers in each of the five core disciplines were the participants in the writing improvement effort. A multi-disciplinary team made up of one teacher from each of the discipline teams was to coordinate the program as a whole and develop assessment tools that crossed curriculum lines, a generic rubric if possible. The plan was to assess the writing of the 9th grade students through a series of writing assignments evaluated according to rubrics developed by the teachers, then to create ways of improving the students' writing in relation to the information generated by the assessment.

At one of the multidisciplinary group's early meetings, a teacher told the story of a student coming into his world history class complaining to another student about a writing assignment he had been given in algebra. The second student expressed surprise and said that he had been given a writing assignment in geometry. They turned to their world history teacher and asked if they were going to write in his class as well. When the teacher confirmed this, one student looked at the other and said, "Hey, it's a conspiracy!" The teachers at the meeting laughed at the story, pleased that their working together might affect their students' learning about writing in their various disciplines. From time to time at our meetings one of the teachers would smilingly refer to "the conspiracy" afoot at Robinson to teach students to write well.

Anyone coming into the reading specialist's small office as she and I pored over the collected student and teacher data and worked to plan the next meeting or evaluate the last might suspect a conspiracy. We talked long hours about what was happening both in the teacher research group, of which we were both members and where we shared with colleagues what was going on in our research process, and the various teacher groups working to implement the writing objective. Our planning and evaluation were interwoven with our attempts to describe what was happening, how it was happening, and why.

Yet if this was a conspiracy, it was certainly inclusive and open, not secretive. It included a large group of ninth grade teachers from five disciplines who also spent time together poring over student papers and analyzing the what, how, and why of writing. We worked as a group to discover what kind of teaching would result in the kind of learning that would give students improved writing skills and how best to measure improvement. The teacher research group, open to anyone who wished to participate, also met regularly and worked together, studying their individual questions related to their own teaching, and examining together what they were finding out.

The conspiracy was not only inclusive, it was also public. Each time a group met and studied the accumulated data, someone would raise the issue of talking to administrators and colleagues about what they were learning. At first this was simply a recognition that the school administrators had a stake in their success. But the teachers also knew that their colleagues wanted to know what they were doing in their meetings, especially those away from school. The social studies teachers, for example, were teaching a new curriculum—world history—and the new assignments and rubrics were becoming a part of that curriculum. Other teachers needed to know about the work being done, and the team members wanted to share the writing lessons and assignments they were developing.

When the first year's work was drawing to a close, the teachers decided that the materials they were developing belonged several places—on Robinson's web site as pages about teaching writing; in a conference on First Class—the school district's e-mail exchange—where the rest of the faculty could participate in and respond to their work; and in the students' school-year planners in a section about how to write at Robinson. Some of the teachers decided to meet over the summer to revise and polish the rubrics, suggestions for teaching writing, and writing assignments to prepare them for the web site. The teacher research group also decided to introduce the faculty to their research articles via the web, and planned a series of voluntary meetings with interested faculty for early in the fall of the next year. The major purpose for making use of the school's interactive computer capabilities was to get feedback from the rest of the faculty on the work.

The Data

Data was generated everywhere. Specifically, the data included:

- Three sets of student writings and the assignments which elicited them, collected over the year—baseline, first, and second semester.
- Field notes, research log entries, and reflections on the activities, meetings, and comments of the various groups.
- Plans, agendas, and records of meetings.
- Documents generated by the participating teachers such as information writing assignments, descriptions of writing process, rubrics,

and writing "tools"—supportive lessons for teachers to use such as graphic organizers and editing checklists.

As data accumulated, two analysis strategies proved very helpful—*constant comparison* and *recurring theme searches*. Comparison of data collected became the basis for future data collection and future planning. For example, when the data indicated that the foreign language teachers were very well informed about the use of rubrics for writing assessment, they were asked to explain how rubrics functioned to teachers in other disciplines and to be consultants for the project. Reading through a pile of data, of whatever kind, became a repeated activity in all our meetings as we searched for recurring themes. Themes such as students' understanding (or lack thereof) of the term "thesis" and the wide differences between teachers' definitions of "thesis" emerged from such searches. The process was to examine both student and teacher data, and then use the information to understand what was needed and to plan what to do next both in implementing the objective and providing staff development.

We developed a worksheet of questions and designed a chart with the help of a foreign language teacher, to assist in managing the data. We were interested in both collecting qualitative data and looking at the rubric data quantitatively. See Figures 1 & 2.

Figure 1
Questions to Help in Data Analysis

Findings from Student Writings

Examine the sample writings from your subject. Look for patterns that seem to be occurring. Contrast differences across assignments and rubric rankings of papers. Think about how the assignments were presented to the students. Were the assignments completed in or outside of class? What about the prewriting activity—what did it involve?

A. Below is a list of possible questions related to the writings that you might want to consider:

- What did you notice about the writings in general?
- What stands out?
- What do they have in common?
- What are the strengths/weaknesses?
- What needs to improve?

B. Below is a list of questions related to the rubric that you might want to consider as you look at the way the papers were scored.

- What did you notice about the rubric scores?
- Are there any consistent problems? Consistent successes?
- Do the high-scored papers have anything in common? (besides the score)
- What do you think caused the score on the low-scoring papers?

C. Additional thoughts about the papers?

Figure 2
Data Collection and Analysis Worksheet

SUBJECT:			Number of papers:			Date:
RUBRIC SCORES	**4**	**3**	**2**	**1**	**Average score**	
CONTENT	____ ____ ____ X 4 = ____	____ ____ ____ X 3 = ____	____ ____ ____ X 2 = ____	____ ____ ____ X 1 = ____	TOTAL: ____ ÷ No. of papers = ____	
UNITY	____ ____ ____ X 4 = ____	____ ____ ____ X 3 = ____	____ ____ ____ X 2 = ____	____ ____ ____ X 1 = ____	TOTAL: ____ ÷ No. of papers = ____	
SUPPORTING EVIDENCE	____ ____ ____ X 4 = ____	____ ____ ____ X 3 = ____	____ ____ ____ X 2 = ____	____ ____ ____ X 1 = ____	TOTAL: ____ ÷ No. of papers = ____	
CONTROL OF LANGUAGE	____ ____ ____ X 4 = ____	____ ____ ____ X 3 = ____	____ ____ ____ X 2 = ____	____ ____ ____ X 1 = ____	TOTAL: ____ ÷ No. of papers = ____	

What did you notice about the writings in general? What are their strengths and weaknesses?

____

____

____

____

At all our meetings there were examples of differences in thinking, ideas that did not fit into our recurring themes, ideas that pushed us to relook our data or collect more. For example, the English 9 teachers and the teachers from the other disciplines thought differently about the place of writing in their curriculums. The teaching of writing was viewed as part of their "content" by the English teachers, but teachers in other disciplines saw it as a way to examine whether or not their students understood content and, increasingly, as the year progressed, as a way to learn content. The discovery of this difference by the group and the time to explore and discuss it avoided the sometimes uneasy feelings in discussing writing evaluation that exist between English departments and teachers in other disciplines. The discovery also contributed to a better understanding of writing to learn on the part of all the participants.

More directly related to my own research was the realization that, although originally I saw the teacher research group as contributing to the school improvement plan directly, the teachers involved, with the exception of the reading specialist and me, were interested in questions not directly related to the school plan. But as I saw that they were investigating their own questions separate from informational writing, I also saw that the process being followed by the various groups and teams working on the writing objective was teacher research, only without the label. The teacher research group was going through an intensive, focused, in-depth study of questions of their own while the teachers involved in working on the school improvement plan were going through a collaborative, sprawling, in-breadth process of teacher research for the school as a whole.

The data kept piling up. Some themes emerged as new ways of looking at old topics in high school improvement efforts. My own log entries contained lots of questions.

- How is research-based staff development different from other staff development?
- How was this cooperative collegial effort able to overcome traditional interdepartmental divisions?
- How can a schoolwide assessment offer learning for students and teachers and be deemed useful by them?
- What is the connection between the need of a school to improve itself and the need to discover how to improve?
- How can interpretive, qualitative research findings, the kind that result from most teacher research, be a valued and useful part of school and district sponsored assessment?

That last question came up many times in my thinking because I had had experience reporting on school improvement plans and found administrators unreceptive to the complex findings resulting from qualitative data, even when they recognized the validity of the research and praised its contribution to the school improvement process. They thought that sooner or later they would be asked to prove results with numbers, and that those numbers would eventually be judged by someone else outside the school—superintendents, school boards, news media—who would also be unreceptive to qualitative or interpretive results. Qualitative teacher research mattered only as an in-house staff development.

I was not able to answer any of the questions in a straightforward way, as it turns out, but I did begin to see, I think, how teachers who conduct research are offering the profession different ways of looking at some concepts that are very familiar—concepts of research, leadership, staff development, assessment, and school planning.

Themes and Findings

Although the reading specialist and I worked together, I made my observations from the point of view of an outsider, a highly involved participant-observer. I tried to understand where all the variables in the data connected into some general ideas that would be of help in understanding what had happened this year and might happen in the future. More and more it seemed to me that it was a process of redefining. At this point I see three different concepts emerging from our work. They are alternate definitions, stated as comparisons, and they sound contradictory, at least as I understand the terms leadership, staff development, and assessment in general use in schools. They are each described using data from the assessment as it progressed through the year.

1. Leadership as coordinating a collegial conspiracy

If someone were to draw up a list of the leaders in this school improvement effort it would look both scattered and interconnected. The reading specialist and I were constant contributors but not always responsible for either making decisions or giving out information. As the project progressed and individual teachers took responsibility for tasks they were especially interested in, it became harder and harder to pinpoint the person in charge at any gathering. The principles at work included:

- **Coordination of effort.** This was evident when the reading specialist carried information from one team member to another, a foreign language teacher helped design a data collection sheet for the whole group, and individual teachers shared lessons that they thought were effective in teaching informational writing. In general, this coordination occurred any time when, in a group setting, an individual crossed over preexisting boundaries, whatever they were, and showed the group a way to work. The composing of the generic rubric exemplifies the coordination efforts. At first, most thought it would and could not be done, but saw how it might help in the assessment. When it was accomplished, after many drafts and much discussion, it was described as a general rubric adaptable to individual teachers' additions and changes, the general and standard coordinated with the particular and individual.
- **Respect for differences.** At the beginning of the year the participants pointed out the differences between teaching science or foreign language or algebra. As the year progressed, teachers of all disciplines remarked on the similarities they found in their students' writing and in their own approaches to teaching across the disciplines. The more coordination, the more mutual respect and collegiality. The safety

and mutual respect of the research setting meant that teachers were able to listen to and learn from each other. Both their individual teaching expertise and their mutual decision making were respected in the group.

- **Accomplishment of mutually agreed upon tasks.** The reading specialist planned for each group meeting to be centered on a task to be accomplished—a rubric to be written, data to be analyzed, or new assignments to be planned. These tasks grew and changed as the groups came up with new ideas to supplement the original plans, but the meetings were not open-ended. This task orientation reminded everyone of the seriousness of the mission and of the school's request and need for their work. They seemed to see this task responsibility as something over which they had control, which was contributing to their teaching, and which had the potential for making their students better writers, all factors which they took seriously themselves.

The reading specialist and I believed in these three principles from the beginning, but they also grew, one from the other, out of the course of the year's work. As we observed and documented the developing project, our own understanding of how to lead developed as well.

In the teacher research group, the teachers were also acknowledged experts on their own teaching and led the discussions of their own research. Some of the teachers in the group commented that they had never before met other members of the group as Robinson is a very large school. They said they were pleased to have the opportunity to get to know colleagues in the setting of the research group where they could look forward to their considered comments on all aspects of their research.

I functioned primarily as a convener and brought information about the research process to share with the group as well as my own research. Even when we were talking about an area where I had more expertise than they did, they remained the experts on their own teaching and researching. Our major mutually agreed upon task was writing up our research. We read drafts to each other and discussed our progress, not with the idea of papers being "turned in" but of being disseminated to colleagues in the school. We were all in this together.

2. Staff development as research by teachers

The writing improvement groups saw their task as collecting and analyzing data, not criticizing the teaching of others and defending their own. Because they adopted a research stance, they were not defensive about the assessment as criticism or beyond their control. They reported what they saw in the student writings, made generalizations across and within disciplines, and offered teaching suggestions that crossed discipline lines. Needed improvements in teaching were discovered as findings and made as interpretations or implications of data.

At first, some teams developed single writing assignments for all teachers in the discipline; others kept to individual teachers' choice. Teachers on the team were clearly not wanting to tell colleagues how to either teach or assess writing. At the end of the year, however, by their own decision, the teachers of each discipline were designing the same assignments for all their students and were interested in what the analysis of the papers would show. They had used their time together to inform themselves about writing process by exchanging ideas and information at their meetings and, importantly, by writing and revising the student prompts, their own informational writing assignments. As they learned more themselves they were more confident about talking with their colleagues who were not on the team.

This process was not based on perceived deficits or on a cadre of teachers given intensive training and then sent to teach their colleagues as messengers of the new knowledge they had received. It was a process where the teachers themselves decided what they needed to know, and when they needed to know it. It was also assumed that they were capable of finding out what they needed to know. Their own differences were respected and they did the same for their discipline colleagues who were not on the team. They were coordinators, they distributed information, they respected differences, and they worked with their colleagues to accomplish self-chosen tasks.

The use of research methodology was the framework for the staff development because examining and analyzing data illuminated needs which were then filled by knowledgeable teachers on the teams. If a team member asked about strategies for helping students learn to organize their writing after seeing the data showing that this was a difficult area for them, another team member would offer a strategy and soon others would chime in with questions or suggestions. The reading specialist and I abandoned our original plan of presentations by outside experts and stacks of articles and handouts. We contributed to the staff development by organizing the meetings of the teams as a process of research, but we also, as colleagues, participated in the search for information and came to each meeting with possible writing "tools," as we all began to call teaching suggestions. They were distributed only when asked for, and accepting any of the ideas was voluntary on the part of the teachers.

As mentioned, the foreign language teachers had already done extensive work on writing rubrics and offered their expertise to others. The English 9 team were asked to write up a Robinson version of the writing process to be included in the students' planners. Individual teachers mentioned parts of the writing process that they found difficult—peer editing was one—and others offered lessons that they had found successful in the problem area—a handout of guidelines for peer editing, for example.

The writing improvement teams and the teacher research group worked separately and, in this large school, although engaged in a similar staff development process, only vaguely knew of each others' existence. In the teacher research group, the teachers devoted a year's effort to studying a question of their own choosing about teaching and learning in their classrooms. They collected data throughout the year, analyzed it individually and as a group, wrote drafts about what they were finding out, and supported each other in writing and revising a final paper on the results of their research. They sometimes gave each other suggestions about teaching, especially if a teacher expressed puzzlement or distress, but their responses were often either sympathy or gentle questions about what seemed to be happening. They acted and spoke as if their task were to help each other succeed by asking the right questions, providing a concentrated interest in each other's research, and offering personal support to individuals.

The teacher-researchers worked individually with colleague support while the groups involved in the school improvement effort worked collegially with individual support. In the larger group, because the research question was essentially the same for everyone, there was more exchange of ideas about teaching strategies. They did not discuss their work as research or focus in on any individual, but they used research strategies.

3. Assessment as understanding of context

Assessment in school plans often includes the assumption that improvement will be shown, progress will be made, and both will be measurable by some method devised by outsiders to the school. This measurement requires the ignoring of context, the pretense that individual differences don't exist or, if they do, that they don't matter. When such issues are raised, often by teachers, they may be viewed as special pleading by ineffective teachers rather than taken seriously as legitimate knowledgeable views of the school's situation.

Research, on the other hand, does not presuppose an outcome of "improvement," but asks how and why and searches for the truth in the context of the whole school. Data is interpreted, and interpretations are complex regardless of what kind of data is analyzed. If only quantitative measures are counted as research, rather than present a clear picture of a school without complications and ambiguity, they obscure the real nature of the problems the school faces in improving teaching and learning.

In the Robinson improvement effort being described here, the assessment research process was complicated, but it did not obscure the truth. The data examined by the teachers clearly indicated areas for improvement. In fact, the teachers involved looked for specific ways to adapt their teaching and make the changes they saw as necessary as a result of their examination of the data. They made no excuses about students' inability to learn or the lack of support in the home. Instead, they spent hours working out new ways of teaching to support student learning and felt the responsibility to share what they found with other teachers.

They were conducting an assessment using research methodology that they saw acknowledged the complicated nature of teaching and learning. They worked with information that showed achievement and needs for improvement in their real and complex interrelationship in the context of classrooms and the school. Understanding this assessment in context, for the teachers involved, included understanding rubrics, test scores, grades and other numerical data, but also observations of students, the words of their discussions and their writing, and contributions to the data from teacher thinking and reflection—an understanding of context. Regardless of what others might believe about measures of achievement, they saw that improvement in teaching and learning is made by teachers acting together as researchers on the data from their classrooms.

Implications

The implications of the work of the Robinson teachers in both the teacher research group and the larger group working on the assessment seemed to me to be about research methodology itself and to be additional questions for further study.

- How can education decision makers learn to see the value in qualitative research as well as quantitative?
- How can schools combine both qualitative and quantitative data in their assessment efforts so that they have a full informative, real picture of student achievement in context?
- How can schools begin to compare teacher research studies and accumulate the knowledge and understandings they offer?
- How can standardization and individuality live together in our efforts to improve teaching and foster learning in our schools?

Some of these questions have tentative answers in the literature about research methodology. In the second edition of *Qualitative Data Analysis* (1994), M. Miles and A.M. Huberman discuss the differences between qualitative and quantitative data and what each can offer an assessment. They see the need for answers to the "how" and "why" questions as well as the need for quantitative results. They believe that the two kinds of data should be chosen for use in coordination with the questions being asked. They see the two kinds of research as complementary—a way to present a full and whole picture. George W. Noblit and R. Dwight Hare (1988) have examined ways that qualitative data can be compared and synthesized so as to make the findings of qualitative research broader. They caution, however, against trying to "add up" the findings of qualitative researchers, and urge researchers to stay true to the specific particular nature of qualitative research from which other individuals can learn.

The work of these researchers and others does not, however, help with the problem faced by teachers and their schools of how to encourage a better understanding of research in their school communities. If a school released test score data alongside teachers' findings and conclusions, the school community would have a way of seeing and understanding how the school is progressing. If teachers' findings and conclusions were available to their colleagues, no matter how particular they were to the classroom from which they originated, other teachers could read and translate what was said, adding to and expanding their own understandings. The unsolved problem is how to foster the ability and willingness of school administrators, school boards, and community organizations to "see" teachers' research as legitimate assessment for decision making, assessment, staff development, and planning.

The overall implication of the research this year is that official school assessments and improvement efforts can be effective if the results make sense to the teachers in the school and are directly related to the learning of students. Given certain conditions, such as those offered to the teachers in this study, teachers will plan and carry out school improvement efforts because of their professional interest in doing a better job. They will openly conspire to assess their work with colleagues and study how to make learning more successful for all.

Works Cited

Miles, M., and A.M. Huberman. 1994. *Qualitative data analysis: An expanded sourcebook*. 2d ed. Beverly Hills, CA: Sage Publications.

Noblit, G.W., and R.D. Hare. 1988. *Meta-Ethnography: Synthesizing qualitative studies*. Newbury Park, CA: Sage Publications.

Appendix A

Resources for Teaching and Assessing Writing Across the Curriculum

Anderson, G.L., K. Herr, and A.S. Nihlen. 1994. *Studying your own school: An educator's guide to qualitative practitioner research*. Thousand Oaks, CA: Corwin Press.

This book combines the story of teachers' efforts to conduct research in their own schools with thoughtful discussion of this kind of research and how it fits into the larger field of educational research. The authors suggest some standards for validity and reliability in teacher research and offer suggestions on how to make it work in a school setting.

Banford, H., and others. 1996. *Cityscapes: Eight views from the urban classroom*. Berkley, CA: National Writing Project.

Eight teacher-researcher authors report on their classroom research and discuss how their research changed their teaching and contributed to their students' learning.

Bean, John C. 1996. *Engaging ideas: The professor's guide to integrating writing, critical thinking, and active learning in the classroom*. San Francisco, CA: Jossey-Bass.

Aimed primarily at college teaching, Bean's text, nevertheless, is equally useful for secondary teachers in various content areas; among the topics addressed are the connections between thinking and writing, design of assignments, and reading, commenting upon and grading student writing.

Bleich, D. 1975. *Readings and feelings: An introduction to subjective criticism*. Urbana, IL: NCTE.

Although mainly a text about how to teach literature from a subjective criticism perspective, Bleich provides throughout his pedagogical and theoretical discussion approaches to evaluating and grading that rest on student participation in discussion and class activities; a useful perspective in light of all the current emphasis upon accountability.

Brown, Jean E., and others. 1993. *Toward literacy: Theory and applications for teaching writing in the content areas*. Belmont, CA: Wadsworth.

Offers useful introduction to writing in the content areas and provides examples of applications in a number of different content areas.

Burns, M. 1995. *Writing in math class*. White Plains, NY: Cuisenaire.

The authors present a clear and persuasive case for making writing a part of mathematics instruction. Five different types of student writing opportunities are described and illustrated with classroom examples, and practical tips.

Childers, P., and M. Lowry. 1997. Engaging students through formative assessment in science. *The Clearing House* (November/December): 97–102.

The authors report on a classroom study they conducted focusing on the design of assignments and their impact on student learning in science and the role of portfolios as an assessment tool of this learning; findings suggested that formative assessment in conjunction with the development of portfolios can have positive effects on student learning.

Claggett, Fran. 1996. *A measure of success: From assignment to assessment in English language arts*. Portsmouth, NH: Heineman.

Designed for English language arts teachers, primarily at the secondary level, this text offers a variety of assignments and assessments tools which should prove helpful to both experienced and inexperienced teachers; assessment tools of students' reading and writing are particularly valuable.

Clarke, D. 1997. *Constructive assessment in mathematics: Practical steps for classroom teachers*. Berkeley, CA: Key Curriculum Press.

In a practical book for teachers, Clarke emphasizes on-going assessment that integrates writing in the form of students' written responses to multiple-step or open-ended questions and problem tasks, self-assessment, student journals, student portfolios, and extended projects. The author suggests a change in the function of assessment from measurement to portrayal of students' mathematical thinking.

Cooper, Charles R., and Lee Odell, eds. 1999. *Evaluating writing*. Urbana, IL: NCTE.

This collection of articles by different authors offers examples of assessing writing-to-learn in four disciplines: science, math, history, and English; suggestions are also offered about working with the writing of culturally and linguistically diverse students and the articles raise a number of interesting issues regarding assessment.

Countryman, Joan. 1992. *Writing to learn mathematics*. Portsmouth, NH: Heineman.

The author emphasizes that writing frees students of the idea that math is just a series of rules, facts, numbers, symbols, formulas, and procedures to memorize and use on tests. Through classroom examples, this book illustrates the use of journals, learning logs, letters, autobiographies, investigations, and formal reports that enhance mathematical reasoning and overall math learning.

DeFina, A.A. 1992. *Portfolio assessment: Getting started*. New York: Scholastic Professional Books.

This text guides teachers who are getting started in implementing and using portfolios as an alternative assessment process. The author offers clear discussion of the value and purposes of portfolios as well as step-by-step ways of integrating them into the classroom; includes sample portfolios, rubrics, and explanatory charts.

Duke, Charles R. 1983. *Writing through sequence: A process approach.* Boston: Little Brown and Company.

Originally designed as a freshman composition text, this book offers practical strategies for engaging in writing regardless of content field, peer review guidelines and rubrics, and advice on making sense of the writing process.

Ellerton, N.F., and M.A. Clements. 1991. *Mathematics in language: A review of language factors in mathematics learning.* London: Deakin University.

This document reviews the body of research and knowledge that is encompassed in the expression "language factors in mathematics learning" and develops a theoretical framework that becomes important to the classroom when we realize that to assess students' learning of mathematics, we must use some form of communication.

Elliott, P.C., ed. 1996. *Communication in mathematics K–12 and beyond.* Reston, VA: National Council of Teachers of Mathematics.

In the NCTM 1996 Yearbook, respected mathematics educators emphasize the importance and provide examples of writing and other forms of communication for implementing mathematics education reform. Contributors to the yearbook illustrate how mathematics classrooms can be discourse communities where students and teachers communicate about the teaching and learning of mathematics.

Eisenhower National Clearinghouse for Mathematics and Science Education. 1996–1997. *New approaches to assessment in science and mathematics.* Vol. 3 (1). Washington, DC: Eisenhower National Clearinghouse for Mathematics and Science Education.

This volume offers 29 projects in science and mathematics that describe, and give examples of uses of writing as well as other alternative assessments in these subjects. Presented in much the same format as an ERIC bibliographic entry, each one of the entries has original sources, grade levels, abstract of project, and relation to assessment.

Gere, Anne Ruggles, ed. 1985. *Roots in the sawdust: Writing to learn across the curriculum.* Urbana, IL: NCTE.

This collection of articles offers suggestions for both secondary and college teachers who wish to emphasize writing in the content areas; useful and classroom-tested teaching practices are central to each article and easily adapted to a variety of content areas.

Gordon, J. 1988. Writing: A teaching strategy for elementary algebraic fractions. *Focus on Learning Problems in Mathematics.* 10 (Winter): 29–36.

The author describes how the learning of elementary algebra can be enhanced by requiring students to write short explanations of their method of solution or why they performed a certain process; examples are provided related to several common algebraic misconceptions.

Graves, D.H., and B. S. Sunstein, eds. 1992. *Portfolio portraits*. Portsmouth, NH: Heineman.

For an excellent cross-level look at teachers' and students' uses of portfolios, this book has it all; the editors have included examples and discussions of portfolios in elementary, secondary, and college classrooms as well as large scale assessment.

Herrington, Anne, and Charles Moran, eds. 1992. *Writing, teaching, and learning in the disciplines*. New York: Modern Language Association of America.

This text, although aimed primarily at college instructors and researchers, offers a variety of viewpoints especially concerning the theory and history of writing in various disciplines; also included are some discussions of practice and specific programs at several institutions.

Howie, Sherry Hill. 1984. *A guidebook for teaching writing in content areas*. Boston: Allyn and Bacon, Inc.

This text offers a comprehensive view of teaching writing in the content areas; topics covered include the writing process, kinds of writing in content areas, vocabulary and spelling, paragraphing and sentence variety, motivating students to write, and evaluation of student writing.

Johnson, T.M., and others. 1998. Students' thinking and writing in the context of probability. *Written Communication*. 15 (2): 203–229.

The article illustrates how one group of teachers applied different levels of a writing framework to describe and assess students' probabilistic reasoning. A major conclusion is that regular written feedback and follow-up prompts from teachers can enhance the quality of students' thinking and writing during mathematical problem solving.

Keith, S. 1988. Explorative writing and learning mathematics. *Mathematics Teacher* 81: 714–719.

The article illustrates how explorative assignments can help expose and identify learning problems; provides some assignments that address these problems and discusses some techniques and benefits of using writing assignments in the mathematics classroom.

McIntosh, M. 1991. No time for writing in your class? *Mathematics Teacher* 84: 423–433.

The author presents ideas to help busy teachers implement four forms of writing that are appropriate for the mathematics classroom: logbooks, journals, expository writing, and creative writing. Includes specific examples and suggestions for classroom activities for each writing form discussed.

National Council of Teachers of Mathematics. 1995. *Assessment standards for school mathematics*. Reston, VA: National Council of Teachers of Mathematics.

NCTM produced this document to assist teachers and others in their development of new assessment strategies and practices that reflect the NCTM's reform vision for school mathematics; standards reflect extensive recent research and the monograph includes an extensive bibliography on assessment.

Northern Nevada Writing Project Teacher-Researcher Group. 1996. *Team teaching*. York, ME: Stenhouse.

For three years a group of teacher-researchers all studied one topic—team teaching—when their state mandated a change in the student-teacher ratio in first grade classes. They examine the ways they changed their teaching in response to the mandate.

Rose, B. 1989. Writing and mathematics: Theory and practice. In *Writing to learn mathematics and science*. New York: Teachers College Press.

The text offers a review of literature that describes efforts to use writing in the teaching of mathematics and provides a discussion of the impact of writing activities on the mathematics classroom.

Self, Judy, ed. 1987. *Plain talk about learning and writing across the curriculum*. Virginia Department of Education.

This collection of articles was one of the first to deal with writing across the curriculum and is still a valuable resource; packed with useful practices in teaching writing in a variety of content areas, readers will find many ideas to adapt to their own teaching.

Shuard, H. and A. Rothery, eds. 1984. *Children reading mathematics*. Oxford, England: Alden Press.

This text provides mathematics educators who are concerned about the ability of children to read and understand written mathematics material ranging from textbooks to home-made worksheets with a review of the research findings in the field of readability.

Simmons, JoAnn McQuire, ed. 1983. *The shortest distance to learning: A guidebook to writing across the curriculum*. Los Angeles, CA: Los Angeles Community College District and UCLA, Office of Academic Interinstitutional Programs.

Addresses issues of content area writing at the community college level; offers practical applications of learning logs, design of essay questions, evaluation techniques, and ways to help students during the writing process.

Stenmark, J.K., ed. 1991. *Mathematics assessment: Myths, models, good questions, and practical suggestions*. Reston, VA: National Council of Teachers of Mathematics.

Pragmatic and readable, this "yellow book" describes ways to test beyond multiple choices. One chapter describes an assessment plan for using portfolios including assignments, holistic grading rubrics, and a management plan. Other chapters emphasize writing as a way of teaching critical thinking in mathematics.

Sterrett, A., ed. 1992. *Using writing to teach mathematics*. Mathematical Association of America.

This collection of essays focuses on writing in the mathematics classroom. The authors describe their experiences using writing in their classrooms and offer specific advice about getting started with writing programs and on matters such as grading, correcting grammar, and the importance of rewriting. Several essays describe student reactions to writing in mathematics.

Tchudi, S., ed. 1997. *Alternatives to grading student writing*. Urbana, IL.: NCTE.

Composed of articles by different authors, this collection offers background information, rationale, and implementation discussions about the variety of alternative ways teachers and students can respond to writing.

Thaiss, Christopher, ed. 1983. *Writing to learn: Essays and reflections on writing across the curriculum*. Urbana, IL: NCTE.

Although addressed to college teachers, the content of this book offers useful insights into the philosophy behind writing to learn; practical applications and examples of students' responses are included.

Waywood, A. 1992. Journal writing and learning mathematics. *For the learning of mathematics*. 12(2):34–43.

This article discusses the development of a pedagogical model for mathematics journal keeping and the practicalities of implementing journal writing in secondary mathematics classrooms; includes sample journal entries.

Webb, Norman L. ed. 1993. *Assessment in the mathematics classroom (yearbook)*. Reston, VA: National Council of Teachers of Mathematics.

The best chapter in this volume devoted entirely to mathematics assessment is Chapter 24 "Assessment in the Interactive Mathematics Project" which describes, among other methods, how to use portfolios in a math classroom. Other chapters describe specific examples of using writing to assess critical thinking and mathematics concepts.

White, Edward M. 1994. *Teaching and assessing writing*, 2d ed. San Francisco, CA: Jossey-Bass Publishers.

For a broad view of teaching and assessing, White is difficult to beat. He places assessment in both a theoretical and practical context and offers excellent background on the development of writing assessment, especially large scale writing assessment.

Wolfe, Denny, and Robert Reising. 1983. *Writing for learning in the content areas*. Portland, ME: J. Weston Walch, Publisher.

This text contains a variety of classroom activities designed to foster writing to learn in the content areas; the reproducible writing tasks and group activities can be adapted easily to almost any content area; a useful resource to have on the shelf.

Zinsser, William. 1990. *Writing to learn*. New York: HarperCollins.

Zinsser was one of the first proponents of writing to learn; this is a fine book on writing in general with particular attention given to using writing in mathematics and science.

Useful Web Sites

www.nsta.org/pubs/tst

Address for the National Science Teachers Association; provides access to a wide variety of publications in which articles on assessment often appear.

http://jchemed.chem.wis.edu/Journal/index.html

Provides access to articles of interest to high school and chemistry instructors.

www.wisc.edu/writing/Handbook/AcademicWriting.html

Offers suggestions concerning science writing, especially lab reports.

www.thegateway.org

The Gateway to Educational Materials—offers a one-stop, any-stop access to high quality lesson plans, curriculum units, and other educational resources for social studies and any other content areas.

www.csun.edu/%7Ehcedu013/index.html

Offers useful links to lesson plans, resources, standards, and curriculum frameworks.

www.beaverton.k12or.us/vose/resources/starter.html

Gives teachers lesson plans and assessment tools for math, social studies and other content areas.

www.enc.org

Site for the Eisenhower National Clearinghouse for Math and Science; click on "Ideas" for standards and frameworks as well as ideas that work; math and science oriented.

www.learner.org.sami/

Features many science and math resources with units, standards, and performance assessments.

www.forum.swarthmore.edu/index.js.html

Gives teachers a huge collection of math resources plus units and lessons; the lessons feature performance tasks, standards, and assessment.

www.kqed.org/fromKQED/Cell/math/mathmenu.html

A good place to see teacher lesson plans that integrate math across the curriculum.

www.c3.lan1.gov/mega-math

This collection of essays focuses on writing in the mathematics classroom. The authors describe their experiences using writing in their classrooms and offer specific advice about getting started with writing programs and on matters such as grading, correcting grammar, and the importance of rewriting. Several essays describe student reactions to writing in mathematics.

www.ericae.net/intbod.stm

Assessment and evaluation resources for a variety of content areas.

www.clearinghouse.net/index.html

For all content areas with its own search engine by unit, subject, or specific word.

www.yahoo.com/Education

An elaborate Internet index for educational topics including assessment, standards, units, and lesson plans.

www.mcrel.org/standards-benchmarks

A standards and benchmarks database with activities links.

www.aasa.org

Maintained by the American Association of School Administrators; gives assessment and standards information plus links to sample assessments.

www.ascd.org

Site for Association for Supervision and Curriculum Development; offers curriculum and assessment resources.

Appendix B

Contributors

Kathleen Ayers is a former teacher of junior high school mathematics; she currently is a member of the Mathematics and Computer Science Department at Boise State University in Boise, Idaho where she is involved in the preparation of preservice teachers. Her research interests include developing and using innovative instructional and assessment techniques both in K-12 and university-level mathematics classrooms.

Kay Berglund teaches elementary science at Norwood School in Bethesda, Maryland. She has mentored hundreds of fifth and sixth grade students and their teachers, as well as their worried parents, through Science Fairs and other long-term projects since 1994.

Candy M. Beal, an assistant professor at North Carolina State University in Raleigh, North Carolina, is a teacher educator who works with students who wish to become middle school teachers. She is a developmental theorist who concentrates on integrative curriculum design, students as interactive learners, and her ongoing research into Russian education. She team-teaches a middle grades language arts and social studies methods "block" at North Carolina State University.

Linda A. Bolte is an associate professor of mathematics at Eastern Washington University in Choyney, Washington. Her teaching experience includes a number of years at the middle and secondary school levels. Current interests include elementary and secondary mathematics teacher education, assessing mathematical knowledge, and reform of college undergraduate mathematics.

Diane Burrell is a mathematics teacher at Hellgate High School in Missoula, Montana with twenty-six years of classroom experience; her interests include mathematics reform and technology in education; she also serves as Senior Project Coordinator for portfolio and writing assessment.

Pamela B. Childers holds the Caldwell Chair of Composition at The McCallie School in Chattanooga, Tennessee, where she directs the writing center and the writing across the curriculum program; she also team teaches an interdisciplinary senior science seminar and serves as a consultant for the national writing across the curriculum network and as treasurer of the Assembly on Computers in English.

Collett B. Dilworth is a professor of English at East Carolina University in Greenville, North Carolina where he teaches courses in writing, English education, and linguistics at both the undergraduate and graduate levels; he also serves as executive director of the North Carolina English Teachers Association.

Anne Wescott Dodd, formerly a secondary school English teacher and principal, is now the chair of the Department of Education at Bates College in Lewiston, Maine. She has a special interest in writing across the curriculum and has conducted workshops for teachers in several school districts.

Charles R. Duke is a former secondary school teacher, director of freshman composition, and teacher of writing who currently serves as Dean of the Reich College of Education at Appalachian State University in Boone, North Carolina; he has directed three national writing projects and has served as a consultant on writing across the curriculum to numerous school districts across the country.

John Fredericks has taught high school chemistry for seven years. He has taught students from sixth grade through college in rural, suburban and inner city schools. He currently teaches at Dallas High School, Dallas, Pennsylvania.

Carolyn Lott is associate professor of curriculum and instruction at the University of Montana in Missoula, Montana; formerly she was an English teacher/media specialist for 25 years and has been active in the Montana Writing Project as a faculty member.

Michael J. Lowry teaches science at The McCallie School in Chattanooga, Tennessee, and serves as a class dean. In addition to teaching biology, chemistry, and physics, he also team teaches an interdisciplinary senior science seminar.

Shirley McCann has worked in public school systems and at the university level for twenty years. She was an area office instructional specialist and middle school curriculum coordinator in Montgomery County Public Schools in Maryland; currently in the Fairfax County Virginia Schools, she is a reading resource teacher; her interests include works with standards, teacher education, and research.

Joseph Milner is Chairman of the Department of Education at Wake Forest University in Winston-Salem, North Carolina where he also serves as director of the North Carolina Governor's School East and as Director of the North Carolina Writing Project.

Marian Mohr was a high school English teacher for over twenty years in the Fairfax County Public Schools, Fairfax, Virginia and she currently assists school systems and writing projects in establishing, coordinating, and maintaining teacher research groups. She has served as co-director of the Northern Virginia Writing Project and as a member of the board of the National Writing Project, and a trustee of the NCTE Research Foundation.

Carol A. Pope is an associate professor of English Language Arts and Middle Grades Education at North Carolina State University in Raleigh, North Carolina; she co-teaches a middle grades language arts and social studies method block for preservice teachers and often conducts workshops and presentations on writing to learn and alternative assessment processes.

Rebecca Sanchez is a curriculum and staff development specialist with the Riverview Intermediate Unit in Shippenville, Pennsylvania. She previously taught tenth grade English at Keystone High School in Knox, Pennsylvania for 22 years; in addition, she has worked as a teacher consultant in the areas of writing, assessment, portfolios, and across the curriculum projects; she also has served as the co-director of the Penn Rivers Writing Project, a National Writing Project site at Clarion University, Clarion, Pennsylvania.

Carol A. Thornton is a Distinguished University Professor in the Mathematics Department of Illinois State University in Normal, Illinois. As co-director of the PUMP Algebra Project and as the result of other professional development efforts, she works 2-3 days a week in schools with teachers and their students.

Sharon Walen is a member of the Mathematics and Computer Science Department at Boise State University in Boise, Idaho; she currently is involved in the preparation of preservice teachers but formerly taught junior high school mathematics. Her research interests include developing and using innovative instructional and assessment techniques both in K-12 and university-level mathematics classrooms.